MOVING PICTURES : FOUR PLAYS

Moving Pictures, Seachange, Stars & Strive

Moving Pictures is an anthology of four plays span
of *Touched*.

'At a time when the Royal Court so often comes u
me as precisely the sort of dramatist that George L___

(Francis King)

Stephen Lowe was born in 1947 in Nottingham. After graduating from Birmingham University in 1969, he spent six years writing, and working variously as a part-time lecturer, clerk, hospital receptionist, newspaper distributor, advertising manager, housepainter, barman and civil servant. While working as a shepherd in Yorkshire he was commissioned by Alan Ayckbourn and joined his company at Scarborough as an actor. His plays include *Comic Pictures* (Scarborough, 1976), *Sally Ann Hallelujah Band* (Nottingham Playhouse Theatre Roundabout, 1977), *Touched* (Nottingham Playhouse, 1977; Royal Court Theatre, 1981; joint winner of the George Devine Award), *The Ragged Trousered Philanthropists* (Joint Stock Theatre Company, 1978; Half Moon, London, 1983), *Glasshouses* (Royal Court Theatre Upstairs, 1981), *Tibetan Inroads* (Royal Court, 1981), *Seachange* (Riverside Studios, 1984), *Keeping Body and Soul Together* (Royal Court Theatre Upstairs, 1984) and two television plays, *Shades* and *Cries from a Watchtower*. He was resident playwright at Dartington College of Arts from 1978-1982 and at Riverside Studios, London, in 1984. He is currently completing a film version of *Moving Pictures* and editing a volume of *Peace Plays* for Methuen.

MOVING PICTURES

Four Plays by

STEPHEN LOWE

MOVING PICTURES
SEACHANGE
STARS
STRIVE

A Methuen New Theatrescript
Methuen · London and New York

A METHUEN PAPERBACK

First published as a Methuen Paperback original in 1985
by Methuen London Ltd, 11 New Fetter Lane, London EC4P 4EE
and Methuen Inc, 733 Third Avenue, New York, NY 10017, USA
Copyright © 1985 by Stephen Lowe
Set in 10 point Press Roman ℞'Tek-Art, Croydon, Surrey
Printed in Great Britain

British Library Cataloguing in Publication Data

Lowe, Stephen, *1947-*
  Moving pictures : four plays. – (A Methuen
  new theatrescript)
  Rn: Stephen Wright   I. Title   II. Lowe,
  Stephen, *1947-*. Seachange   III. Lowe, Stephen,
  1947-. Stars   IV. Lowe, Stephen, *1947-*. Strive
  822'.914   PS3573.R5433
  ISBN 0-413-58780-0

A Warning: an explanation: a couple of confessions, and a hope: all jumbled together in bad prose

Twenty years ago, at school in Nottingham, I played M. Jourdain in Molière's *The Bourgeoise Gentilhomme,* and whilst, perhaps fortunately, I can no longer recall the subtle nuances of my own performance, the recollection of one of the aspiring M. Jourdain's epiphanies has remained with me. It is a very funny scene, where, attempting to rise into the 'highest culture', he is first taught the terms verse and prose, and discovers to his amazement and delight that he has been effortlessly speaking prose all his life. Art, for one blissful moment, seems to him to be easy. And I have a sneaking suspicion that as I hammed my way towards ecstasy playing him, I thought so too. Years later, my first professional acting job was to play his teacher, and I learned otherwise. And, of course, M. Jourdain himself is in for a rude awakening, as are we all, and there are sometimes a few laughs to be had from that, and sometimes some very difficult silences.

This is by way of saying that as I sit attempting to write this introduction, this particular parcel of prose, the discovery I come to yet again, is that I am not, unlike my old friend, a master of prose, but more importantly for you (dear reader) I am not a writer at all, of prose, or poetry, or anything else between. And it seems only fair to warn you in advance in case you approach the task of reading my work with any expectations of literature. My pretensions, or aspirations, are in quite a different direction. As soon as I left university, having failed to complete my last attempt at prose in a postgraduate thesis, I had written onto my passport that I was a playwright. Since then I have been trying to live up to that moment of conceit that is only really possible when you've never had a play performed. As time goes on, the difference between literature and theatre has struck me with increasing intensity, and I'd like to quote in clarification from another playwright for whom I have the greatest admiration. In his book *To Present the Pretence* (a work I recommend to anyone interested in the theatre) John Arden articulates the crucial distinction.

A playwriter is simply a person who puts pen to paper and sets down dramatic dialogue. But the playwright pursues an ancient and complex craft analogous to the crafts of the Cartwright, the Millwright, the Shipwright or — in old Scots — the Wright, pure and simple. The origin of the word is Old English Wyrht = a work, or Wyrcan = to work. The playwright works drama just as the millwright works mill-gear.

Ironically, my true surname is not Lowe, but Wright, which I had to change when I joined Alan Ayckbourn's company in Scarborough as an actor. I took my mother's maiden name, and with it a professional identity. Wright, anyway, had always seemed to me a boring common name when I felt I clearly should have been called something more exotic, like Büchner or Shakespeare. This was during a period of seven years and twenty odd plays that no-one seemed remotely interested in doing. But now, having for the last ten years worked solidly in the theatre, I have become a great respector of just this commonality of wrights. A key factor in my continuation as a playwright is that such work involves so many other people's creativity working in different forms — a number of which I have had the opportunity to practise in the past.

I have never been bored wrighting for the theatre, though often I've been depressed and frustrated by the state of the art, and probably no more than now, in the present political climate. But the language of theatre is as relevant as ever, and that 'empty space' remains there, only waiting for us to decide to work together within it. And its potential for expression in this collective language is well nigh infinite. Whenever I turn again towards that space where the magic that we need can be rediscovered I feel a real excitement, the nervous excitement of journeying towards the unknown that I experienced as a child at pantomimes before the curtain went up. And a thrill of coming to a space that argues possibilities, change, transformations.

The first play I ever recall doing (as an amateur, a lover, of the theatre) was when I was seven and it was called *Fat King Melon*. No doubt kids up and down the country are still doing it. I hope so. I played the king who, having fallen in love with what would now be considered as an anorexic princess, diets to fulfil (his mistaken belief about) her dream of the ideal man. Meanwhile, of course, she is fattening herself up to be attractive to him. Such is life. I was padded up with a pillow, but I couldn't get the gradual stages of dieting to work satisfactorily until I discovered that if I ripped the pillow (leaving a trail of feathers behind me) it worked. I remember being told even then that it made no sense, having the king waddle around like a balding chicken, that it was in some sense, not 'real'. But it worked. And years later, I began to see why. Because it dealt in a desire of the character that made possible a visual transformation, and it acknowledged the theatre language itself as it did so. I didn't have Brecht to quote from at the time, but they let me get away with it anyway, and I've been trying to get away with it ever since.

Re-reading these plays again, I'm struck by how far M. Jourdain and his epiphanies, and King Melon and his transformation have influenced them. They have involved me in a theatre of embarassment, of self-awareness, of people struggling to change, to break out, with people trying to connect. And I've been struck by how, like Fat King Melon, they seem preoccupied with the problems of love, in one form or another. Whether that will match your perceptions of the plays I can't tell. I don't recall that being consciously in my mind at the starting point, but then again one often forgets the point of embarcation and are left in memory with only snapshots of the beaches to restimulate our feelings. I hope my plays are more than that, that these 'personal islands' will come alive for you and connect with your personal landscapes, that the creative effort you make to try to visualise beyond the words on the page will be rewarded by something that truly works as moving pictures.

Stephen Lowe. December 1984.

MOVING PICTURES

A comedy

For Tom

Moving Pictures was first performed in an earlier version, under the title *Glasshouses,* at the Royal Court Theatre Upstairs, on 3 April 1981, with the following cast:

ARTHUR	Richard Butler
DORA, *his wife*	Margery Mason
JIM, *their son, aged seventeen*	Nick Dunning
JACKIE, *their daugher, aged fifteen*	Sylvestra le Touzel
CATHY, *Jim's girl-friend*	Karen Drury
LEFTY (*named Frank in the 1981 version*)	Bernard Kay
ELSIE, *his wife*	June Watson
PETE, *their son*	Martyn Hesford

Directed by Annie Castledine
Designed by Annie Smart
Lighting by Gerry Jenkinson
Sound by Mic Pool

The play covers a time-span of twenty-one months, from August 1963, and is set in Nottingham.

ACT ONE

Scene One

The Bedroom. An old, cheap, three-quarters bed. Dark. Lit by a small 'window'.
DORA stands on one side facing her husband, ARTHUR. Behind them in the shadows stands their son, JIM, holding a mirror.
She suddenly drags the sheets off the bed, revealing the whiteness. ARTHUR, turns away, apparently disinterested.

DORA: Help! You bugger.

JIM: He woun't lift a finger, you know that.

DORA: I wish they were knocking him down wi' the house. He weighs on my chest like a ton of bricks.

JIM (*indicating mirror*): We takin' this?

DORA: Never. Seen too much that 'as. Too little. Either way I don't want it tellin' tales.

JIM (*puts his arm round her*): Come on, gi's one of your Doris Days, Dora Cooper.

She smiles.

DORA: Get away.

She looks out of the window.

You know, in America, only posh folk live in skyscrapers like that. Ten floors up. We'll be the envy of all of Sneinton. Be able to look down on the lot of 'em like a load of toffs. (*Pause.*) Be able to breathe a bit up there, stead of the dark and damp.

ARTHUR has sat down on the bed, and opened up a copy of the Daily Mirror.

JIM: It's goin' to be lovely, Mam. I promise you.

DORA: Where's the van? Bloody Council keep you hangin' about for years. Can't do wi' bein' kept waitin' no longer.

JIM: Worse comes to the worse, we can carry the stuff across the road.

DORA: You 'ave to 'ave a van. Waited twenty years to move, and I'm havin' a van. Phone the Co-op for us and find out where they are.

JIM: We've still the bed to take down.

DORA: I'll get him to do that, if it's the last thing I do. Go on. Gi' us the spanner.

JIM: Let me do it, Mam.

DORA: Find that van.

He hands her the spanner. He lingers at the door, watching. DORA knocks ARTHUR on the arm, and throws the spanner down in front of him.

ARTHUR: If I had an ounce of manhood in me, I'd be down Colwick watching the races.

He picks up the spanner, and watches her drag the mattress off the bed. He idly studies the frame.

Never shift them buggers. Out the question. It in't goin' wi' us. Let 'em knock the 'ouse down round it.

He turns away.

DORA: How many times? (*She darts round in front of him.*) It's for Connie's gal. I've promised it to Connie's gal!

ARTHUR: I'm going to. I'm going to. All right.

He toys with a nut.

DORA: Daft as well as deaf. I never 'ave no bloody luck.

ARTHUR (*giving up*): No. No go.

DORA: Gi' it me.

JIM: Let me do it, Mam.

DORA: I thought you'd gone. Get me that van before a white one comes to take me away.

JIM exits.

DORA: Show you, you bugger.

She grabs the spanner and with a tremendous effort loosens the nut. She holds it up triumphant.

ARTHUR: I loosened that one for you.

DORA *struggles with another nut, and eventually drops the spanner through the frame.*

ARTHUR: Told you. Woun't listen to me.

She climbs under the frame. ARTHUR *takes a pen out, and begins marking off the runners.*

Hard-going. Eastern Princess. Good mare.

He sits back on the frame. DORA *rises behind him with an aluminium chamber pot.*

ARTHUR (*not looking*): Why you coun't leave one bulb in, I'll never know.

DORA: I'll brain you, you bastard, and they'll gi' me a medal.

ARTHUR: Yo' listenin'?

He turns. She waves the pot at him.

DORA: No more. No more of this. None of this lark in the new house.

ARTHUR: You packed up here. Not me. It in't my fault. Hide it in the blankets if you're scared of folk seein'.

He turns away.

DORA: No more.

LEFTY, *their neighbour, enters.*

LEFTY: Got champagne in there, have you? Am I breakin' up a party?

DORA: If you'd come a minute later, you might have got an invite to a funeral.

LEFTY: Not today. Not a big day like today. Your kid said you might need a hand.

DORA: You all done are you, Lefty?

LEFTY: We're not takin' ought, are we? She's havin' all new. Never-never. Just stuck the lot out for junk. Now what's the job?

DORA: I've got to get this bed down. I've promised it Connie's gal, who's getting wed.

LEFTY (*walks round in front of* ARTHUR): Let the dog see the rabbit.

ARTHUR: Roped you in, 'as she?

DORA: You'd think it'd shame him, woun't you?

LEFTY: No.

ARTHUR (*standing*): Leave the bloody thing.

LEFTY: Seen a few years' service.

DORA: It was me mam's before us.

ARTHUR: It ain't goin' wi' us, you know.

DORA: I dream of them new single divans.

LEFTY: All over then is it?

DORA: You must be kiddin'. Bin so long I can't recall what *it* is!

ARTHUR: Suit yourself.

LEFTY: Just bang the rust off and it'll be a doddle.

He hammers the rust off.

ARTHUR: You want to watch 'im near beds.

LEFTY (*applying the spanner*): It's comin'. It's comin'.

ARTHUR *laughs to himself.*

ARTHUR: Should 'ave seen 'im in the war. Them I-tie women.

LEFTY (*holding up the nut, victorious*): There. Done. (*To* ARTHUR:) My war's finished. (*To* DORA:) I waved the white flag years ago.

ELSIE (*off*): Where you hidin'?

ARTHUR: Some war for some buggers.

DORA: You should tell her.

LEFTY: I've tried to.

ARTHUR: Say no more. Nod's as good as a wink to a blind man.

*He turns away to continue his betting,
and does not notice the arrival of*
ELSIE. LEFTY *gets on to the next
nut.*

ELSIE: I'd know them grunts and groans
anywhere. All noise, and no joy.

DORA: He's doin' all right, Elsie.

ELSIE: He was always a sight too fond of
other folks' bedrooms.

LEFTY: You're goin' back a bit, aren't
you?

DORA: I'm goin' to miss 'im for a hand
around the 'ouse.

ELSIE: He's yours. Do you want him
gift-wrapped? I see you got yours
stuffed. Stick 'im on the balcony to
fright the pigeons? You should 'ave
come out to Clifton wi' us. You'd have
got a garden.

DORA: It's too far for him from work.

ELSIE: Lefty and 'im should move in
together. Then yo' and me could set
ourselves up wi' a bit of quality.

LEFTY *has finished the final nut.*

LEFTY: You are a joker, you are, Elsie.

ELSIE: Don't see yo' laughin'.

LEFTY: Where do want me to stick it,
Dora?

ELSIE: None of your smutty talk here.

LEFTY: What did I say?

ELSIE: I know your games. Took me a
bit of time. But I've learnt 'em.

LEFTY: Don't be daft, woman.

DORA: Leave it here, Frank. Our Jim'll
carry it out.

LEFTY: Right. Back in a jiff. Bit of a
surprise.

ELSIE *watches him go.*

ELSIE: Only surprise he could gi' me
would be if he'd joined the Foreign
Legion. I'd knit him a balaclava.

DORA: You don't mean that.

ELSIE: Where's me needles?

DORA: Time to start afresh. Wipe the
slate clean.

ELSIE: I'll wipe him clean. And the lads
are bloody useless as well.

ARTHUR *lights up.* ELSIE *takes a fag.*
Bless you.

ARTHUR: Last off me you'll scrounge.

ELSIE (*taking no notice*): First sign of
work and our Doug's off on his bike
to Skeggie, wi' that tart.

DORA *lights one of her own
cigarettes.*

DORA: They goin' steady, are they?

ELSIE: Better not be. Her from up St.
Anne's Road. Common as muck up
there.

Silence.

Is it underfloor heating in the flat?

DORA: Not in the bedroom.

ELSIE: No, well, that's what you've got
Prince Charming for. Did you order
that wall-to-wall carpeting?

DORA: Not yet.

ELSIE: When you lay it, leave a couple
of inches round the edges. It grows
with the heat. That woman wi' the
carbuncle goes in the Dog and Bear
she were tellin' me.

JIM *enters, followed by his sister,*
JACKIE, *and* ELSIE*'s son,* PETE.

DORA (*to* JIM): What did they say?

JIM: They're goin' to be a bit late,
that's all.

DORA: How late?

JIM: About an hour. Don't worry, Mam.
They'll come. Half the town's on the
move. Bound to be a bit chaotic.

PETE: That goes for our van as well,
Mam.

ELSIE: Bloody Co-op. I'd never bloody
shop wi' them if I had cash, I'd tell
you.

DORA: All this hanging about. Falling over each other.

JIM: Gi' us a hand, Pete.

PETE: Right.

They clear some space by dismantling the bed.

JACKIE: Dad bein' his normal helpful self, is he?

DORA: What do you think?

ELSIE: Seen your dad?

PETE: No.

DORA: That's the first time that bed's been in bits since the bomb fell on Mafeking Street, and the vibrations broke it.

JIM: Sure it was the bomb, Mam?

DORA: What does that mean?

JIM: Well, we know how you Nottingham gals looked after our American allies.

ELSIE: I'd slap him down, I would.

DORA: I wasn't like that.

ELSIE: Straight as a dye she was, your mam.

JACKIE: You've upset her.

JIM: I was only kiddin'.

ELSIE: Your mam kept herself for him.

JIM: More's the pity.

DORA: I don't know why he says things like that.

ELSIE: No respect.

JACKIE: It's cos he's daft.

JIM: You should know.

DORA: Don't start you two. Not today. Please.

JIM: It was only a joke, Mam.

LEFTY enters, carrying an 8mm movie camera.

LEFTY: Da-da-dada-dada! OK, lovely ladies. Big smile for Lefty. Here's your chance to make it to Hollywood.

ELSIE: Don't they show you up, eh? Like bloody kids with their toys.

LEFTY: Fabulous. Todd AO. Look at this, boys.

JIM: What is it? 8mm?

LEFTY: Ye'. And it's got zoom and everything.

JIM: Can I have a look?

LEFTY: Sorry, mate. Skilled technician stuff, this.

ELSIE: What you doin' with it, then?

JACKIE: You goin' to film all of us?

LEFTY: That's the idea.

JACKIE: Great.

She bumps into her dad.

ARTHUR: What's goin' on here? Party? Come in here for a bit of piece and quiet.

LEFTY: Tell him he can do his Jimmy Cagney.

PETE: You can't film in here, Dad.

LEFTY: I know that. I thought I'd do us all on the street, waitin' for the van to come.

DORA: I hope you've got a lot of film, then.

JIM: Come on, Mam. Don't worry. It'll turn up.

ARTHUR: Where yo' get that?

LEFTY (*mouthing*): Dixons.

ARTHUR: How much?

LEFTY reluctantly holds up four fingers.

ARTHUR (*laughing*): What? Forty quid?

ELSIE: Bloody hell. They must have wet themselves when they saw you come through the door.

ARTHUR: I could have got you a sixth off at Boots.

LEFTY: Tell him they don't sell these at Boots. Not with zoom. Tell him.

JIM: Why bother?

ELSIE: Last time you wander off wi' your wages. I'm not doin' up the new house on my money alone.

LEFTY: All right. All right.

ARTHUR: Could have got you a sixth off.

DORA: Shurrup, Arthur.

LEFTY: We might as well get the use of it, now I've bought it. I mean, we ain't goin' to be here for ever, you know.

ELSIE: Dead smart, seein' as how we're moving in an hour.

LEFTY: I don't mean here. I mean . . . It'll be good for the kids. Someat to remember us by.

ELSIE: Cheerful sod. He's tryin' to bury me now.

ARTHUR: Forty quid. Has it got sound?

JIM: Look, you've all got an hour. Go for a last drink down the Dale, and then have your picture took.

DORA: Well, we can't stay here for sure. In the worst room of the house.

JACKIE: I'm goin' round Mrs Henshaw's. To get done up a bit.

She exits.

ELSIE: Well, I'm for the Dale. But I'm not havin' this film mallarky. I'm takin' no memories wi' me.

She exits.

LEFTY: I thought it were a good idea.

DORA: It is a good idea. Bring 'im wi' you.

LEFTY: Try and keep him away.

DORA: I'll have a word wi' her.

She stands for a moment, before she leaves.

Ta-ra.

She goes.

ARTHUR: Well shut of 'em. Yap yap yap all the time. Get on your bloody nerves.

JIM: If you leave us the camera, we'll take you all comin' out of the pub. Gi' 'em someat to laugh at when they see it.

LEFTY: I'd better keep it wi' me.

JIM: You should be in some of them.

PETE: I'll look after it, Dad.

LEFTY: All right.

ARTHUR: Five minutes. Peace and quiet.

JIM: Let's shift this lot.

They carry out the bed in sections.

LEFTY (*to* ARTHUR): Come on, corporal. Marching orders.

ARTHUR: What yo' on? Half an hour. Starters orders. Come on.

LEFTY (*hands him a copy of the* Daily Mirror. ARTHUR *studies form*): Pointless, Arthur. Only done it for the exercise. (*He taps him on the arm.*) No bookies, Arthur! Knocked it down. He's half way over to bloody Leicester now. Opened a new shop.

ARTHUR: Ye', them's what I picked.

LEFTY (*grinning*): Fancy that.

ARTHUR: Half a dollar?

LEFTY: For Christ's sake, Arthur! No bookies! We can't get no bet on!

ARTHUR *winks, and mimes a telephone.*

LEFTY: Speak to me, Arthur. I'm not deaf.

The boys return for the last section.

JIM: I was conceived on this bed.

PETE: Bit late now to throw it out. Damage's done.

ARTHUR *has found a piece of paper and holds it up. The boys watch him.*

LEFTY: What is it? What's the game?

ARTHUR: Bookie's new number. He knows we're good for it. I'll gi' him a blow.

LEFTY *takes the paper to check the number.*

LEFTY (*to himself*): You'll gi' him a blow. I like that.

ARTHUR: You get the drinks in; I'll get the bet on.

LEFTY: If you say so, Arthur.

ARTHUR *turns and notices his son.*

ARTHUR: Listening at keyholes for your mam are you?

JIM: Come on. Let's go and work out some shots.

JIM *and* PETE *exit.*

ARTHUR: To work. Don't want to hang around here. It's like a bleddy cemetery.

LEFTY: You're crazy, Arthur.

ARTHUR (*turning*): Who's got the bookie's number?

LEFTY *holds it up.*

ARTHUR: You ring him, then. My round, anyroad. Save time that way round.

He exits.

LEFTY (*laughing*): Won't admit there's ought wrong wi' you, will you? You don't change.

He stands for a moment in the empty room before leaving.

Scene Two

A street. Rain. Distant thunder.
   JIM, *head-bare, wearing a white, short mac, stares out, triumphant.* CATHY, *a well-dressed, attractive girl, follows, carrying a colourful umbrella.* PETE, *in duffle-coat, brings up the rear.* CATHY *tries to hold the umbrella over* JIM. *He does not notice. They all stare out.*

JIM (*suddenly*): DAVID!

He throws his arms up in celebration. CATHY *averts disaster with the umbrella. Silence.*

PETE: He's not in.

JIM: Oh, yes, he is. His genius is still trapped in them thin walls.

CATHY *takes* JIM*'s hand.*

CATHY: You'd think they'd put up a plaque, wouldn't you?

JIM: A prophet in his own land.

PETE: They'll knock it down soon, and put up a block of flats.

CATHY: Like they did with your house, Jim.

PETE: Ye', where they goin' to put your plaque, Jim?

JIM: Is that meant to be some sort of joke?

CATHY (*quickly*): The garden could do with a bit of a tidy-up.

JIM: Let it grow wild, full of 'pansies, red geraniums and mignonettes'.

PETE: What's a mignonette when it's at home?

JIM: What the fuck does it matter what it is?

CATHY: But they shouldn't let those weeds take over his lawn.

JIM: LAWN? They might have lawns where yo' come from, but this in't Wollaton. This is where the people live. They don't have lawns here. They have jungles, jungles of life.

PETE: You're comin' it a bit strong, aren't you?

JIM: What's the matter with you two? This is Lawrence's house, the house of *Sons & Lovers.* His mam died here, his mam who shared his urge for freedom, but who stayed locked up wi' only a coarse, drunken demon for a jailor. Can't you imagine what it was like in there? I bloody well can.

He walks off a distance.

PETE: You'll get used to it.

CATHY: He feels very deeply.

PETE: My shoes let in water.

CATHY *crosses to him and tries to cover him with the umbrella.*

CATHY: You'll catch pneumonia.

JIM: He caught TB, but it didn't stop him writing.

CATHY: And it won't stop you, either.

He looks at her.

JIM: Cathy, we have to fight to free ourselves. To break through. That's what Lawrence is all about. Making the great escape. (*Pause.*) Making love.

CATHY (*smiling*): You're so wild, Jim.

JIM (*laughing*): What's the matter? Aren't they like this at your tennis club?

CATHY: No. Invite me to meet your family, Jim.

JIM: Gi' 'em time to get properly settled in.

CATHY: You're not ashamed, are you?

JIM: Of what?

She moves to kiss him, lightly. They embrace.

PETE: What's goin' on? I'm turnin' into a goldfish here.

JIM (*suddenly*): Let's go inside.

PETE: Wha'?

JIM: There might be someat left from his days. Just to stand in his bedroom. We can't miss out on this.

CATHY: Somebody's lookin' through the curtains.

They all turn quickly upstage.

JIM (*whispering*): Go on, Pete. Go and ask 'em.

PETE: What? You dragged us here. It's nought to do wi' me.

JIM: Did I force you? Did I twist your arm?

PETE (*reluctantly*): I'm not sayin' it in't interesting, Jim. But I mean, come

on, enough's enough.

JIM: That's it then, is it? That's what your friendship's worth, is it?

CATHY: If he doesn't want to go —

JIM: Hang on. I just want to get this straight. Being my blood brother means nothing to you, right?

CATHY: Blood brothers?

PETE: What you goin' on about that for? We were kids then. Polythene tee-pee and I-Spy feathers.

JIM: Go ahead, mock. That's all you ever do. I just want to say one thing. No matter how daft it seems now, that mingling of blood forms a sacred bond and there's no way I'd ever break it.

PETE: I don't even remember him cutting his finger. I cut mine. It went septic.

JIM: Last chance.

Silence.

Fine. I just want you to know that my bond still stands, even though you've broken yours.

Silence.

CATHY: Is that it, then?

JIM: You go.

CATHY: I wouldn't know what to say.

JIM: I'll tell you.

CATHY: I still wouldn't be able to say it.

JIM: Listen, you dream of being an actress don't you? So, do your Hayley Mills. Hayley Mills would just walk straight up and bang on the door.

CATHY: You hate Hayley Mills.

JIM: What the fuck has that got to do with it?

CATHY: It's embarrassing.

PETE: Why don't you go?

JIM: Because.

PETE: Because what?

JIM: Right. You have 'something to expiate. A pettiness.'

He turns and walks off.

PETE: The bus stop's the other way.

JIM: Fuck you.

He goes. Silence.

CATHY: Has he gone?

PETE: No. He's hiding behind the hedge, like he always does.

Silence.

CATHY: Should I go and ask them?

PETE: He doesn't really want to go in, anyway.

Silence.

CATHY: Did your finger really go septic?

PETE: It was only a game. A kids' game.

They follow JIM *off.*

Scene Three

ELSIE*'s garden. A rectangular patch of green 'lawn'. Downstage,* LEFTY *is measuring up a plank, propped against* DOUG*'s motorbike. He is whistling 'We'll meet again'.* PETE *enters, carrying a small bag of tools.*

LEFTY: Where were they?

PETE: She'd stuck 'em in the loft.

LEFTY: Carried these to some jobs in me time. Good saw. Clean your teeth twice a day, last you a lifetime, eh?

PETE: Ye'.

LEFTY: Din't find me left-handed screwdriver?

PETE: No, Dad.

LEFTY: They used to send us apprentices out for them. Rubber hammer. Spotted paint for a rocking-horse.

PETE: Ye'.

LEFTY: Hold us that end.

He props the other end on the bike, and begins to saw.

PETE: Doug's going to love you for that.

LEFTY: It's bloody broke, anyway. (*He saws.*) Not your cup of tea this, is it?

PETE: It's all right.

LEFTY: You do well to be a white collar.

PETE: Just filing at present.

LEFTY: You have a future though. I were good at this. End up mowing bloody lawns for the council. Yesterday, doing colliery banks. Big, electric mowers. You rope 'em round yourself, and up to your mate at the top, to stop it all toppling over. Nearly sheer banks, you see.

He saws through the wood. PETE *is bored.*

Monday'll be all right. Clipping hedges.

PETE: You know Mam's telling the neighbours you're a landscape gardener.

LEFTY (*embarrassed*): Why does she do that, do you think?

PETE: She's out to embarrass you.

LEFTY: No. It's just her little joke, innit? Makes no odds. I don't know any of 'em, anyway.

He stares at the end of the plank.

Allers cut on the outside of the line. You can allers sand down to a snug fit.

ELSIE *enters.*

ELSIE: What you two up to?

LEFTY: Just thought we'd get started on them fitted wardrobes.

ELSIE: I've told you, I'm having the professionals in.

LEFTY: Come on. I used to do this stuff all the time, when I had me business.

ELSIE: Used to. Aye. Used to is right.

There's a lot of things you used to do you're not going to do in this house.

LEFTY: Let up, woman.

ELSIE: Don't go calling me woman.

LEFTY: Oh, sod it.

LEFTY *moves off.*

ELSIE: Where you slopin' off to?

LEFTY: Goin' to see a man about a dog.

ELSIE: Very funny.

LEFTY (*turning*): Come on, get your hat and coat on. It's Saturday night.

ELSIE: You're not throwing any more of your money over that counter.

PETE *sits on the bike, trying not to pay attention.*

LEFTY (*relenting*): What do you want of me, Elsie? (*Silence.*) All right, I'll stay in. Keep you company. (*Softly, aware of* PETE:) Maybe we might have a house-warming.

ELSIE: We've been here three bleddy month.

LEFTY: Bit of heat built up then, an't there?

ELSIE: What yo' leerin' at?

LEFTY: Yo'.

ELSIE: You're hopin', aren't you?

LEFTY: It's free entertainment, innit?

ELSIE: Don't you be too sure.

LEFTY: We could measure up in the bedroom together, eh?

ELSIE: Honest, Frank, I worry about you. I swear there's someat wrong with you.

LEFTY: There's nought wrong wi' me and I can prove it.

ELSIE: You can't prove you're alive.

LEFTY: Should I drop me trousers? I can still show you and your neighbours a thing or two.

ELSIE: Put it on the mantlepiece, I'll smoke it in the morning.

LEFTY (*suddenly exhausted*): I could fetch you one.

ELSIE (*calling out*): Are you listening to this?

PETE *puts his head down over the handlebars.*

Them days are over, Lefty.

LEFTY: I said they were. I said they were.

Silence. LEFTY *begins to walk across the lawn towards the house.*

ELSIE: Now where?

LEFTY: I have to wash me hands.

ELSIE: Oh, we are gettin' la-de-dah, aren't we? Goin' to the little boy's room.

LEFTY: I mean it. I've got to wash me hands.

ELSIE: Ye', well don't go tramping through to the upstairs. Makin' a mess. Use the kitchen sink.

LEFTY (*angrily*): I'll wash 'em down the lav, if you like.

ELSIE: Ye'. Good idea.

He exits.

PETE: Don't go on at him, Mam.

ELSIE: Bloody good job I 'ad our Doug to stand up for me. You'd have been no use.

PETE *begins to tidy away the tools.*

Little cherub. You'll allers be Mamma's little baby, you know. My little ray of sunshine.

She turns back to survey the garden. The lights slowly fade down under ELSIE*'s speech, leaving her in a solitary spot.* PETE *clears the stage.*

Start out here as soon as Spring comes. Me own lawn. Nice little patio. Swinging chair. Pond. Goldfish. White ones. Don't want to be common. Climbing roses. Creepies. Got to get that hedge to grow. Doug'll have to shift that bloody bike. It'll have me

privet growing through its handlebars
soon. Neighbours'll think we're dead
common wi' a bike stuck out the back.
If he'd just find a decent gal. She's not
coming on my lawn in her high heels.
The grass grows. Why don't the bloody
hedge?

As the light fades on ELSIE, *creep in
a slow spot on* DORA. *Their two
speeches overlap slightly.* ELSIE *exits
at the end of her speech.*

Scene Four

DORA's *flat.*
DORA *perches on a wooden chair,
holding a full length curtain over the
'window'.*

DORA (*hidden*): I had thought of putting
up some lace wi' 'em, then I thought,
no, spoil the view; folk can't see in,
so we might as well get the joy. Good
length. (*She lowers it.*)

Slow light up behind her to include
JIM *and* JACKIE *on the settee. He is
reading* Portrait of the Artist *and she
is getting made-up with the help of
a mirror balanced on her knees.*

Look at that. The whole world mapped
out like patterned carpet. Trent Bridge.
Boots. Lace Market. Won't be long
now, Jackie, will it? You're lucky to
get in wi' Elsie's crew. Top overlooker.
Gets her gals all the best piece-work.
Better than mine. I've been on Y-fronts
for a year. She's havin' it away wi' the
boss, is mine. She's not on her gals'
side, that's for sure. (*She notices*
JACKIE.) We've got a bathroom now
you know. Mirrors. (JACKIE *takes no
notice*.) I'd better hand-sew these.
Could run 'em up at work, but they
go up the wall. I'll run 'em tonight,
when he's out. No. No net up there.
Let the sky in.

*She gathers the curtains up. Slow
light to include* ARTHUR *dozing in
an armchair.*

Oh, it's all looking a picture. (*She sees*
ARTHUR.) 'Cept for him. (*To*
JACKIE:) You're gilding the lily a bit,
aren't you?

JACKIE: Don't worry, Mam.

DORA: I'm not worried. You take your
freedom. I was kept locked up when I
was a kid. First time I got me head,
look what I got.

The doorbell chimes.

Visitors, and I an't even put a comb
through me hair. We in't expectin', are
we?

JIM: I asked Cathy to come round.

DORA: Why didn't you tell us –
Bringin' your gal home?

JIM: You'd only 'ave gone to a lot of
fuss.

DORA: Bet her mam has her hair
brushed, when the bell goes.

JIM: I don't want to make a big thing,
Mam. Let her take us as she finds us.

DORA: No airs and graces.

JIM: That's it.

He exits.

DORA: You can allers bring your fellers
home if you want.

JACKIE: What fellers?

DORA: I'd better wake your dad up.
Can't have folk seeing him sleeping
it off.

JACKIE: Leave him, Mam, 'til I get off.
He'll only have someat to say.

DORA: He's not a pretty sight.

JACKIE: He's no better woke up.

DORA: Oh, God. I've got to wake 'im.
Can't 'ave him snorin'.

She shakes him. CATHY *and* JIM
enter.

JIM: Mam.

Awkward silence.

ARTHUR (*putting his head between his hands*): Man can't get five minutes' peace.

DORA: Hello, duck.

JIM: Cathy,

DORA: How are you, Cathy?

CATHY: I'm fine, thank you.

DORA: Lovely. In't she lovely?

CATHY (*after a pause*): How are you, Mrs Cooper?

DORA: Coming on nicely.

CATHY: New curtains?

DORA: To go with the carpet. (*She looks down.*) It's still got a few inches to grow.

CATHY *looks confused. As she turns to* JIM, DORA *hands* ARTHUR *a shirt.*

JIM: Don't ask me. I only live here.

DORA: Get that on!

CATHY: You've done a lovely job of it.

DORA: Would you care for a bit of salad? I've got a lettuce.

CATHY: No, thank you, honestly.

ARTHUR (*noticing her for the first time*): Who's this?

DORA: Jim's dad. My husband.

JACKIE: You should have left him.

Silence.

CATHY (*smiling*): Mr Cooper.

ARTHUR (*eventually*): How's yer dad? All right is he?

CATHY *nods.*

ARTHUR: He's lucky.

Silence.

DORA: Shuv up, Jackie. Room for both of you to sit down there. It's almost a three seater.

CATHY: Hallo.

JACKIE *grins.* CATHY *and* JIM *sit.*

ARTHUR: Lav free?

DORA: Bathroom. Yes.

ARTHUR *exits.* DORA *smiles at* CATHY.

JACKIE: I'm off before he comes back.

JIM: You know she goes in pubs, Mam.

DORA (*to* JACKIE): You don't, do you?

JIM: Gets Paddies to buy her Pernods.

DORA: Buy her a what?

CATHY: It's a very expensive drink.

DORA: Is it? Is it nice?

JACKIE: He's mekin' it up, Mam. (*To* CATHY:) See you again.

She exits.

DORA: How's your mam and dad, all right?

CATHY: Planning their holidays.

DORA: Somewhere nice, I bet.

CATHY: Tenerife.

DORA: Oh, they say Spain's lovely.

JIM: Where we goin', Mam? Skeggie?

DORA: I don't know. What wi' all those mods tearin' around on their scooters. I'd love to go abroad, I would.

CATHY: These new package trips are almost as cheap when you add it all up.

DORA: You have to fly, though, don't you?

JIM: It's the safest form of transport.

DORA: I lived through the Battle of Britain. Don't talk to me about that.

There is the sound of the lavatory flushing.

CATHY: You can get pills to relax you.

DORA: I'm still takin' 'em for me thyroid. Anyroad, it's just romancin'. He wun't go abroad. He dun't have much faith in foreigners since they lost the war.

ARTHUR *returns.* DORA *watches him like a hawk.*

JIM: Take him to Italy. He can replay his old battles there.

DORA: Would be nice before you kids disappear to the winds. Could get Elsie and her old war-horse. That might tempt him. Hark at me, gabbing away, and I an't even made you a cup of tea.

CATHY: No, thank you.

DORA: You must have a cup of tea.

CATHY: Well, OK, then. Thank you.

DORA: See? I knew you wanted one. Don't stand on ceremony here, you know. Not that politeness in't nice, but it in't as nice as a cup of tea, is it?

CATHY: No.

DORA: Right.

She exits.

CATHY: What shall we do tonight?

JIM: We've got a job on. Mam's not sure the underfloor heating's working, so we have to take off all our clothes and spend the evening lying on the floor.

CATHY: Talking like this in front of your dad — it's weird.

JIM: You love the thought of it, don't you, but you don't like to hear the words.

CATHY: Why did he never learn to lip read?

JIM: He dun't even admit he's deaf. It's us who are deaf and daft, according to 'im.

Silence.

CATHY: Do you really hate him?

JIM: I hate what's he's done to Mam.

Silence.

CATHY: How's the novel?

JIM: I can't write. I try. I just can't. It's all hollow. I thought being an artist made you a doctor in the madhouse. But it don't. I'm just one of the patients like everybody else.

CATHY (*gently*): We'll stay in, if you want, but . . .

JIM: Ye', but. No. But's fine. I just need somebody to talk to.

CATHY: That's why I'm here.

JIM: Ye', but you're not here in the middle of the night, are you?

DORA enters.

DORA: I guessed, no sugar?

CATHY: Thank you.

ARTHUR stands up, and puts his clean shirt on.

DORA: Where you two off, then, tonight?

JIM: We thought we'd stay in and watch the telly.

DORA: Oh, right. (*Pause.*) Well, your dad and me'll pop out for one a bit later.

ARTHUR: Where's me tie?

DORA: God, he's making a quick start. Make you a nice home and you can't wait to get off to your scruff pub. Here y'are. (*She hands him a tie from off the back of the chair.*) He's got two ties, you know. But he only wears his MP one. Military Police. Not the other. He dun't care for politics.

ARTHUR: Knot.

DORA: Come here.

He sits down and she ties it.

JIM: Don't do that, Mam.

DORA: Don't marry a weak man, Cathy. I could have had a guards officer in the war. Scotch bloke, but he was all right.

JIM: Leave him, Mam.

DORA: I can't let him go out looking like he's come through a hedge backwards. What would folk think of me? Look at him. He was a boxer at one time.

JIM: Ye'. He used to box kippers down the fish market.

DORA: He knows he was. In the army. A boxer. Can you believe that?

CATHY: I don't know.

DORA (*tapping* ARTHUR *on the arm*): Weren't you a boxer?

ARTHUR: What?

DORA: You. A boxer. (*She mimes.*)

JIM: Don't bother, Mam. Nobody cares.

DORA: Boxer. Come on. Boxer.

ARTHUR: What? Not tonight. Next Wednesday, Middleweight. Who wants to know?

DORA (*desperately*): No. You. A boxer.

JIM: Don't work yourself up, Mam. Forget him.

ARTHUR: Don't tell me he's interested in boxing. Not him. Bloody ballet dancing, maybe.

DORA: Leave him alone, in front of his gal.

ARTHUR (*laughing*): Nancing about. Here, duck, you tell him to get his hair cut. Don't listen to me. Daren't own him in the bloody street, I tell you.

JIM: Can't breathe in this place for him.

ARTHUR: Here's ninepence. Go and ask 'em for the basin cut.

JIM: Come on. Let's go.

JIM *stands up.*

ARTHUR: What's the fuss? Only joking. Nobody can take a joke.

DORA: He'll be off out in a bit.

JIM: He haunts this place and he in't even bloody dead yet. More's the pity.

DORA: Don't say that.

JIM: Don't say you don't think it.

Silence. JIM *exits.* CATHY *stands.*

ARTHUR: Too bloody touchey by half.

DORA: Give my love to your mother. Maybe we'll get to meet one day.

CATHY: I'm sure she'd like that.

She nods goodbye to ARTHUR.

ARTHUR: I woun't waste your time wi' him. He's out his bloody head like the rest of this family.

CATHY *exits.*

Decent gal. He's done all right there.

ELSIE *stares at him.*

Are you coming out or what? It's no skin off my nose. Just don't muck me about all the time.

DORA: I should have strangled you, when I had the chance.

ARTHUR: Good to see you smiling for a change. You know where I am, when you make your mind up.

He turns to go.

Blackout.

Scene Five

ELSIE*'s garden.*
Sound of lawnmower. Lights. LEFTY *kneels to examine it.*

LEFTY: Should be straight lines. Why aren't you straight? Must be someat wrong wi' the bloody thing.

ELSIE *enters.*

ELSIE: If you can make a mess of our bloody lawn how come you can't go back to work, and do it for money? Go and tell that daft sod of a doctor you're running up and down all day wi' your mower.

LEFTY: I've told him. I've told him to send me back.

ELSIE: Bet you have. Bet you begged 'im on your bended knees. Bloody don't know what's wrong wi' you. I could tell 'im. Bloody useless, that's what's wrong wi' you.

LEFTY: Just the move made me nervy, he says. Be all right.

ELSIE: That was nine months ago. What you havin', a baby?

LEFTY: Takes time to adjust to the change.

ELSIE: Be tellin' me you're going through the change of life, now. All hot flushes. It's amazin', innit, that whatever's up wi' you, don't stop you being on heat all the time. Pity you an't got change to jaggle in your pocket for your old fancy women.

LEFTY: You always make me out I'm in the black, Elsie. It's allers me. I allers have to pay for it.

ELSIE: Ye', well you're going to have to now. We've got commitments on what wi' holidays an' all. I need you workin' and your packet. So, it's a sellers' market now. You're on my street now, sunshine. You can't go walkin' up and down here, waving at women in windows. So you'd better get back to work, double quick. Them who don't pay, can't play.

LEFTY: You shun't be like that, Elsie.

ELSIE: Who made me? You sit and ponder on life wi' out your slap and tickle. That'll gi' you some incentive to make money that will.

She exits. LEFTY *stands.*

Scene Six

The cinema.
As lights fade on LEFTY.

FILM COMMENTARY: And here, on this tranquil Mediterranean beach, our two friends, Hilary and Clara, can at last unwind from the pressures of the modern world. As they leave their clothes behind them, they enter into their naturist paradise. The sea laps gently at their feet. Now there's all the time in the world for sun worship and the most complete of all tans.

Flickering cinema projection light.
CATHY, JIM *and* PETE *can be dimly seen.*

Time to swim, and to engage in other open air pursuits. Here they are, joining in the fun of beach badminton with some German naturists.

PETE (*laughing*): Do you think the cameraman's naked, as well?

JIM: I think the whole thing's obscene. All this pretending you can have a free world without a trace of sensuality whilst all the time selling your film on tits and bums to the raincoat brigade.

CATHY: You don't think they're being honest?

JIM: Look, anybody could make a more honest film than this.

PETE: Says who?

JIM: Says me. I could do better than that any day.

PETE: Oh ye'?

FILM COMMENTARY: The evening brings party time. A time for dressing up. A hat or perhaps a necklace of shells. And on with the dancing.

JIM: Listen, if you want to show a film about the natural life, show them making love in the sand.

CATHY: You couldn't do that.

JIM (*enthusiastically*): We could. Just a short film. But one that really affected something. Like I want my writing to do. We could use your dad's eight mill. . . .

PETE: He'll love that.

FILM COMMENTARY: Here, in freedom, the whole family can play together.

JIM (*passionately*): Maybe that was what's been wrong. Why I coun't write me novel. It's not a novel, it's a film script. Christ, that's what Lawrence would be doing if he was here now — he'd be making movies about sex.

FILM COMMENTARY: There can be nobody, no body, that can cause shame. Here, from the youngest baby, to his mother and father, his grandparents, and even his great grandparents.

PETE *is cringing in his seat.*

PETE: God, if our mam starts strippin' off in Rimini, I'm on the first plane back.

JIM: We can't leave it to this shit to speak the truth. We could make a short film, that would be truly Lawrentian. A film that will hit people with the truth of their own sexual natures.

PETE: What would you know about that?

JIM: What?

PETE: Nothing.

FILM COMMENTARY: In this film, we have given you only the briefest glimpse of a world where you may be naked as nature intended. But it may indicate that our cause is a just and reasonable one. Please, help us with our fight for the freedom to be free.

Music. Cinema intermission lights up. JIM *leans forward absorbed in thought. Silence.*

CATHY (*to* PETE): Why don't you go outside and see if your girlfriend's there?

PETE (*nervous*): She said half seven or not at all. She has sometimes to read books . . . er . . . *The Bible* . . . to her sick great grandmother.

CATHY: What's the matter with her?

PETE: Cancer.

CATHY: Oh dear. (*Pause.*) Is she nice?

PETE: Don't know. Never met her.

CATHY: No, I mean your girl.

PETE: All right. Is this film subtitled or dubbed? I can't stand it when they talk and it's not with their own lips.

JIM: Got it. We'll film on location in Italy. The two lovers, me and Cathy,

meet on holiday. Black and white at first. Heightens their loneliness and despair. Then they fall in love, make love, and somehow, the whole film changes, it bursts into colour, as they break through from the madness of the world they're been trapped in.

The lights begin to dim. Italian music from 8½.

JIM: Great idea. Come on, Fellini. Show us the way. These Europeans are so much freer in these things. It's a great idea, don't you think?

CATHY: I suppose so.

JIM: I can see it now. Love lies in the sand.

Scene Seven

The beach at Rimini.
    As the music builds the three of them step forward and begin to strip down to beach wear. CATHY *lies down and* JIM *kneels over her to apply sun tan lotion.*
    Downstage, LEFTY, *stripped to the waist, hankie over head, stands focussing the camera.*
    Upstage, ELSIE *and* DORIS, *in their summer outfits, sit at a patio table.* ARTHUR *stands, trousers rolled up, barefoot. He sports a cheap seaside hat, and a short-sleeved shirt.* JACKIE *stands with her bikini and a transistor radio.*
    As the light fills out to cover the stage in brilliant sunshine, no one moves as they all stare towards LEFTY.
    Music ends. Silence.
    Eventually:

ARTHUR (*in fine voice*):
    O sole mio,
    Sta in fronte a te,
    O sole mio
    Sta in fronte a te.

DORA: Shh!

JIM (*softly*): It's now or never,
    My love won't wait.

ELSIE *sighs.*

LEFTY: Just hold on. Don't move. This is going to be a good one.

CATHY *and* JIM *look as though they are going to burst out laughing.*

CATHY: What's he doing?

JIM: Fuck knows.

PETE: I don't think me dad's quite grasped the technique.

LEFTY: O.K. That's it. Relax.

DORA: Thank God. I was getting hot flushes holding me breath like that.

LEFTY: Look top notch that will.

ARTHUR: That it?

ELSIE: Just a sec. What you got us standing here for like stuffed dummies? It's a bloody movie camera, innit? A movie camera!

LEFTY: Ye', well . . .

ELSIE: The whole bloody point is that we move, innit? I mean, correct me if I'm wrong, but in't that the bleedin' point?

LEFTY (*clearly confused*): Ye' but it looked good.

ELSIE: Might as well have had a bleedin' snapshot.

LEFTY: Don't go on, woman.

ELSIE: Don't call me woman.

DORA: It dun't matter, Elsie.

ELSIE: Course it matters. Let's get somebody who can use the bloody thing. Get the value out of it.

LEFTY: It's ever so technical. Nobody else can do it.

ELSIE: Pete!

JIM: Your master's voice.

PETE: Why do they always have to drag us into it?

ELSIE: You can use this, can't you?

PETE (*wearily*): Ye'.

LEFTY: No, he can't. I mean, he dun't know how to use the zoom for example. Do you?

ELSIE: Gi' it to him. Let's have someat to show the neighbours we've actually been here.

JIM *applies the lotion to* CATHY.

CATHY: Oh, this is heaven.

JIM: The new religion. The worship of the purely sensual. You'll have to confess this. Ten Ave Marias.

CATHY: Hail Mary's.

PETE: Just sit round the table, and eat your ice cream.

DORA: Grand, in't it?

ELSIE: You can't beat the I'ties when it comes to ice cream.

DORA: They say Devon ice cream is very nice.

ELSIE: Clotted.

They sit down. LEFTY *wipes his face with the handkerchief.*

LEFTY (*to* ARTHUR): Bit hot in't it?

ARTHUR: Course you can. (*He takes him to one side and hands him a bottle.*) Aperitifo. Gi' you an appetite.

LEFTY: Not with the pills, Arthur. Doctor. You know.

ARTHUR: Horse piss. Dear at half the price. Get it down you.

LEFTY *begins to drink.* ARTHUR *notices* JACKIE *as she passes him on her way down to join* CATHY *and* JIM.

Just wearing a couple of hankies. One sneeze and away.

DORA (*noticing*): He never leaves her be.

ELSIE: Where she been all day then?

DORA: I think she's found some friends.

ELSIE: They can have too much freedom, you know.

DORA: No, they can't.

JACKIE *lays out her towel.*

JIM: You want to be careful with these Italian mods.

JACKIE: It's them who needs to be careful.

She switches on her transistor which is playing an Italian version of the Beatles.

JIM: Turn it down.

JACKIE: Lord and master.

She turns it down and lies back. PETE *is now ready with the camera.*

ELSIE: So what do you want us to do?

PETE: Nothing.

ELSIE: He's as daft as his dad.

PETE: Just smile. Talk to each other.

LEFTY *turns back with interest.*

ELSIE: I'm not talking to him.

PETE: Look, you don't have to say ought anyway. It dun't pick up sound. Just mouth things, and wave your arms around like the Italians.

JIM *turns to watch them, as the two women begin an elaborate mime.* ARTHUR *leads* LEFTY *away down stage.*

ARTHUR: Leave the women to it, shall we?

LEFTY: What?

ARTHUR (*laughing*): On guard duty, are you? Scared they'll get their bums pinched? Well, you should know about the native customs. Come on. We've got a bottle to finish.

They sit and LEFTY *sets to drinking.*

JIM (*in despair*): Look at 'em. Desperately trying to be happy. It's like living in a madhouse.

CATHY *reaches out to him.*

JIM (*quietly*): You're killing me. I want to make love to you. Sorry. Sorry to mention it.

CATHY: If we could just become engaged.

JIM: You really want to put the chains on wi' the ring? I don't believe in that.

He gets up and crosses to PETE. LEFTY *is knocking the drink back fast.*

ARTHUR: Bloody I-ties. Got to 'and it to 'em. They know which side their spaghetti's buttered, turning a battle field into a seaside town.

LEFTY: Was we here, Arthur? Them ruins — did we do that, or was it the Romans?

JACKIE *turns over.*

JACKIE: Go on. Let him.

CATHY: I thought you were asleep.

JACKIE: Just 'cos I lie on me back don't mean I'm asleep.

CATHY: You listen to your brother too much.

JACKIE: I do more than that.

CATHY: What does that mean?

JACKIE (*laughing*): It's no big thing. Believe me.

She closes her eyes.

PETE: OK, Mam. Finished.

ELSIE: Thank God for that.

JIM (*to* PETE): I've cracked the next section.

PETE: Great.

They turn back towards CATHY. *The two women settle back for a siesta.*

JIM: We can use some of that film of them.

PETE: What for?

JIM: It in't just enough to show the lovers. You have to see how they might turn out if they don't break through. We'll just keep cutting away now and again to the parents.

ARTHUR: No point trying to get a bet on round here. I-tie horses are the same as their tanks — they only run backwards! (*He laughs.*) We saw 'em, din't we, crashing through them back streets.

LEFTY: Was it round here? It dun't look like I pictured it.

JIM: We just want some free shots of the lovers. Just looking into each others eyes. Then we'll do some individual shots.

He notices she is distressed

(*Kneeling:*) Are you all right?

CATHY: I don't want us to end up like them.

He embraces her. PETE *is a little unsure whether to film or not, and hovers around.*

ARTHUR (*noticing the women sleeping*): Dropping like flies round here.

LEFTY: Is this the front then, Arthur?

ARTHUR: Siesta. Soldiers laying down their arms to siesta. What did they know about war?

LEFTY: Siesta. Time for bed. Get away from the front. Through the back-streets. Find the gals.

JIM: Just take us above the waist.

PETE: Right.

LEFTY *becomes drunkenly transfixed by the embracing couple.*

ARTHUR: All this mother Mary stuff. La Madonna. Mama mia. You don't win wars worshipping women.

LEFTY: Ye', find the girl. The mother. I'd know her if I saw her. Gi' me some pleasure. All them dead. Mates. Oh, the sweat on her neck. Black hair down her back.

ARTHUR: Don't get me wrong. Nobody respects my missis, *mia moglie,* more than me. Broke the mould when he made her. Had me family, did me duty. No idle taking me pleasure. Not wi' her.

LEFTY: Them brown eyes looking at me. Oh, me lovely.

ARTHUR: Well, you don't get to be an M.P. without control. Din't let you in, did they? (*He laughs.*) Latin blood in you and no mistake. Good job I was looking after you, or you'd have come back wi' someat worse than your demob suit.

LEFTY: I turn away from her look. She dun't say ought. The walls could do wi' a lick of paint.

ARTHUR: Don't pretend you're not listening. Think you are bloody ashamed. Shit hole of a brothel that was. All them tarts like leeches all over you. Puttane! Puttane!

LEFTY: A kid in a cot in the corner.

ARTHUR (*laughing*): Your bloody face when I kicked my way through that door. Lance Corporal stripes on me arm. 'You lad, name, rank and number? Out. On the double. Hand on me holster. No fucking around.'

LEFTY: She knelt down, Arthur. I thought she were going to pray. Undid me. I coun't credit it.

ARTHUR: 'Glasshouse for you, sunshine.' Oh, you were multo vino weeping, the puttane weeping, whole bloody cathouse weeping. 'Out of Bounds.' Your face. Thought I'd locked you up and thrown away the key.

LEFTY: Oh, she were lovely. She looked up at me. Her hand down there, wi' me, the victor, chocolate and lire in me breast pocket. Breast.

ARTHUR: Mind yo', you were a bit bloody quieter in the morning. All thank you, then. Well, that's what mates are for.

He lies back.

LEFTY: No, my love, it in't right you on your knees. Bed. Lift her up. Lay her open on the bed. Take me boots off? 'No, leave your boots on, man, or the kids'll have 'em.' Who paid? Somebody along the line maybe,

maybe I passed me money along the line. Lie down. Blanket. No sign of blood, long time past, who can tell what squaddy that was. I mutter someat, she dun't understand, cover up the slowness of comin', stammer someat, maybe money, chocolate, gi' it to the kid in the cot shaking his cot looking at me and his mammy, what can *I* gi', and she mumbling mmaa soft sounds as maybe love is maybe it is her eyes open mmmaaa mmmmaaa and the kid takin' up his mam's cry. Mamma. Mamma. Come on, kid. Close your eyes. Mamma. Banging. Banging at the door. Somebody kicking at the door. Can I stay here? Why don't you leave me here? I've paid me dues. I've killed. Leave me. If you look at me, I come alive. Kicking. Mamma! Lefty! Close me eyes. See him disappear Mamma no one can see me now stay here Lefty!

He is crying. Sound of scooters approaching. He looks up frightened.

Excuse me. I have to go home now. Me mam's calling me in for tea.

He rises unsteadily and exits. Piercing sound of a scooter horn. ELSIE and DORA begin to stir. JACKIE rises.

PETE: Off for a little stroll are you?

JACKIE: These legs aren't made for walking on. I don't want to wear them down.

PETE: She thinks she's Mae West.

JIM: Let's get on with it. Relax, Cathy. It's not a Hayley Mills number. She's a woman who's broken through. Monica Vitti. Let the sand know the difference.

He kisses her. ARTHUR sits up, and watches them. JACKIE passes her mother and ELSIE.

ELSIE: Where you knickin' off to?

JACKIE: Just goin' for a ride, that's all.

ELSIE: Get away wi' blue murder.

DORA: Hadn't you better put someat on?

JACKIE: What?

DORA (*tentatively*): Crash helmet? Dress?

JACKIE: Shan't be long.

She exits.

ELSIE: Daft as a brush you are.

DORA: These chairs'd look nice on your patio.

ELSIE: They would, woun't they? They'd stand the weather. Them swing efforts'll be soppin' wet all the time.

DORA: They sell 'em at the Co-op.

ELSIE: Are they dear?

DORA: I din't bother looking.

ARTHUR passes the film-makers on his way to his wife.

ARTHUR: Men died on these beaches, so you could shame us.

He staggers past them.

JIM: Shoot the bugger.

PETE: Yer what?

JIM: Film him.

PETE: O.K., boss.

He films him. ARTHUR sits down at the table.

ARTHUR: Dinner time.

DORA: We're not at home now, you know. Just click your fingers and away we go.

ELSIE: Might get one of them dishy waiters running over. Ever so obliging they are.

DORA: Elsie.

ELSIE: Could oblige me. Picture it. Young shoulders on your clean sheets. Smart little parting down the middle. Look so nice and neat on the pillow.

DORA: It's the hot weather giving you a turn, duck?

ARTHUR: E pronto!

DORA: Shurrup! Showing us up.

ELSIE (*suddenly*): Eh, where's Lefty? He's gone and lost the poor sod! Why coun't he keep an eye on his mate? He knows he's poorly. Where the bloody hell is he?

DORA: It's all right. (*To* ARTHUR:) Where's Lefty?

ARTHUR: Ready when you are. Just say the word.

ELSIE (*beginning to panic*): He'll never find his way back. Not in a strange place. He hardly recognises his own house as it is.

DORA (*desperately*): Where's Lefty?

ARTHUR: Pasta. Lasagna. Vermicelli. Ought. Gracias.

DORA (*shaking him*): Lefty!

ARTHUR: I'm easy. Multo vino.

ELSIE: He's probably got him drunk as well. The doctor said with them pills. He'll be out his bloody 'ead with panic, Dora.

DORA: We'll get the police.

ELSIE: We dun't even talk the language.

DORA (*indicating* ARTHUR): He does!

ELSIE: Ye', but he dun't talk ours. Help me.

DORA: Jim! Pete!

JIM: What is it? We're busy.

DORA: Get here.

JIM: Sod it!

The children wander over.

ARTHUR: Vino locale da tavola. Cheap but good.

ELSIE: He's lost wi'out me. I should never have let him just wander off.

DORA: Don't go blamin' yourself.

ELSIE: I'm a bastard, I am. I really am.

PETE: What's the matter?

DORA: Have you seen your dad?

PETE: Well, he's over . . . Oh Christ!

ELSIE: Do someat. Be bloody useful for once. He's your dad.

PETE: He can't have gone far. You cover the front, Jim. I'll track up these backstreets.

JIM: Right.

The lads run off.

ARTHUR: Dinner! Shootin' off all over the shop.

DORA: Shurrup. Do you speak Italian?

CATHY: French.

DORA: That's no good.

ELSIE: Nobody ever thinks about the poor sod. I should have pinned a label on him, with the hotel's name on it, so somebody found him, they could bring him back. Reward.

CATHY: They'll find him.

ELSIE: Just when you begin to enjoy yourself. It was me talking about them young I-ties like that. God heard me. He's punishing me.

DORA: God's got better things to do than that. It's nobody's fault.

Silence.

ELSIE: Where's his camera?

CATHY: I'll get it.

She goes forward to pick it up.

ELSIE: I pray he's all right. I coun't live wi' meself.

ARTHUR: Multo vino. Pronto.

DORA: I could kill you, you bastard.

Blackout.

Scene Eight

ELSIE's *garden.*
Christmas music.
A cold, December day. Upstage, the
patio table and chairs are lying around as
though just unwrapped from the card-
board Co-op boxes that surround them.
As the light slowly comes up, LEFTY *sits*
on the motorbike, rocking to and fro. He
grips a copy of the Daily Mirror.

LEFTY: All bunched together. All
bunched together. Lefty on the inside,
looking for an inch of space to make a
break. There's a gap. The Nottingham
lad gi's her a bit of stick, and they're
through. He's on a . . . black horse . . .
a black mare . . . Yellow stripe.
Coming through. Coming on like a
dream. Couple of furlongs. Pacing
beautiful. Two, three, four lengths
ahead now. Comin' up to the flag.
She's coming. She's comin' home.

He sighs, and begins to check his
paper. Noise from within the house.

(*Climbing off.*) Black mare. Yellow
stripe.

PETE *and* JIM *appear carrying a*
large box. As they enter –

PETE: I've got the money for the editor.

JIM: Great.

PETE: Mind you, it's only a hand-wind
on.

They notice LEFTY.

LEFTY (*grinning*): Brrrmmmm!
Brrrrmmmm! Nice bike.
(*He shivers:*) Brrr. Brrr. Catch cold.

He covers the bike in its wrap.

JIM: Where?

PETE: Down there. By the bike.

JIM: Weighs a ton.

LEFTY: Boxing Day. That's why they
call it Boxing Day. 'Cos of the boxes.
Get it?

PETE: Got it, Dad.

They place the box down, and begin
to open it.

LEFTY: Black. Yellow stripe.

He studies his newspaper.

JIM: How you managed to con me into
doing this? It's your brother's responsibility, not mine.

PETE: Ye', well, Doug's got enough on
his plate.

JIM: 'As he told your mam yet? She
won't be pleased when she hears
there's a wedding.

PETE: 'As he 'ell? But when she finds out
why, she'll go up the bloody wall.

LEFTY: Princess Delilah.

They look at him.

That's my present, innit?

PETE: I woun't get too excited, Dad.

JIM *consults his diagram.*

JIM: They should all be numbered.
A1.B2.

PETE: Ye', well, they're not.

JIM: Does he want to marry her?

PETE: Have you seen her brothers? No,
maybe he wants to. I don't know.

DORA *and* ELSIE *enter.* ELSIE
carries a tray with a glass of water and
pills on it.

ELSIE: You boys OK?

PETE: Fine, Mam.

LEFTY: Fine.

She starts arranging the chairs.

ELSIE: See, they'll fit nice, won't they?

DORA: They'll look lovely.

LEFTY *wanders over to see what they*
are doing.

ELSIE: Thank you, Lefty.

LEFTY: For what?

ELSIE: For these. It's the best Christmas
present you've ever bought me.

LEFTY (*confused*): Are they?

ELSIE: Bless you.

She kisses him.

LEFTY: S'all right.

He wanders back to the boys.

PETE: Gi's a hand, shift this bike round.

JIM: Sure.

PETE: Doug swears it was the bike made her pregnant.

JIM: Now there's a novel idea.

PETE: No, 'parrantly it broke, when we were all in Rimini. He were plannin' goin' to Skeggie wi' his gang, but he coun't cos the bike was fucked up —

JIM: So he . . . er . . .

PETE: Exactly.

JIM: And now she's done the same to him.

PETE: With knobs on.

JIM: Sounds a fair deal. Listen, we'll have the big push at Easter.

PETE: Wha'?

JIM: Film the lovers before they meet on the beach at Skeggie. In black and white.

PETE: They'll never believe Skeggie's Italy.

JIM: They will. It'll work a treat.

LEFTY: Do you want a hand? I'll gi' you a hand.

PETE: No, thank you, Dad. You just relax. Enjoy yourself.

They begin to assemble the frame.

LEFTY: I'm willin' to work.

JIM: 'Scuse me.

ELSIE: Don't get under the workers' feet now. Come on, out of it. (*She crosses to him with the tray.*) You see what I have to put up wi', Dora. He's got to have a place he can be out the road.

PETE: He's all right.

LEFTY: I'm all right.

DORA: Have you guessed what it is yet?

LEFTY (*unenthusiastically*): Yes.

DORA: What is it then?

LEFTY: It's a greenhouse.

ELSIE: Good. Well done. A greenhouse. They cost a packet, them do.

LEFTY: I bet they do.

ELSIE: And you're going to grow us lots of nice things, lettuces, tomatoes, to make all the money back again.

LEFTY: I don't grow. I'm a builder and decorator.

ELSIE: Once upon a time. Now you're a market gardener.

LEFTY: I don't like gard'ning.

ELSIE: Yes, you do.

LEFTY: Do I?

ELSIE: 'Course you do.

LEFTY: I've never liked working out of doors.

ELSIE: You don't have to. That's why I brought you the greenhouse. Nice little cosy place of your own.

LEFTY: Hm.

ELSIE: Aren't you pleased?

Silence.

DORA: 'Course he is.

ELSIE: Here. Come on. Take these.

LEFTY *swallows the pills down with the water.*

LEFTY (*grimacing*): Yuk!

ELSIE: Are the pills nasty?

LEFTY (*winking at the lads*): No. It's the water.

ELSIE: Ye', well, you'll just have to get used to it. If you two want to kill him, just gi' him someat to drink.

PETE: We know that, Mam.

LEFTY: That's fine wi' me.

ELSIE: We need you well.

LEFTY: Thank you.

ELSIE: And don't you two go knocking my hedge down now it's started to grow.

PETE: No, Mam.

ELSIE (*to* DORA): I think I'll put it up, just to see what it looks like. But I won't leave it out 'til the spring.

She begins to put the 'umbrella' up.

LEFTY: You listen to your mam. She means well.

PETE: You'll be all right, Dad.

ARTHUR *enters.*

ARTHUR (*to* DORA): Word wi' me mate, then we're off.

DORA: Elsie says for us to stay lunch.

ARTHUR: Five minutes.

He nods to LEFTY, *and they move to the downstage area.*

DORA (*to* ELSIE): I an't really planned on stoppin'.

ARTHUR: Picked the winners yet?

LEFTY *surreptitiously hands him his* Daily Mirror.

ARTHUR (*slipping him a bottle of rum*): Here. Special. To keep you warm 'til the start of the flat.

He checks his selection.

PETE: How you going to film the love scene?

JIM (*grins*): I'm working on it.

PETE: Ye'. I bet.

JIM: Needs a lot of rehearsal, that's all. It's a tricky bit.

ELSIE *puts up the umbrella. It reads* 'Martini'. DORA *and* ELSIE *step back to admire it.* LEFTY *takes a secret drink. He laughs.*

LEFTY: Remember we used to drink the water from the lorry's radiator. In the desert. You've never let me down, Arthur. (*He drinks.*) Bbbrrrrr!

Fade to blackout.

ACT TWO

Scene One

DORA*'s flat.*
Jazz: Miles Davies. Lamplight.
CATHY *and* JIM *are in embrace on the cushions on the floor. Their clothes are in a state of disarray.*

JIM: No. No. Not that way. Not this time. Come on. Please.

CATHY: Oh Jim, don't ask me. Please.

JIM: It'll be safe. I promise. I've been to Boots.

CATHY: I'm not ready, Jim.

JIM: You don't fool me. You want it as much as I do.

CATHY: I do, yes, I do. But let me come to it in my own time.

JIM (*rolling away*): Oh, God.

Silence.

CATHY: It isn't that I don't want. I do. But there's other things to consider.

JIM: What, you mean, like your mam and God? I don't think I can hang around that long.

JIM *looks at her. She's near to tears.*

CATHY: Why do you always make me feel so guilty, Jim? I feel guilty with you for not going through with it. And if I do do it, I know I'll feel guilty with my parents. I never have any other feelings, except guilt.

JIM: How do you know what you'll feel until you've actually taken the risk? That's what our film's all about. They don't feel any guilt. Why should they? They've done nothing wrong. It's only your middle-class repressive world that says breaking through is wrong, because it dreads change. If we had the money to make the film, I could show you what I'm on about. But it's like every way I turn I'm trapped, and you don't help. We'll never make it.

CATHY: We're nearly there. Don't give up.

JIM: What are you talking about?

CATHY: The film. Everything.

They kiss, quietly.

JIM: If only I had some money. Then we could make it.

Silence.

CATHY: You know I have some.

JIM: I'm not sayin' ought.

CATHY: You know what I was putting it away for.

JIM: It's up to you. I'm not forcing you.

Pause.

CATHY: I'll get it out the Post Office.

JIM: You've made a wise choice, kid. Now, I'm going to make you a star. Just relax.

CATHY: Jim.

JIM: It's all right. I understand. I can wait.

CATHY: I feel so hot. Like I'd just strayed in from the sun.

JIM: I love you when you're all red and sweating.

CATHY: Do you love me?

JIM: Yes.

They kiss.

CATHY: Where are the tissues?

JIM: I'm lying on them.

CATHY: I love you, too.

They embrace.

Cross fade into:

Scene Two

ELSIE*'s garden.*
    PETE *holds up a small goldfish bowl, with two white goldfish. His mother stands by his side, carrying a copy of the* Daily Mirror.

ELSIE: Come on. I'm not here for me health.

PETE: That's the point, Mam. It's still too cold to put 'em in the pond.

ELSIE: Rubbish. Spring's here. It says so in the paper.

PETE: They're tropical fish, you know.

ELSIE: Get away. Nottingham born and bred. They'll survive. Chuck 'em some crumbs now and again, and they'll keep paddlin' round. I wish I could have had shut of our other two lovers as easy. He's a bloody idiot, your brother.

PETE: It happens, Mam.

ELSIE: It has to happen to me, don't it? It has to be my bloody doorstep they darken. My doorstep he'll have to carry her over. And carry it'll be, come an Easter wedding. She'll be too big to walk on her own. I woun't 'ave bought that dog you know, if I'd know. It'll be like a bloody doss house.

PETE: It won't be for long. They'll find somewhere.

ELSIE: Where?

PETE: They're up for a council house.

ELSIE: They're knocking more down than they're building. I'll have them hangin' on me bloody apron strings, just when I was lookin' forward to getting shut of you all. I cheered up for a minute when I thought I was losin' a son, but, no, it's me has to gain a bloody daughter-in-law. And a bloody grandkid. I'm not old enough to have a grandkid.

PETE: This pool needs a really good clean-out first. They'll choke in here.

ELSIE: Oh, sod you. Do what you want. Buy some bloody pigeons as well. Fill the house. What's it got to do wi' me. I only live here.

She turns to go. LEFTY *appears behind her.*

LEFTY (*quietly*): Can I have me paper?

ELSIE: We need you back at work,
m'lad.

PETE: It in't his fault, Mam.

ELSIE: Who's is it then?

LEFTY: I'll work.

ELSIE: If we had his money we woun't
be in this mess.

LEFTY: Money. You ask me. I'm the
breadwinner. Fish. Little pellets of
bread you throw in. Then they come
to the surface and you can net 'em.

ELSIE (to PETE): You should be in a
factory 'stead of workin' for National
Assistance. Who wants to work for
them?

PETE: I'm more useful there.

ELSIE: Useful! There's none of you
useful. If someone could make my
hedge grow, I'd be happy.

LEFTY: I'll buy you a hedge soon.

ELSIE: If Doug fixed that bloody bike,
he could sell it.

LEFTY: I don't mind it.

ELSIE: He makes no effort. Goes round
in a daze like his dad. It's muggins
here has to comb through the paper
every day looking for flats.

LEFTY: Gi me the paper. I'll earn
your money.

ELSIE (to LEFTY): Where's that daft
camera of yours? Should be worth
a couple of bob.

PETE (quickly): Save that, Mam, 'til
after the wedding. Might as well get
the use out of it.

ELSIE: You two are obsessed with
takin' pictures of things I'd rather
forget.

LEFTY: Zoom lens. Close up of the
horses. Photo finish.

ELSIE: Won't need a zoom lens for her.
You'll need Todd AO to get her in the
picture. Hope there's no bloody wind
or she'll take off like a zepp'lin.

She turns to go in.

LEFTY: Paper!

ELSIE: Ought for peace and quiet.

She hands it to him, and exits.
PETE *stands watching him.*

LEFTY: Who's a zepp'lin?

PETE: It dun't matter, Dad.

LEFTY: Doodle bugs we had. No
zepp'lins. And barrage balloons. She
means barrage balloon.

PETE: That's right.

LEFTY: I'll get you money. I know I
can do it.

PETE: 'Course you can.

LEFTY: All be lovey-dovey then.

PETE: Ye'.

LEFTY: Get us a drink, Doug.

PETE: Pete.

LEFTY: I think better wi' a drink.
Helps me see straight.

PETE: No, Dad.

LEFTY: Arthur'll be round soon to see
me. If it's money you want, ask me.

LEFTY *goes back towards his greenhouse.* PETE *watches him for a
moment.*

Cross fade into:

Scene Three

DORA*'s front room.*
Sound of DORA *hoovering. Saturday
afternoon. Late January 1965.*
*As before. Settee and chair now have
lace-edged white linen headrests.* JACKIE
and JIM *sit on the settee, reading – he,
a large library book on Eisenstein, she,
a record magazine.*
ARTHUR *sits in his chair, his feet
in a bowl of water. He is reading the
newspapers.* DORA *hoovers under her
children's feet.* ARTHUR *raises his to let
her move the bowl. She hoovers and*

replaces it. He is watching something. He rolls the newspaper up. It is a fly. He begins to wave it around. JIM *and* JACKIE *take note. He taps* DORA *with the paper. He indicates the fly. She takes the paper. She tries to find it. As she does so her anger shows as she screws the paper round in her hands. She sees the faces of her children, as they turn back to their reading. She gives him the paper back, switches the hoover off, and leaves the room.*

JACKIE: Are you goin' to look after 'im if Mam dies first?

JIM: Yer what?

JACKIE: He woun't be able to look after himself. Puttin' milk on cornflakes gi's him a headache.

JIM: What you talkin' about? She in't goin' to die first. He an't given her a chance to live yet.

Silence.

Would you?

DORA *enters, carrying a bundle of lace. She stands for a moment looking at* ARTHUR. *He does not notice.*

JACKIE: Come and sit down, Mam. You're on your feet all day.

They make space for her between them. Throughout the scene, she hardly takes her eyes off ARTHUR.

JIM: Cosy, innit?

DORA: You make it as nice as you can.

Silence.

JIM: Have you ever seen *Battleship Potemkin,* Mam?

DORA: I've seen the Ark Royal.

JIM: No, it's a film, Mam.

DORA: *Gone With The Wind* did for me.

JIM: What?

DORA: You never appreciate the decent bloke. Leslie Howard. He's got ears like Clark Gable. That's about all. Thought I could make someat of

him. Florence Nightingale. Must have been mad. Nought but a nurse and a skivvy ever since.

She begins abstracted work on sewing the curtains' hems.

DORA (*to* JACKIE): You could do these as well as me. Nobody ever lifts a finger round here.

JACKIE: Why you botherin' wi' lace, Mam?

DORA: You 'ave to bother. Can't have folks lookin' in.

JACKIE: They'd have to be in a plane to see in here.

DORA: People can look up as well you know. I'm the only one in the block wi' out lace.

JACKIE: You lose the view.

DORA: I've seen enough of them factories from the inside. (*She jabs her finger with the needle.*) Oh. I'd have been shut of 'im years ago, if it an't been for you kids.

JIM: We weren't stopping you, Mam.

DORA: And who was s'posed to dig 'im out the pub early for me? I lose me whole day off waitin' for him.

JIM: It took me half an hour to find him. He was down the Peel.

DORA: Bloody tinker's pub. Playing brag, was he? Only thing he's good for. He's good for nothing else.

JIM (*grinning*): Ye'. well he won't so hot today. He lost.

DORA: Serves him right.

JIM: He looked like grim death when I found him. As though he was going to challenge the others to a duel for cheating, only he coun't work out how they were doing it.

DORA: Nobody can cheat 'im. Not wi' his concentration being deaf. But he woun't have it nobody could beat him fair and square.

JIM: That's the beauty of it. They *were* cheating him. One of Dad's cronies, that dwarf from down the market, gave me the nod as we left. These three Irish paddies twigged he was deaf. So they were takin' him' to the cleaners. Hardly Brett Maverick stuff, but it worked.

JACKIE: What were they doin'?

JIM (*laughing*): They were telling each other their hands, so only the best went up against Doc Holliday here.

DORA: They were doin' what?

JIM (*laughing*): They told each other what cards they had. Simple but effective.

DORA: I can't believe it.

JIM: Gospel.

DORA: Nobody'd do that to an old soldier.

Silence.

JIM: What's the matter?

JACKIE: What did you do?

JIM: What do you mean, what did I do? If he won't so pigheaded, and learnt to lip-read, he'd have sussed that trick out in five seconds.

JACKIE: Din't you tell him?

JIM: What, and have him call 'em out to a gunfight at the OK Corrall? They were big lads. He in't the lightweight champion of the Eighth Army now, even if he thinks he is.

JACKIE: You should have done someat.

JIM: Why?

DORA: He's your dad.

JIM: No fault of mine.

JACKIE: You should have stuck up for him.

JIM: Let him fight his own bloody battles.

DORA: He fought for you many a year.

JIM: I woun't even born then.

DORA: Makes no difference. It was you he fought for.

JIM: What you talking about? We sit here, day in, day out, watching what he does to you, and you want me to get me face pushed in for his honour?

JACKIE: He's deaf. He can't help it.

JIM: Can't he?

DORA: He din't ask to be deaf.

JIM: Din't he? Did he ever listen to a word anybody said when he could hear? He's chosen his bed, and he can lie in it. I spent seven years as a kid on me knees praying for him to hear again before the tissues completely crumbled away. That's all the time he's having out of me. He's had your blood. He in't having mine as well.

DORA: You *are* his blood.

JIM: Never.

DORA (*distressed*): I din't bring you up to hate your father.

JIM: You didn't have to. It's as natural as hating the Nazis.

DORA (*crying*): No. That can't be right. I din't know my dad. But I would have loved him, no matter what he was like.

JIM: Come on, Mam, what's all this?

JACKIE: Now look what you've done.

ARTHUR (*suddenly*): What the bloody hell you doing, upsetting your mam?

JACKIE: It's all right, Dad.

ARTHUR: I'll not have it. Better you're off out, than you go upsetting that lady.

He steps out of the bowl.

DORA (*wildly*): Leave him alone. You're always picking on him.

JIM: Christ Almighty!

ARTHUR: Nought to do with me. Out the question. The lot of you.

JIM turns away in a rage. ARTHUR sits and covers his face in the newspaper.

DORA *stands, staring at her family. Silence.*

As the lights slowly fade, the lights go up on the down stage right area on LEFTY.

Scene Four

ELSIE's *garden.*
Light up on LEFTY's *greenhouse which is tightly packed with a large earth-tray, and the motorbike.*
LEFTY, *now in short sleeves, is riding the bike. He is rocking himself into something of a frenzy as he incants the names of the horses.*

LEFTY: Home stretch. Black Pageant on the inside. Comin' on strong. Don't gi' up now. Come on, Debbie's Gal. You can see it. Stretch out. Legs. Stretch for it. Closin' up by you. No. You've got him. Here it comes. You've got him. Yes.

He sits back, fighting for his breath.
ARTHUR *enters behind him.*

LEFTY: Debbie's girl. 4.30.

He marks his paper. His hands are shaking. ARTHUR *touches him lightly on the shoulder.* LEFTY *is startled.*

ARTHUR: Easy, 'oppo. It in't Eliot Ness.

LEFTY (*ecstatic*): Arthur!

ARTHUR: Bloody hot in here. Workin' on your tan, are you? Like a bloody cathouse.

LEFTY: Doghouse.

ARTHUR: I can see you are. Dun't that bugger let you out for a run, then? Allers stuck in here.

LEFTY: Drink!

ARTHUR: You spoilt her, you see. They allers bite the 'and that feeds 'em.

LEFTY *mimes drinking.*

ARTHUR: You know we won, then? Not that daft, are you?

ARTHUR *takes a bottle of ale from a*

brown paper bag, concealed under his coat. LEFTY *grabs it.*

LEFTY: Keep watch.

ARTHUR: Three out of five this time, laddie. Gettin' better all the time. One of these weeks you'll pick all the buggers past the post, and the triple's come running home.

LEFTY *has uncovered his bottle opener, and is busy downing the pint.*

ARTHUR: Steady on, son.

LEFTY (*grinning*): Medicine.

ARTHUR: What you on then?

They go through a comic mime, swopping the paper for the bag of ale. ARTHUR *studies the selection. There is a spaniel barking inside the house.*

LEFTY: She's got a dog. I keep the door closed. I don't like dogs. It's who feeds 'em. They dun't like nobody else.

ELSIE (*off*): Stay there, Charles. Mummy will be back in a jiffy.

LEFTY *furiously digs up the earth tray with his trowel, and buries the bottles.*

ARTHUR: What the bloody hell's going on?

LEFTY: She's here.

ARTHUR: Some sort of game is it? Find the treasure?

LEFTY *gets them underground, just before* ELSIE *enters the greenhouse.*

Mary, Mary, how does your garden grow, eh?

He sees ELSIE, *who carries a dog's tray in her hand.*

ELSIE: How the bloody hell did you get in here?

ARTHUR: Fair to middlin'. He's chirpier. Blood in his cheeks.

ELSIE: He's not comin' out to play so don't waste your breath.

ARTHUR: Having such a lovely nurse to look after him.

ELSIE: Flannel. Don't wash wi' me.

ARTHUR: No tea, thanks. Got to be off.
See a man about a dog. See you next
week, Lefty.

He goes.

ELSIE (*grudgingly*): Must be some good
in him, trooping out here every week.

LEFTY: Me and him was in the army
together.

ELSIE: Still think you are, half the
bloody time. Here, look what Charles
has given you. (*She empties the
dogshit into his tray.*) Come on, dig
it in. I want tomatoes off you, m'lad.
We're all banking on you.

She goes. LEFTY *picks up his trowel.*

Scene Five

DORA'*s front room.*
Cross fade up on PETE, *in his working
suit, staring out.* JIM, *revealed, sits
behind him, perched on the edge of his
father's armchair. He wears his school
blazer.*

PETE (*distressed*): It was just seein' em
both, I suppose. The other side of the
glass. It's bad enough when it's folk
you don't know, come cap in hand,
but when it's me own mam and dad.
He thought we were the bookies. He
kept scrawling names of horses on the
forms, and sliding 'em under the glass.
Grinnin' away. He din't know who
I was. When I saw her come into the
office, draggin' him like a dog on a
lead, I just din't know . . .

Silence.

JIM: Coun't she've hung on 'til you got
home to tell you the doctor had laid
him off for good?

PETE: She din't come to tell me. She'd
been round the Panel screamin' blue
murder at them stoppin' his money.
Then she'd come straight round to us,
to see what we had goin'. She saw me
as a soft touch. She went up the

bloody wall when I told her what the
rate was. I mean, I can't work miracles.
I wish I could. I should have done
someat for him. There's nought I
could do. I feel such a failure. He
looked so bloody lonely.

JIM: Dad still goes to see 'im.

PETE: Them visits're all that keeps 'im
alive. Funny how the war, all that
killing, should be the only thing that
keeps them goin'.

JIM: It's someat, though.

PETE: I kept catchin' me face in the glass
when I looked at 'im. I'll end up
like 'im. I know I will.

JIM: No, we won't. Neither of us'll end
up like our dads.

PETE: It's all right for you. You'll be off
to college come September. It's us
who are left here. Wi'out anybody.

JIM *suddenly stands up and begins to
push the chairs back.*

JIM: Come on.

PETE: What?

JIM: You're right. We can't wait for wars
to gi' us contacts in our old age. We
have to free ourselves now of
everything they've ever laid on us.

PETE: I'm not wi' you.

JIM *begins to take his shirt off.*

(*Nervous:*) What you doin'?

JIM: Come on. Take your clothes off.

PETE: What for?

JIM: *Women in Love.*

PETE: Women? What have women got to
do with you and me?

JIM: Lawrence. Gerald and Birkin. In
Women in Love. A nude wrestling
match. You and me. Break through
the conventions that kill us men.
Know each other.

PETE: I don't want to know you. Well, I
do, but . . . I don't want to fight you.
Why do I want to fight you?

JIM: You don't fight me. You fight *with* me. We struggle for life together. You can't do it on your own. We have to fight to bring each other into life.

JIM *is down to his underpants.*

PETE: Ye', fine, but we don't have to actually . . . fight. I mean, I mean, we . . . not actually . . .

JIM: It's a ritual bond between us. It has to be acted out or we don't recognise it. It'd be just words otherwise.

PETE (*desperate*): Look, the last time we did someat like this, I almost bled to death. These games allers hurt me more than they do you.

JIM: That's the pain of living.

He starts to take his underpants off.

PETE (*panicking*): All right. I'll fight you. But I can fight you just as well wi' our clothes on. Put your clothes back on, please.

JIM *strips.*

JIM: We can't bare our souls if we won't bare our bodies.

PETE (*looking away*): In the book, they had a log fire and they were pissed. That's why they did it.

JIM: Well, we've got central heating. Only the externals change. The challenge remains the same.

PETE: This is crazy, Jim.

JIM: Of course it is. Where else can you look for hope in this so-called sane world? (*Pause.*) Do you want to end up like your dad? It's now or never.

Silence.

Trust me.

PETE *begins to strip, slowly.*

PETE: I don't think I want to do this, you know.

JIM: Me neither. But it has to be done.

PETE: Nobody can see in, can they?

JIM: No.

He strips and turns to face JIM. JIM *stretches out his hands to grapple.* PETE *turns away. He turns but looks away. He holds out his hands. They wrestle.* PETE *hardly puts up a fight. He clings on to* JIM *as they topple over to the floor. They are locked in an embrace.* JIM *breaks it viciously.* PETE *cries out.* JIM *stands, and angrily walks away. He begins to get dressed.*

(*Furious:*) What the hell are you playin' at? You have to fight. You din't fight.

PETE *remains on the floor, crying silently.*

I din't hurt you. Come on. It's over. It didn't work for you. It failed. Let's forget it.

PETE: What was supposed to happen? What was we s'posed to feel?

Silence.

JIM: It's nothing to do with sex. It's above all that. That's what Birkin could never make Ursula understand. It's completely different. Finer.

PETE: What?

JIM *is dressed.*

JIM: Get your clothes on. Somebody will be coming home soon.

He leaves the room. PETE *stands, and begins to dress.*

Scene Six

ELSIE's *garden.*
    Cross fade from PETE, *to his father,* LEFTY *in the greenhouse. He rocks ecstatically on his bike over the racing page of the* Daily Mirror. *The sound of a wedding party.*
    Music: Presley's version of 'Jezebel'.
    Light up on garden. A mild, Easter afternoon. The 'sun umbrella' is open, and the table strewn with half-eaten sausages, streamers, bottles and paper cups.

ELSIE *enters, in her wedding C & A finest, carrying* LEFTY*'s pills and a piece of wedding cake.* JACKIE *follows her out, and lights a cigarette.*

ELSIE *crosses to the greenhouse, and enters, catching* LEFTY *at the height of his ecstasy.*

LEFTY: Come on. Come on. You'll make it.

ELSIE: What the bloody hell's goin' on here?

LEFTY *panics, and desperately tries to hide the newspaper but she grabs it from him.* JACKIE *stands outside to hear what's going on.*

LEFTY: Gimme. Gimme! Mine!

She sees the pin-up on page three.

ELSIE: What the . . . What are you doin'? Were you lookin' at this little tart? Lustin' after this young gal, Lefty, were you? Is that what you were doin'? Lefty.

LEFTY, *relieved, nods wildly.*

LEFTY: Ye'. Ye'. Lovely, in't she?

ELSIE: Oh, I knew you were sick, Lefty, but not this far gone. You dirty little bugger. I'm speechless. Right, well I'm not havin' any of this goin' on at the bottom of my garden. No more page threes for you. (*She rips it up.*)

LEFTY: Gimme. It's for you.

ELSIE (*picks up the rest of the paper*): I'm not gi'ing you the chance of spying so much as an ad. for long coms, Lefty.

LEFTY: I need it. Please.

ELSIE: Thank God you din't come to the Church. God knows what capers you'd have got up to. It was bad enough wi' her wi' her belly out.

LEFTY: Gi' me.

ELSIE: Get them pills down you. Might make you half way decent in case anybody comes to look at you.

She leaves the greenhouse.

(*To* JACKIE:) They're all sick underneath. That's someat you don't know yet, but should.

She exits.

LEFTY (*following through the door*): Mammy. Mammy.

He sees JACKIE *and she smiles at him. He darts back inside the greenhouse. She follows him into the greenhouse and takes a magazine out of her shoulder bag.*

JACKIE: Take it. Lots of young girls in lovely clothes. You can have it. I've read it.

LEFTY *flicks through it.*

LEFTY: No.

JACKIE: It's O.K. . . . Honest.

LEFTY: A newspaper. Just a newspaper.

JACKIE: These gals are in colour. They look lovely.

LEFTY: A paper, please.

JACKIE (*shrugs, and rummages in her bag*): Suit yourself, but I don't know I've . . . Eh, you're in luck. I was saving this to do the Cliff Richard comp., but, (*reluctantly:*) that's all right.

He almost snatches it from her, and turns away. She backs out as JIM *and* CATHY *enter, followed by* PETE, *and the camera equipment.*

JIM: Din't they look grand? By golly, they did look grand, din't they? Fair made me weak at the knees. I had a little cry in me hankie. Gordon Bennett. Let's get out of here, before the rockers start biking on the lawn.

PETE: Hang on. I'm best man. I might have other duties to perform.

JIM: You goin' to stay and deliver the baby, are you?

CATHY: Cynic.

JIM: Come on, we've got to get back to the flat.

CATHY: What for?

JIM: The love scene.

CATHY: What?

JIM: We're going to film the love scene tonight. Mam and Elsie're planning to go on the town. There'll be nobody there for hours.

Elvis Presley is taken off to accompanying boos.

ELSIE (*off*): Someat for the old 'uns!

CATHY: Does it have to be tonight?

JIM: We'll never get a better chance. Then to Skeggie for the bank holiday to do the opening and it's in the can.

Russ Conway is now playing 'Penn.s From Heaven'.

PETE: I can't manage them lights you've knicked from school, and the camera. I'll need a hand.

JIM: No sooner said than done. (*To* JACKIE:) Come on, Jackie.

JACKIE: Yer wha'?

JIM: We need you to gi' us a hand with the film.

JACKIE: Oh, you're singing a different tune now. All that time on holiday you woun't let me wi'in a mile of your precious movie. But as soon as you're stuck, it's little sister time. You've had all the hand you're going to get off me.

JIM: Oh, shurrup. Come on. Cathy would like another gal there with her, woun't you, Cathy?

CATHY: Yes.

JIM: There you are. I'm not asking you for me.

JACKIE: What do you want me to do?

JIM: You're continuity girl.

JACKIE: What's that when it's at home?

JIM: You have to check we're wearing the same clothes in different takes.

JACKIE: But it's a love scene. You won't

be wearing any clothes.

CATHY: Won't we?

JACKIE: Oh, well, it might be a laugh, anyroad. But not all night. I've got other plans.

The spaniel is yapping.

ARTHUR (*off*): Bloody dog.

ELSIE (*off*): He's all right. Not used to people.

DORA (*off*): Arthur!

ARTHUR enters, slightly drunk, and glares at the children.
Silence. He makes a beeline for the greenhouse. DORA runs on behind him, and catches his arm.

DORA: Arthur!

ARTHUR: What now, woman?

DORA (*fighting for breath*): They're playing . . . 'Pennies from Heaven'. (*Mimes piano.*) Playing 'Pennies from Heaven'.

ARTHUR: Not me. I haven't. Hardly touched a drop. You have. Not me.

DORA: I'm not saying ought about that. Your song. 'Pennies'.

ARTHUR: Ye', I'm with you, Dora. All right. Good girl.

He turns away.

DORA: You're not, you bugger. Wait.

She takes some coins from her pockets, and holds them out.
'Pennies'.

ARTHUR: I gave you last night. What you done wi' it all?

She shakes her head, and throws the coins in the air.

DORA (*exhausted*): 'Pennies from Heaven'.

JACKIE is writing something on a piece of paper.

ARTHUR: Don't go throwin' the buggers away. I sweated to get them.

DORA: God help me.

ARTHUR: If you don't want 'em, I'll 'ave 'em.

JIM: Why bother, Mam?

JACKIE *hands* ARTHUR *the note. The music has changed to* 'Summertime'.

ARTHUR: What's this? 'Pennies From Heaven'?

DORA (*nods*): Yes.

ARTHUR: What, now?

JACKIE: Ye'. Go on, Mam. Dance wi' 'im.

DORA *holds her arms out.*

ARTHUR (*almost shyly*): You lead then.

JIM: This I've got to have.

He takes the camera and films them. ARTHUR *hums the first few bars. They dance.* ARTHUR *stops.*

ARTHUR: I can't remember any more.

He turns into the greenhouse. DORA *turns, embarrassed, to the children. She kneels to pick up the loose change.* CATHY *helps her.* JACKIE *turns away. The boys check through the equipment on the grass.* PETE *slings the camera round his neck.* ARTHUR *walks round into* LEFTY's *vision.*

LEFTY: Arthur! I knew you'd come.

ARTHUR *signals to keep it quiet; indicates people outside.*

LEFTY (*whispering*): Drink!

ARTHUR: You're hot stuff, Lefty. All bar one last week. Soon be able to buy yourself a bigger greenhouse.

LEFTY: Gimme!

ARTHUR: Celebration, eh?

He hands him the smuggled whisky. LEFTY *drinks.*

ARTHUR: Paper, eh? Come on.

LEFTY *hands over the newspaper.* ARTHUR *searches for a notepad, and*

his glasses. LEFTY *is at work on the bottle.*

DORA (*to* CATHY): He respects me, you know.

CATHY: I'm sure he does.

DORA: That's what his mam taught him to do. I sometimes wish she hadn't, but there we are. There might 'ave been more love, then.

CATHY: Do you believe in love, Mrs Cooper?

DORA: I believe that love, and love-making, must be a lovely part of life. I just an't known it, that's all. (*Pause.*) You go maudlin' at weddings. I prefer a nice funeral, I do. I'll go and see if Elsie's ready to go up town.

She exits.

ARTHUR (*suddenly*): What's your game, Lefty?

LEFT (*grinning*): Winners.

ARTHUR: Don't bugger me about.

LEFTY: Sssshhh! Winners, eh? (*He mimes jockeying.*)

ARTHUR: I know they're all winners. If we bet 'em last week, before they past the post, we'd have made a killing.

LEFTY: Last week?

ARTHUR: Gi' me the proper list. I an't got all day to play sucky buggers.

LEFTY: Last week?

ARTHUR: Where's today's paper?

LEFTY: Today's paper?

ARTHUR: I don't like jokes about 'orses, Lefty. Ought but 'orses. Where's the bleedin' paper?

LEFTY: Her. She takes 'em. She rips 'em up.

ARTHUR (*looking round*): What you done wi' em? You playin' hide and seek? What you dun wi' em? Ate 'em?

LEFTY *grabs hold of* ARTHUR's *shoulder, trying to make him lip read.*

LEFTY: Her. She steals 'em. It in't me. I woun't let you down.

ARTHUR: Now then, son. Hands off. None of that. Just cos you're losin' *your* marbles, don't try to loosen mine.

JIM: What's goin' on in there?

LEFTY: It's her. Listen. Fuck her! Fuck her!

PETE *and* JIM *run over to the greenhouse, in time to catch the scuffle as* ARTHUR *fights off the panicking* LEFTY. PETE *takes his father and sits him down.*

ARTHUR (*dusting himself*): I can fight me own fights, thank you.

LEFTY (*hysterical*): Don't let the dog in.

PETE: It's all right, Dad.

ARTHUR: Went for me bloody throat. Taken leave of his senses.

PETE: Steady, Dad, steady. Who gave him this whisky?

JIM: Guess.

ARTHUR: Nought to do wi' me. I wash me hands of him. I do.

PETE: No wonder he's going wild. On top of them pills.

ARTHUR: You can't help some people. That's it. out the question.

He leaves the greenhouse. The girls stand outside.

PETE (*emptying out the bottle*): It'll kill you, Dad.

LEFTY: No.

ARTHUR (*to the girls*): Waste of bloody time. She's done for him. He used to be someat at one time. Not any more.

PETE: Sit quiet, Dad.

JACKIE *crosses to the greenhouse.*

JACKIE: What's goin' on?

JIM: God knows. You know what he's like.

JACKIE: Is your dad going to be all right?

PETE: I don't know whether I should leave him.

JIM: There'll be folk about.

PETE: Ye'.

JIM: Let's go 'for someat else happens.

CATHY: I have to pick me coat up.

JIM (*quietly*): It'll be all right. I promise.

CATHY: Yes.

She exits.

JACKIE: I'll nick some bottles on me way out.

JIM: Good idea.

PETE: Dad.

LEFTY: Sir!

PETE: It's me.

LEFTY: Don't let the dog in. It pees in here. It pees in the corner. There's allers a big puddle there.

PETE *stands in front of him.*

PETE: Dad.

LEFTY: There's money on its way. Honest. I pay my way.

PETE: Dad. You remember you're in Doug's bed tonight, 'cos of the wedding?

LEFTY: Whose wedding?

PETE: Doug's. Dad, Mam's staying the night at Dora's so the honeymoon couple can have your double.

LEFTY: I'll have a double.

PETE: No you won't, Dad.

LEFTY: No, you're right. I'm with you.

PETE: Doug's bed. There'll be folk around, Dad. You'll be all right.

LEFTY: Doug's wedding? Was I invited?

Silence.

You come to take me picture? For the album? Want me on me own. Good idea. I'll put a show on for you. Come on. Camera.

PETE *focuses the camera.* JIM *watches through the glass.*

Gi' you a bit of a song, shall I? Put on a show for you. Fire away. Shoot. (*He sings:*) 'I'll be seeing you . . . in all the old . . . bars and races . . . I'll be seeing you . . . bars and races. All day through.' Is that enough?

PETE: Fine.

LEFTY (*cheerfully*): Only I can't remember no more.

PETE: I'm off now, Dad.

LEFTY: Don't let the dog in. (*Smiling:*) He's flooding me out.

PETE *leaves, and sees* JIM.

PETE: Let's get out of here.

JIM: Did you film him?

PETE *looks at him, and walks off.* JIM *stands, looking through the glass. He follows* PETE *off. Inside,* ELSIE *'pulls the plug' on the record player. Boos and cries.* LEFTY *sits down. He hums 'I'll be seeing you'.*

Fade to blackout.

Scene Seven

DORA*'s front room.*
Darkness.

CATHY: I don't see why we couldn't stay in the bedroom.

JIM: We need the room to move around. Gi's some light.

A couple of cheap stands of spot illuminate the central area of the carpet, where JIM *and* PETE *drop the mattress. The furniture has been pushed back.* CATHY *stands on the edge of the lit area, with an armful of bedding. Around the stands are bottles of wine, and glasses.* JIM *and* PETE *are momentarily blinded. They*

step out of the area. JACKIE, *who is sitting on the floor, starts giggling, otherwise silence.* JIM *takes the bedding and throws it roughly over the bed. He takes a drink. Silence.*

JACKIE (*slightly drunk*): Now what?

Silence.

JIM: Good.

Silence.

Lighting OK?

PETE: Bit dark.

CATHY (*horrified*): A bit dark?

PETE: You need a lot of light.

JIM: But it'll do?

PETE: Ye'.

JIM: Good.

Silence. CATHY *takes a drink.*

JIM: Right, now . . . This section is black and white, right?

PETE: I know.

CATHY: Black and white?

JIM: Ye', but we're going to dye it blue, so it stands between the two worlds of the isolation, and then the break-through.

JACKIE (*giggling*): You should call it 'Blue Movie'.

JIM: Shurrup you.

Silence.

CATHY: Can we get it over?

JIM: Do you want to rehearse first?

CATHY: No.

JIM: Good.

Silence.

JACKIE: It's a thrill a minute, filming, innit?

JIM: Right. OK. What we do is, er . . . Pete, you'll move around us. Take a series of short, free shots, maybe some out of focus, against the light, faces, arms and things. (JACKIE *giggles.*)

And then we'll shoot the actual taking off of clothes later.

CATHY: You mean, we don't have to take our clothes off?

JIM: Oh, ye', but we film the main bit first, and then we put them on again, and . . . take them off later.

CATHY: I don't see the point.

JIM: It's a film. You never shoot in sequence.

CATHY: Why not?

JIM: Because you don't!

JACKIE: On your marks. Get set. Go!

JIM: Shurrup! Right. Let's not make a song and dance of it.

He quickly strips and jumps into bed.
CATHY *begins to strip, slowly.*

PETE: I think we'll be all right wi' the light, but it's difficult to tell. I think so.

JACKIE: I can see fine.

JIM: Why don't you piss off if you're not going to be any use?

PETE: I'm scared stiff of overloading the adaptor.

CATHY, *having stripped to bra and panties, climbs into bed.* JIM *rolls over to her.*

JIM (*quietly*): You've still got your things on.

CATHY: Nobody will see. We'll be under the blankets.

JIM: Listen, it in't a fucking Hayley Mills number. There'll be times when we're not under the blanket.

PETE: Are you ready?

CATHY: Yes.

JIM: No! Listen. We have to be honest about this. That's what the film's all about.

PETE: It'll be all right. I can shoot round it.

JACKIE: Shoot round what?

JIM: No you can't. It'll look stupid. Like all them other films. You'll be wanting to cut away to waves and fireworks, and fucking rockets shooting in the air.

CATHY: Don't swear.

JIM: There has to be naked bodies. There has to be.

CATHY: I don't see why. Everybody'll know what's happening.

JIM: They can't just know it in their heads. They have to experience it. It has to be erotic. They have to experience what's happening.

CATHY: Nothing's happening. Not really. We're acting. Aren't we?

JIM: Of course we're acting. But −

While they have been arguing, JACKIE *has stripped off.*

JACKIE: Here, shove over.

She climbs into bed.

JIM: What the fuck are you doin'?

JACKIE: I'm a stand-in. So to speak.

JIM: You're pissed. Get out. I've got enough to put up with.

JACKIE: That's what you think?

JIM: Get out.

JACKIE: Look, nobody's going to tell my bum from Cathy's. 'Specially as they don't see hers. Sophie Loren has stand-ins all the time. You never see her bum.

JIM: Wha'? That's brilliant. Now you're beginning to sound like my sister.

CATHY (*almost hysterically*): She *is* your sister!

JIM (*to* PETE): And we just intercut close-ups of Cathy's head and shoulders.

CATHY: You can't do this with your sister, Jim.

JIM: Why not? Seein' as I can't do it wi' you. It's a great idea.

CATHY: Pete, tell him, he can't do that. I mean, he just can't do that.

JIM: Let's get rolling.

JACKIE: Ye'.

PETE: I don't think you can do that —

JACKIE: Shall I just lie back and yawn?

JIM: Smart-arsed little bitch!

He rolls over on top of her.
CATHY leaps out of bed.

CATHY: For God's sake, Jim, stop it!

JACKIE and JIM embrace.
CATHY strips off.

CATHY: Come on. Get her out!

JIM: Are you sure?

CATHY: Of course, I'm sure. Get her out!

She climbs back into bed.

JIM (*to* JACKIE): Come on, you, get your clothes on, and act your bloody age.

JACKIE: I'm stayin' here.

JIM: Out.

JACKIE: It'll be a much better film with the three of us. Good box office.

JIM: Get her out, Pete.

JACKIE (*grabs* PETE's *leg*): The four of us! That'd be terrific. Come on, Pete, don't be frightened.

PETE (*as he loses balance*): Jesus Christ.

CATHY: Not His name. Not His name. Please.

PETE: Sorry it just slipped out.

JACKIE: I'll put it back for you, duck.

JIM (*to* CATHY): Don't cry.

CATHY: It's supposed to be beautiful.

JIM: It will be. Just give me a chance.

PETE (*overwhelmed by* JACKIE): Mind me Bolex.

JACKIE: With pleasure.

PETE: Jackie, please!

JACKIE: It's a new world, Pete. Come on, risk it. You may never get the chance again.

JIM: ACTION!

He embraces CATHY. PETE *almost manages to drag* JACKIE *out of bed.*

PETE: Gi' me a hand, Jim. She's blind drunk.

JIM (*to* CATHY): Relax.

CATHY (*crying*): I love you.

JIM: I love you, too.

JACKIE: I love you, baby. 'Love, love me do, you know I love you —'

PETE: I can't —

CATHY suddenly screams and jumps out of bed.

JIM: What is it?

CATHY: You've stopped acting!

JIM (*following after her*): Of course I'm acting.

They can all obviously see his erection.
JACKIE laughs.

JACKIE: That's not acting.

JIM climbs back into bed.

JIM: Listen, that is acting. That's real acting. You're bound to get a bit caught up in it, aren't you?

CATHY: Oh, Jesus.

PETE: Help.

JIM: For crying out loud, why is it so difficult to make a little film? I mean, what's the —

There is the sound of a door banging.
They all freeze.

DORA (*off*): He's allers been a baby. Makes such a bloody fuss.

ELSIE (*off*): You'd think I poured it over him on purpose.

DORA (*off*): I'll get him a clean shirt.

ELSIE (*off*): It was only a port and lemon.

ARTHUR *enters, stripping off his shirt which has a red stain down the front. He is almost blinded by the light.*

ARTHUR: Sorry. Wrong house!

He turns to go. The two girls dive back into bed.

DORA (*off*): It's his bloody tie he's fussed about.

ARTHUR (*turning back*): What the bloody hell?

PETE (*weakly waving the camera*): Film.

ARTHUR: OUT!

DORA (*off*): What's he bellowin' about?

She enters, carrying a fresh shirt and tie, followed by ELSIE. ARTHUR tears the blankets back to reveal the children.

ARTHUR; Brothel! My house! Bloody brothel!

JACKIE *curls up, laughing hysterically.* CATHY *clutches for the sheets.*

DORA: What you doin'?

ARTHUR: In the truck. The lot of you. Come on.

JIM: Mam, it in't what it —

ARTHUR (*to* DORA): Cover your eyes up, woman.

DORA: Don't talk daft, man. I brought them into the world.

ELSIE: It's one of them orgies. They're having a bloody orgy.

JIM: It's nought like that.

ARTHUR: Out, woman. Leave me to sort out these little buggers.

ELSIE: This is what happens, when you gi' em too much freedom.

DORA: What? What happens?

ELSIE: Come on, open your eyes, Dora. You think the sun shines out their bloody arses, well, now you can see.

ARTHUR (*to* JIM): Tell your tart to get some clothes on. Makes me sick looking at you.

JIM: Tell him to shut up, Mam!

ELSIE (*to* PETE): And what you bloody doin'? Least, I could understand it if you were in there wi' 'em. Wha' you doin' wi' your clothes on?

ARTHUR: Get out this room, woman, and take your daughter wi' you. Leave me to handle the men.

JIM: If everybody'd just shut up for a minute.

ELSIE: I'd gi' a sigh of relief if I saw you wi' a gal.

PETE: What does that mean?

ELSIE: Any more shame and I could slash me wrists.

JIM: We're just trying to make a film, that's all.

PETE: I'm the cameraman, Mam.

ELSIE: Christ! They're makin' a filthy film.

CATHY: A love film.

ARTHUR (*to* DORA): You've ruined 'em. Rotten. Lettin' 'em run wild. I knew you would.

JIM: He has to put his filthy paws over everything.

ELSIE: You're like your dad. You all disgust me.

PETE: Don't say that, Mam.

ARTHUR: I brought you up wi'out the stick. 'Cos she went on and on. All love and pink lav paper. Look where that gets you.

CATHY *is trying to dress under the blankets.* JIM *is wriggling into his jeans.*

JIM: It's just a scene from a film, Mam. We won't doin' ought. She's my sister.

ELSIE: Now he remembers.

JIM: It's just part of the film.

CATHY: A love film.

DORA: You should have told us.

JIM: I was goin' to but I din't know if you'd understand.

DORA: I see.

ARTHUR: Don't talk to him. Out the bloody question he is. Talk his way out of ought. Not an ounce of respect for his mam in him.

DORA (*to* ARTHUR): You've got it wrong. Listen to me!

ELSIE: What a bloody day, eh? Kids. God's punishment.

CATHY *tries to dress* JACKIE.

CATHY (*to* ELSIE): Help me.

ELSIE (*turning away*): Nought to do wi' me.

JACKIE (*crying*): I don't want to get up.

ARTHUR: The gal, I never thought ought of. Could see the way she was goin'. Some women it's in their blood.

JACKIE (*hysterical*): Bastard.

CATHY (*to* PETE): Help me.

JIM (*to* DORA): Tell him not to talk like that.

DORA: Arthur!

ARTHUR: But your mother. She's one of a kind. An antique. Show her respect.

DORA: I don't want respect, Arthur. I just want you to look at me.

PETE *is doing his best to help* CATHY.

PETE: What do I do?

CATHY: Just hold her.

DORA (*to* ARTHUR): LISTEN TO ME!

ARTHUR: You should have heeded me. You've failed me. Failed me in my son. That's not right. After all I've given you.

JIM, *now wearing his jeans, stands.*

JIM: He can't talk to you like that, Mam.

ARTHUR: Get out of my sight.

JIM (*grabbing hold of* DORA): Leave him, Mam. Leave the bastard. He kills everything.

ARTHUR: Hands off her. You're not fit to touch her shoes.

JIM: Leave him, please!

ARTHUR: Don't show your back to me.

CATHY, *having given up on* JACKIE'*s underwear, has managed to slip her dress over her.* ARTHUR *grabs* JIM'*s shoulder to turn him round.* JIM *spins, thinking he is going to be hit and strikes his father hard in the stomach.* ARTHUR *falls on the edge of the bed,* JIM *follows him, maniacally.* DORA *and* PETE *manage to drag him off. His father is hurt and stays down.*

DORA: For God's sake, Jim. Leave him. For my sake.

JIM: I should have done for him years ago.

DORA: Please!

Silence.

JIM (*crying*): You'll never be free, Mam. He'll keep you locked up.

DORA: You don't understand.

JIM: I understand he's killing you.

DORA: You're a kid. For all your brains.

Silence.

Go away. All of you. Leave it to me. It'll be all right in the morning. Somehow. Go away.

JIM (*softly*): Come with us, Mam.

DORA: Go on. You'll all live. It's not the end of the world. Cathy!

CATHY: Come on, Jim.

DORA: Somebody help me get him on the bed proper.

JIM: Let him rot.

He picks up his shirt, and coat, and exits. JACKIE *has been wandering round looking for her shoes. She finds them.*

CATHY: We were doing nothing wrong. I know we weren't.

DORA: No.

CATHY *takes* JACKIE *out after* JIM. PETE *helps* DORA *get* ARTHUR *on the bed.*

PETE: Is he all right?

DORA: The beer will have cushioned the blow. Long as he don't spring a leak, he'll live.

PETE: What about the lights?

DORA: Leave 'em. Leave everything. Just go.

PETE: Mam?

ELSIE *does not turn round.* PETE *exits.*

ELSIE: Well, I've seen it all now.

DORA *covers* ARTHUR *with the blankets.*

What sort of house do you run here, Dora?

DORA: I don't run any sort of house. People live here, that's all. A family.

ELSIE: Some family. The lad's in bed with his sister, and then beats his old man up. His mam don't even blink an eye. The *News of the World* would have a field day with this.

DORA: Well, the *News of the World* would get it wrong. Come on, Arthur. Open your eyes. There's nought wrong wi' him. He'd be screamin' blue murder if he had so much as a scratch. He'll just stay curled up wi' his eyes closed, 'cos he can't think of ought to say. Blot us all out. Every night of my life.

ELSIE (*shaking her head*): Well, far be it for me to tell you how to run your family, but —

DORA: Your lad was here an' all, you know.

ELSIE: Egged on.

Silence.

DORA: I'm tired. How do you think you switch these bleddy things off?

She finds the switches on them, and turns them off one by one.

ELSIE: Arthur'll kill him in the morning.

DORA: No, he won't. That's the worst of it. He'll be as proud as punch.

ELSIE: Proud?

DORA: He's been wanting to make him fight for years. He'll claim Jim as his own now. That's the way his mind works. That's the worst of it.

ELSIE: Well, I hope you're not proud of him.

DORA: I'm not proud, no. But I'm not ashamed, neither.

ELSIE: I thought I knew you. All them years of living next door.

DORA: Just goes to show, dun't it? You take Jackie's bed. Do you want an hot water bottle?

ELSIE: No.

The light is down to the last small lamp.

DORA: He'll probably be all right. It's quite mild.

ARTHUR *is snoring.*

I'd better take his shoes and trousers off. You get to bed.

ELSIE *exits. Lights fade as* DORA *undresses* ARTHUR.

Scene Eight

The street.
   Night. Outside the block of flats. The sound of a door swinging to. JIM *appears, and charges across the downstage in a fury. He stops in his tracks at the far side, counts up the floors of the block, and stands staring at the eighth.*
   CATHY *follows, supporting* JACKIE *who is tripping over her shoes.*

CATHY (*letting go of* JACKIE): Jim!

JACKIE *totters on a few steps more, losing a shoe.*

JACKIE: Fuckin' shoes! Wha's a matter wi' 'em?

CATHY: It might help if you did them up.

JACKIE *stands on one leg and falls over.*

JACKIE: Timber!

PETE *enters, and picks up the shoe. He, and* CATHY *cross to help her.*

JACKIE (*laughing*): She fell at his feet.

CATHY: Come on, for God's sake.

JACKIE: I like it here. In the gutter. That's where people like me are supposed to live, innit? (*She laughs.*) Fallen women. Bloody hell, it's a bit cold on the bum.

PETE: You'll get piles.

CATHY: It might help if she had some underwear on.

JACKIE: Who needs 'em? It only makes for more work. Takin' 'em on and off.

PETE: What we goin' to do wi' her?

JACKIE: You're not doing nought wi' me. I work. I earn me money. Don't come to me wi' your help.

PETE: Here's your shoe.

JACKIE: Put it on then, Prince Charming. But no looking up me dress. That's why he put the shoe on himself, you know. That's not true, is it? He loved her. Scruffy little tart though she was.

PETE *kneels and puts the shoe on.* CATHY *crosses to* JIM.

JIM: I should have killed that bastard.

CATHY: There's nothing you can do.

JIM: I've got to get her out of there.

JACKIE (*standing up*): Call her out on the balcony, then shin up her hair, and slay the dragon.

JIM: Shurrup, you!

JACKIE (*to* CATHY): You think he's Prince Charming. You must be daft.

JIM: It's your fuckin' fault we're in this mess. It was yo' being in the bed that caused all the fuss.

JACKIE: It's allers the gal gets the blame innit? Well, I've had enough of that. Who got who into bed first, eh, big brother? I'm not havin' all this guilt. I'm not takin' it lying down. Unless I want to. All this crap you men put on us. Fuck off!

JIM: Fuck off yourself.

JACKIE: Well, I'm not stayin' here wi' a load of kids.

She starts walking off.

CATHY: Where you going?

JACKIE: Out.

CATHY (*to* JIM): You can't just let her go.

JACKIE: He can't stop me. I've got real friends.

JIM: Tart.

JACKIE: Sticks and stones. I tell you, it's all kids' games wi' you.

JIM: You're doin't it just to spite Dad. Spitin' him by provin' him right.

JACKIE: You don't understand nothing, do you? I feel dead sorry for you.

JIM: Piss off.

JACKIE (*to* CATHY): Look after him. Somebody's got to.

She goes.

PETE: Where *we* goin'?

JIM: Why does she stay with him? She could just walk out the door. Freedom's just outside the bleddy door. (*Quietly:*) Oh, Mam. (*To* CATHY:) You'd better be gettin' home. *Your* mam'll be worried.

CATHY: Are you all right?

JIM (*quietly*): No, I'm not.

PETE (*crossing*): You can come and stay wi' me, Jim.

JIM: No.

PETE: Why not?

JIM: I'll be all right. (*To* CATHY:) You'd better get home.

CATHY: I'll go with you.

JIM: Where?

Silence.

PETE: You can both have my room.

CATHY: What about you?

PETE: I could do wi' a walk. If I get back I can allers doss down on the sofa.

CATHY: It's beginning to rain.

PETE: I don't mind a walk in the rain.

CATHY: Jim?

JIM: He'll not stop me making this film, you know. Nothing will stop me making it now.

He and CATHY *exit.* PETE *stands for a moment. The rain begins to come down faster.*

Scene Nine

ELSIE*'s garden.*
Dark. Heavy rain. A dog snapping.
LEFTY *careers from the house into the safety of his greenhouse. His hand is bleeding.*

LEFTY (*out of breath*): Good dog, good dog guard dog. On guard duty. House out of bounds. Officers only. Privates – No Entry (*He giggles.*) Privates. Who's that sleeping in my bed? No, not my bed. Officers Only. Not my wife. Some fat tart. She won't my wife. What was that officer sayin'? 'Next door?' Won't no tart next door. Empty. No point in staying there. Not when it's empty. Better stay in your glasshouse, Lefty. Or you'll only end up in trouble. Arthur'll bring you a drink. Arthur'll bring you a glass of water. 'Arthur?' (*Pause.*) 'Lance Corporal, sir!' (*Pause.*) He's not comin'. He's thrown the key away. Water. (*He sucks his hand.*) How am I? I don't get through the day, doctor,

sir. I'm here in the morning. People see me in the morning. But then come dinnertime I'm not here. And it's getting earlier. Some folk don't see me after tea. (*He sees the wedding cake.*) Cake? No, thank you, sir. Don't eat much. No point if folk don't see you. I'd eat if it helped, but it dun't, so I don't. Gi' it the dog. Dogs love you if you gi' 'em cake. And horses. Here, come on, beauty. Come on. (*He holds the cake out in the palm of his hand to the motorbike.*) That's my gal. You'll come through for me, won't you? Yes, you will. You'll make me garden grow. Horse shit. Better than dog shit. Bottles'll sprout up over the shop. (*He laughs.*) Good gal. Daddy'll sleep in the stable wi' you tonight. You'll keep me warm won't you? Cake all the way if you're first past the post in the morning. You'd like that woun't you? Come on. Cold. (*He lies down.*) You'll keep me warm, won't you?

Blackout.

Scene Ten

The beach at Skegness.
From the far distance, sounds of a seaside/fairground/rock and roll music, and the occasional sound of motorbikes revving up.
A cold, grey, Easter day. The remains of a battered Punch and Judy booth, and a couple of smashed deckchairs upstage.
CATHY *picks her way through the debris.*
JIM *studies the scene.* PETE *carries the film gear.*

CATHY: Those rockers must have ridden their bikes across this lot.

PETE: They've blitzed the Punch and Judy. (*He picks up a piece of wood.*) Hello, Judy, come and have a look at my big stick. Bang. Bang.

Sound of the bikes. Both CATHY *and* PETE *look apprehensively towards* JIM.

JIM: Perfect. Peeling paint. Shattered glass. A bombed out world. Desolation Row. Hiroshima Mon Amour. And the lovers will just wander among its insanity.

PETE: Can we get on with it? All hell's going to break loose in a bit.

JIM (*absorbed*): The film will be like a strange circular dance returning to those images of our parents — trapped in the isolation called family. Oh that's it. We'll end with Lefty dancing alone in his greenhouse. It says it all.

PETE: What?

JIM: And stillframe on him for the final credits.

PETE: You want to use that of my dad?

Silence.

You're jokin', aren't you? I mean, we an't buried him yet, and you want to. . . .

JIM: Look, he was the one always goin' on about being remembered. That's why he bought the camera in the first place.

PETE: Oh, great. Easter Sunday, and Jim's goin' to gi' my dad life after death. For a joke. God, it must be eatin' your heart out you two crept off so early 'cos otherwise you might've filmed him curled up on that floor. That would have been even a better ending, woun't it?

JIM: It's not for a joke, Pete.

PETE *turns and walks away.*

That it then? Take your bat and ball home. And spoil it for the rest.

PETE (*puts down the equipment*): Here, keep it. Take it back to me mam when you've finished.

CATHY: Where you going?

PETE: Not home. There's nought to stay there for.

JIM: We don't need you.

PETE: I know.

JIM: Pete, I'm sorry about your dad, but you're just not listening to me. I have to make the film the way I see it.

PETE: If I'd've filmed you and your dad fighting, would you have rushed to put that in?

JIM *turns away.* PETE *leaves.*

CATHY: He's not going to hide behind a hedge, you know.

JIM: We don't need him. We can do it with just the two of us. Once when all the actors and crew walked out on Antonioni he shot the rest of the film himself, with just his star, Monica Vitti. Endless shots of Vitti walking through an empty town. *The Eclipse.* Fantastic movie. It's going to be a wonderful ending.

CATHY (*quietly*): Why have you changed the ending, Jim?

JIM (*reluctantly*): I've changed my mind. I change, the film changes. That's how it works.

CATHY: Why have you changed? Why do they end up again in a world of black and white? I thought they'd broken through.

JIM: To what? What is there to break through to? You mean all that romantic crap about love-making while the sun shines? That's for kids that. I've put all that at the beginning of the film. Holding hands, all wide-eyed and innocent, by the deep blue sea. Then they make love, and they see the truth. Love's a con. A false dream. You're more alone after than before. But at least you're free of your illusions. You can look around at your mad black and white little world and face the facts. There's just man alone. Nothing else. The rest is lies.

CATHY (*softly*): It wasn't like that for me.

JIM: No, well it is for me. And it's my film.

He turns back to his camera.

CATHY: It was the first time for us. You were upset. It dun't mean it's the end of the world. You can still use colour, can't you?

JIM: We'll film you walking past the smashed up shops.

She turns and begins to walk away.

(*Suddenly desperate.*) Cathy! Don't go.

She turns back. Silence.

Please. I can't make it all on my own.

Silence. Fade.

Scene Eleven

ELSIE*'s garden.*
DORA *and* ELSIE *are sitting by the pond.*

DORA: Well, your fish are doin' all right, at any road.

ELSIE: Like the rest of me inmates. All they bloody do is eat. Practically stopped swimmin' so they can save their energy for meal times. That and . . . you know. The other day, I'd come out here for a bit of peace and quiet, and I looked in and I thought, Christ, they've bloody died. They were dead still, one a couple of inches above the other. I thought, they're going to turn on their backs and float up with their little fins stickin' in the air. But do you know what the buggers were up to? There was this ever so tiny little thin thing going from the tail of one to the other. The bloody things were havin' it away. In my pool. It shook me. I thought bloody hell, even me goldfish are getting more out of life than I am. I was that mad, I was going to chuck a stone in.

DORA: You should learn from them. Get yourself out a bit.

ELSIE: What? I tell you, if I see a frog in there, I'm goin' to kiss it. Well, you never know, do you?

DORA *laughs. A baby cries, off-stage. The lights slowly come up to include the rest of the garden.* ARTHUR *is busy digging up the empties from* LEFTY*'s earth trays.*

There it goes. All the bloody time. I don't know how she's got the face to take her kid back to the same vicar just six weeks after the wedding. I've never been so shamed. She's ruling the roost, she is. I'm stuck out here all the time. I'm sick to death of it.

JIM *and* CATHY *enter.*

JIM: How was the christening?

DORA: It was a lovely service.

JIM: I brought your camera back, in case you want to take some pictures of the baby.

ELSIE: I can't use the bugger.

JIM: No, well, I thought Pete.

ELSIE: He an't turned up.

JIM: Oh, I thought he might be here. Anyway I've finished the film, so . . .

ELSIE: When do we get to see this masterpiece then?

JIM: Er . . . I don't think you will.

ELSIE: Why not? Your mam says it's a love film. We like a good cry.

JIM: I'm not sure it's right for folk to see.

DORA (*to* CATHY): Have you seen it?

CATHY: Yes.

DORA: Why can't I see it? Do you think I woun't understand it?

JIM: It isn't that. It's just . . . seeing it. Well, it dun't say what I wanted it to say. Well, it says what I wanted it to say, but I don't want it to say that now. Now that I see it. If you follow me.

ELSIE: Clear as mud.

DORA: Well, what do you want it to say?

JIM: I don't know.

DORA: I'm sure it's ever so good. Is it good, Cathy?

CATHY: Yes.

DORA: I'd love to see it.

Silence.

JIM: What's Dad doin'?

ELSIE: Diggin' up all the bottles Lefty had spirited away in there.

DORA: And we know where he got 'em, don't we?

ELSIE: Well, then he's entitled to the money back on the empties, in't he? What does it matter now? Maybe it bought Lefty a bit of joy. He never put down roots here, you know. I don't know why. It was the move killed him.

DORA: Arthur misses him. They had a lot of good times together.

JIM: Him miss him? You must be kiddin'. He probably don't even know he's dead.

DORA: You've got your dad wrong, you know. He dun't show his feelings. He dun't believe a man should do that. But he has his feelings all the same.

ELSIE: Has anybody told him that he's got feelings? Maybe he's just forgotten.

DORA (*to* JIM): Go and say hello to him.

JIM: What?

DORA: He's seen you through the glass. You an't never spoken to him since. It hurts him. Just say hello. Don't cost much.

JIM: Come on.

DORA: For me.

CATHY: Go on. You were talking about the people in your film not talking. That what was holding them back was not being able to hear what each other said.

DORA: Well, that's because you coun't afford sound, in't it?

Silence.

JIM: OK. Just don't make a song and dance out of it.

He crosses to the greenhouse.
JIM *enters the greenhouse.* CATHY *drifts back to the women.*

DORA: We haven't been seeing a lot of you lately. I've missed you.

CATHY: I thought it best to stay away while he did his exams.

DORA: So we'll be seeing more of you now.

CATHY: I'm not sure.

PETE *arrives.*

ELSIE: Eh, up, all the prodigal sons are turning up. I knew you'd have to come home to your mam sooner or later.

PETE: It's just for the day, Mam. Have to get back to London.

ELSIE: We'll see about that.

PETE: You all right, then?

ELSIE: Am I, hell?

PETE: Good. Jim brought the camera back?

CATHY: He's finished the film.

PETE: How was it?

CATHY: He's not happy with the ending.

PETE (*pause*): Really?

ELSIE: You'd better take some of that brat before they put him to bed.

PETE: Right. Might as well get the work out of the way.

He checks the camera.

DORA: It's nice out here, innit? I'd have liked a little garden.

CATHY (*to* PETE): He was hopin' to catch you.

PETE: Was he? Why?

CATHY: He was talking about the end of *Women in Love.* Needing a friend, as well as a . . . woman. I haven't read it.

PETE: I have.

CATHY: What does it mean?

PETE: Maybe it's a game. Who knows?

DORA: Your hedge is coming on a treat.

ELSIE: It is, in't it? You know, if you lie back, nobody can see you.

They lie back on the grass. PETE *crosses to watch* JIM *and* ARTHUR *in the greenhouse.* ARTHUR *turns and notices his son.*

ARTHUR: Gi' us a hand takin' these bottles back to the beer-off.

PETE *begins to film them.* CATHY *watches him.*

DORA: They can see you from that bedroom over there.

ELSIE: Folk are too busy in their bedrooms to go looking out the window. Well, some folk. 'Sides, it'll grow, now it's got going.

The baby starts crying again.

ARTHUR: I'll gi' you half a dollar.

ELSIE: There it goes. What sort of name is Sasha, I ask you? Is that a gal's name or a lad's name?

DORA (*pauses*): It's a French name, I think.

CATHY: Yes, it is.

ARTHUR: No, come on. Partners. Fifty-fifty. Whatever you get.

ARTHUR *holds out his hand towards him.* JIM *slowly takes it. They shake hands. His father sniffs, and turns away to his work.* JIM *realises* PETE *is filming. He stands watching him.*

PETE: Just filming some new footage, Jim.

JIM *nods. He tracks the camera from* JIM *to include* CATHY *and the rest of the garden. No one else moves. Freeze.*
Music: The Beatles. 'Help me if you can . . .'
Fade to Blackout.

SEACHANGE

For Tina
and thanks to the staff and students of
Dartington College

'We are closed in, and the key is turned
on our uncertainty . . .
We had fed the heart on fantasies
the heart's grown brutal from the fare
more substance in our enmities
than in our love . . .'

Yeats, *Meditations in Time of Civil War*

Starting Out

In the summer of 1980, I travelled with my family on a boat from Instanbul down the Aegean coast, criss-crossing from the Turkish mainland to the Greek isles. We boarded at an Instanbul in a state of considerable political unrest, but, imitating well-trained tourists, we weaved our way among the military, and the demonstrators, to mosque and palace.

As we left Instanbul, and travelled through the Straits of Messina at night, I could see the flame of the Unknown Soldier flickering on the mainland of Gallipoli. But the still air failed to carry the smell of its ashes across the sea, or perhaps the aroma of kebab and the sweat of the determined holiday-makers deterred its passage.

With the aid of the heat and alcohol, I fell into a haltering conversation with a Turk, a lecturer like myself, and we talked, inevitably, of education, and then slowly, delicately, of politics and socialism, using the excuse of language difficulties as a screen for silent reflection and assessment. And, always, the flame flickered in the distance, as we talked of Anglo-Turkish relationships, and, inevitably, of war.

His grandfather had run the garrison at Gallipoli, had ordered the laying of the barbed wire under the water. At his death, many years later, he told his children of his horror, as he watched the allies thrashing in the water, or swarming out of the sea onto the warm inviting, and equally deadly, beach.

I spoke for the first time in years of the legend of my wounded grandfather, dragged back from the beach onto a Red Cross ship and safety, only to meet death when it was sunk by a plane.

And of how he was a champion swimmer, spending every Sunday swimming what I knew later as the most polluted of rivers — the Trent. I wondered if, at that moment, we cut through the clear water of his grave.

My friend took himself off to bed, perhaps to tell the ghost of his grandfather of this simple meeting. I stayed with the wine to talk to mine, and grandfather and I that night shared an equally uncertain intimacy, born this time of those who love each other through blood, but are only too aware of how the sea of time divides them.

A week after our visit along that coast, the Generals took over the land, and this friend, along with many others we met there, found the Generals' promise of security a constant threat to the dream of freedom they contemplated.

I returned to the increasing insecurity of my own land, determined to write a play about my grandfather, and tried to glean what facts I could from memory.

Certain circumstances, both personal and political, prevented me, until two years later, in the spring and summer of 1982, I was reminded forcibly, like everyone else, of boats and death at sea, as our 'armada' sailed out into the South Atlantic towards that well known 'incident'. The ship's deck with the dark waters below was under all our feet.

Workshopping with students at Dartington College of Arts, I wrote, and they performed, the first version of this piece, the narrative of which was completed before the war itself ended.

We were all on the Ship of Fools and clearly had to look elsewhere than to the captain and the crew for real guidance back to sanity. And amidst all that shouting we had to listen very quietly for the voices that might hold the key to hope.

To find the truth one could no longer trust the facts of politicians and the pathetic distortions of the media, but we had also to listen to both personal myths, and wider legends. It was at this point my grandfather spoke to me again.

Stephen Lowe
Riverside, June 1984

Seachange was first performed at Riverside Studios on the 4 July 1984, with the following cast:

JOHN	Terence Wilton
TOM	Kenneth Colley
EILEEN	Sheila Reid
DOCTOR	Christopher Guinee
DORIS	Elizabeth Bradley
PAUL	Michael Packer
HELEN	Michele Copsey
CASS	Caroline Embling

Directed by David Leveaux
Designed by Brien Vahey
Lighting by Rory Dempster
Music by John White
Assistant Director Irina Brown
Wardrobe Kate McFee
Casting Director Simone Reynolds
Stage Manager Melanie Bryceland
Assistant Stage Manager Mark Layton

Set built by John Leonard and Peter Price
Furniture built by Philip Parsons

PROLOGUE

JOHN *mid-30s, white summer clothes.*

JOHN: A death at sea, perhaps a murder, haunts me to tell its story. Makes me wonder if there's any meaning to futility. How do we value an act of folly?

Silence.

At the turn of the fifteenth century, a poet wrote a tale called 'Das Narrenschiff'. The Ship of Fools. Some historians say that such ships actually existed, in the period between the medieval acceptance of Folly as part of communal life and its eventual isolation into those asylums that so typify the emerging Age of Reason. Others claim it was merely an artistic device, a literary metaphor, or conceit.

Pause.

Myth, however, has it that sailors were paid to take away the mad, and thus these ships travelled from port to port, picking up their human cargo, occasionally giving showings to any interested audience. Folly had already voyaged sufficiently from normal life to provide an entertaining diversion, like a visit to the theatre, or to the zoo. Except they didn't have zoos then. Zoos grew out of the notion of asylums, and which between the walled-in theatre and the madhouse was mother to the other, I can only conjecture.

Pause.

But let us be careful not to diminish the worth of these ships. There was more to them than mere containment. The mad were in fact on a voyage, and the voyage had a destination with a sense of purpose, which was to bring the lost souls back to sanity and, naturally enough in a devout society, they visited shrines, centres of religious experience and healing, and the most significant of all these shrines for Folly was a small German town called Nuremberg.

Silence.

But what do we know of the experience of the passengers on the Ship of Fools? There are only fables of their embarcation, and a few images of their voyage from those who paid to see their antics. But no legends of their arrival, or their return. Perhaps they never did return. Perhaps at the penultimate port of call before Nuremberg, their protectors, these sailors, doctors, perhaps they led them off the ship, so near to sanity, and escorted them, humanely, to the final camps.

Pause.

Or perhaps we find that more comforting to believe than their return.

ACT ONE

Scene One

Silence. Music/sounds of a ship ready for sail. Slow light up on the other passengers ready for departure, but isolated, single in their preoccupations.

JOHN: What can we agree about on starting out? We are in a theatre, an asylum of memory. We are setting out to sea. It is the early summer of 1982, already history. Our ship picks up its human cargo for a slow cruise through the Aegean. I am one of many individuals who boarded at Istanbul, Constantinople, Byzantium.

The ship's horn. A burning hot summer's day. JOHN takes off his jacket.

The sea is as flat and green as an English lawn. The scene reminds me of the literary conceit of the Edwardian cricket match. All it needs is for a team of Christs in whites to stroll the surface of the water.

Pause.

Ghosts rise without my invocation or desire. I want only to be done with the image of the past, and the temptation of the future. I want to be only here. Now.

He turns and moves towards a table as HELEN, *a young woman in shorts and T-shirt, moves towards it, carrying her yellow plastic rucksack. She notices his papers spread out. He reaches for them.*

Allow me.

He reaches to tidy them up, but she turns away and sits elsewhere. He watches for a moment, and then stares at the letter in his hand.

Oh, mother. (*Pause.*) Why can I never leave a letter unopened? Even when I know it only brings another's pain uselessly into my own privacy.

He crosses with it to the rails.

EILEEN, *a nervous-looking woman in her mid-forties, dressed in a two piece summer outfit, sits and begins to apply sun lotion carefully to her nose. The ship's* DOCTOR *stands nearby watching.*

'Dear mother. We pass through the Straits as I reply. The coast of Gallipoli stares back at me, but we won't stop until we reach Troy. So, as you wish, I'll scatter your petals of remembrance into the oblivion of the deep blue sea.'

DORIS, *in her eighties, sighs loudly, and turns slightly in her deck chair.* JOHN *walks along the edge of the ship, scattering the petals that fall from the envelope.*

Grandfather, you made your futile gesture here. Now I've made mine. And let that be an end to it.

He turns head down back to his table and, echoing the moment with HELEN, *he comes face to face with* TOM, *in full Great War infantry uniform and soaking wet. Silence.*

TOM (*amiably*): Do yo' know what we's supposed to do in this sort of circum-stance? Do I bounce you on me knee like a grandson or do we shake hands like men?

TOM *holds out his hand.* JOHN *slowly curiously reaches out towards it.* TOM *pulls it back.*

Best not. Sea water. Salty, dry your skin. Can I dry mine, before I catch me death again? I won't in battle dress, anyroad. Stuck below deck as a stretcher case. Just longjohns there.

He begins to strip.

Bleedin' hell, but I hate this outfit. I remember watching it float down the ward as the water rushed in. It gave me a strange delight.

JOHN *turns away.*

Subject not your liking?

JOHN *does not respond.*

Are these mine?

JOHN *turns back to see him indicate the clothes folded over the back of a chair. JOHN shakes his head, baffled.*

Check your mam's letter.

JOHN (*reading*): 'Dad dressed in the fashion. Mam says he was smart in his strawyard, pink striped shirt, brown suit.

TOM: Thought they were.

He starts to drop his pants as a young girl, CASS, *crosses in front of him.*

Whoops-e-doodle!

He tries to cover himself, nearly falling over. He laughs.

I woun't've wanted to shock the little lady, wi' someat she an't even dreamed of. Still, no fear of that now. Could do me whirling dervish stark naked and she woun't bat an eye.

He wanders after her and watches her as she shyly, checking no one is watching, strips down to her costume and lies on her towel. TOM *watches in shock and fascination.*

Well, she's got no shame has she?

JOHN: They're all like that now, grand-father.

TOM: Are they indeed?

JOHN: It doesn't mean anything. We all bare more of our skin, but keep within as dark as ever.

TOM *stares at her.*

TOM (*quietly to* CASS): Sorry lass, I din't mean to judge you.

PAUL, *aged 19, in a sports coat and flannels, camera around his neck, hovers upstage, his eyes constantly flickering back to* CASS.

There was a nurse, raven-haired like you on the ship. Angel she was. Mind you, my bones are as white as hers now. Me and her lie together for eternity, but not wi' the fulfillment of desire.

JOHN (*suddenly*): Enough.

TOM: Wha'?

JOHN: I don't want to hear about your death.

TOM: Sorry. Am I spoilin' your holiday?

JOHN *looks away, clearly on edge.*

Has the revolution come then?

JOHN: Pardon?

TOM: The likes of my family on the upper deck.

JOHN: No, we've all been bought off with outings and a cup of tea.

TOM *watches him, quietly. He nods to himself sadly.*

TOM: Gi's a cup then.

Pause.

JOHN: Of course.

TOM: Tea and biscuits out of Gallipoli. Now, there's a dream.

TOM *stands caressing his clothes, as* JOHN *nervously attempts to pour the tea.*

These were for best, of course. Me stepping-out clothes. Clothes for love talk and new jobs.

JOHN *struggles with the packet.*

Trail the packet in the water. Let the barbed wire do the tearing.

JOHN *spills the biscuits.* DORIS *wakes with a start and, clearly disorientated, moves to the rail.* TOM *stares at her.*

Did she end up looking like her?

JOHN: Who?

TOM: Your gran. My lady.

JOHN (*pause*): I don't remember.

TOM (*indicating* CASS): She were more like this one, when I last saw her.

TOM *notices* PAUL *watching her. He clearly does not approve.*

JOHN: Biscuit?

TOM (*turning back*): Very civilised. All dressed up like Sunday tea. I used to take your gran on the river at Whit. Trail your hand in the water. Thanks for the outing, son.

JOHN: It's nothing to do with me.

TOM *sits.*

TOM: What is to do wi' you?

JOHN: Pardon?

TOM: What do you do to warrant sun and sand?

JOHN: I write plays.

TOM: Must pay well.

JOHN *laughs.*

TOM: You probably got that off me. I were interested in the theatre. Used to shift scenery for Variety.

JOHN: I know.

TOM (*singing*): 'She's my lady love, she's my own, my lady love . . .' Always wanted to be a singer. Never got the break. Still, it come through for you.

JOHN: You were a socialist weren't you?

TOM (*firmly*): Am! (*Pause.*) And you?

JOHN: Our land's at war again. A minor skirmish this time. But the country's still waving in the wind with its flags and bunting, as the kids queue up for blood letting.

TOM: The leeches are still with you?

JOHN: As fat as ever.

Silence.

TOM: You look tired, my son. Have they told you it can't be done?

JOHN: Don't mock me, grandfather. You weren't so smart.

TOM: Have you got children?

JOHN (*pauses*): A daughter.

TOM: Ye', it was my daughter killed me. Your mam shot me wi' her little finger. Pointed it at me, like the gal in the picture. 'What did you do in the war daddy?' But I don't blame her.

I rail against them bastards who got a kid to kill her father.

JOHN *breaks away from the table. As he moves away he passes* HELEN *who accidentally knocks her books off the table, reaching for her pen.*

He bends to pick them up and hands them back. She makes an almost imperceptible nod.

What do you want — a shipboard romance is it?

JOHN *stands by* HELEN *not looking at* TOM.

What do you want of me?

JOHN *does not reply.*

(*Rising.*) You must have called me up for someat.

JOHN: I didn't call you up!

TOM: How come I'm here then?

JOHN *shakes his head, impatiently.*

JOHN: How do I . . . You're just the product of idle association. From the reading of your daughter's letter.

TOM *waves the letter angrily.*

TOM: Then burn it. If you desire nought of me, burn the bleedin' thing and send me winging back to Hell again.

JOHN *takes the letter from him, and stares at him.* CASS *suddenly sits up between them and puts her hand up against the sun.*

She gasps and then checks quickly to see that no one's noticed. TOM *kneels by her.*

JOHN (*fascinated. Softly*): Does the blood still beat through your body in that particular passion?

TOM: I'm feared for the gal, that's all. She needs looking after.

JOHN: You don't fool me, Grandfather.

TOM (*challenging*): What about you? Aren't the ashes still hot in your grate?

JOHN *looks down at* HELEN, *and then turns away.*

(*Softly to* CASS:) Oh, my angel. Oh, this can't be.

TOM *moves his hand across her face – almost touching her. He sighs. He stares down at his crutch.*

I always thought only the hermit crab stirred there. Oh. Even the heat of a hopeless craving is better than the grave. I'll do ought the lad asks to stay. They say wanting makes slaves of us all, but also great builders. What will we resurrect from the ashes this time round?

He stands to face JOHN *who slowly puts down the letter. They hold position apart from* EILEEN *who steps forward to* DORIS *with the book she is reading. The sound of cicadas into the next scene.*

Scene Two

The ruins of Troy.

EILEEN: 'The new city, Troy VIIa, was a continuation of its predecessor in all essential features, although many signs of its insecurity have come to light, and soon it was immediately razed to the ground by fire. There is every reason to believe that this catastrophe corresponded to the famous Trojan War, which according to Homer, opposed Agamemnon's . . . Acheans –

DOCTOR: Achaeans.

EILEEN: – To Priam's Trojans. The date is controversial. The most likely opinion giving it, like Herodotus, as a little after 1250 B.C. . . . .

The DOCTOR, *a middle-aged man in uniform, turns to* JOHN. *They both wear sunglasses.*

DOCTOR: A time of heroes.

JOHN (*mildly*): The local mafia.

He watches HELEN, *as she puts on her sunglasses and moves away.*

PAUL *hides under his jacket trying to change film.*

DOCTOR: Not according to Homer.

JOHN (*smiling*): Official propaganda.

DORIS (*to* EILEEN): I think I have been here before.

EILEEN: *Déjà vu*?

DORIS: Or do I think of Rome? All ruins look the same.

EILEEN: Do they?

DORIS: Pillars. Grass. Cats. Sniffing dogs like bags of bones.

CASS *kneels, softly enticing a dog towards her.* TOM *watches her protectively.* PAUL *surfaces.*

DOCTOR: Ah, Orpheus!

PAUL: Sorry?

DOCTOR: Paul, isn't it?

PAUL: Yes.

DOCTOR: What do you make of it all, Paul?

PAUL: All what?

DOCTOR: Do you consider the destruction of a whole civilisation for a lover's lust to be acceptable?

JOHN *turns to watch* HELEN, *who stands nearby.*

PAUL (*hesitant*): Well, I don't know much about the classical, not really but . . .

DOCTOR: Ah.

PAUL: I just wondered –

DOCTOR: Yes?

PAUL: Do you know where Philadelphia is?

DOCTOR: Philadelphia?

PAUL: Only I can't find it on the map.

DOCTOR: You're on the wrong boat. The transatlantic was the one behind.

PAUL: Oh, yes, I see, ye', very good. No, what I meant was the original

Philadelphia that St Paul visited after Ephesus – It's Greek for the place of brotherly love.

DOCTOR: I believe that's in Utopia.

PAUL: Oh, where's that?

DOCTOR: It's Greek for no place.

PAUL: What?

DOCTOR: It does not exist.

PAUL: But it's in the Bible.

DOCTOR: So is heaven, another Utopia.

HELEN *stares at the* DOCTOR, *then turns away.*

TOM: You living are so certain.

DOCTOR: If you really want brotherly love, you might try the Falklands.

DORIS *looks up.*

DORIS: Where are they?

EILEEN: What, dear?

DORIS: These Falklands. Perhaps I've played there.

She digs into her bag to produce a battered world map. PAUL *stands, confused.*

DOCTOR: If I can be of any further service.

PAUL: I have no need of a doctor.

He turns away, to take concealed photos of CASS *who waits patiently for the dog to approach. The* DOCTOR *speaks confidentially to* EILEEN.

DOCTOR: He believes God will cure him. No doubt sees his acne as a test for a future Job.

EILEEN *does not respond.*

DORIS: Where are they?

DOCTOR: Somewhere off South America.

DORIS: Do we go there?

DOCTOR: Not on this trip, dear.

EILEEN (*studying* DORIS'*s map*): There they are.

DORIS: No, I've not been there.

EILEEN: How can you be so sure?

DORIS: There's no red cross. I always mark the theatres with a red cross.

EILEEN: Are you famous?

DORIS: It depends where I am.

TOM (*to* JOHN): My fame's marked wi' a red cross. The first hospital ship sunk by a plane. I coun't have dreamed my death when I was a kid, 'cept perhaps as a far fetched fantasy. The shield of St George cracked wide open by the breath of a flying dragon. There's a tale for your lass.

JOHN *apparently pays no attention.*

Only goin' to tell stories wi' a happy ending, are you?

JOHN: She wouldn't listen.

TOM: It's you who won't listen. Come on, I can give you the inside story.

JOHN (*sharply*): No.

TOM: Why not?

JOHN: Why do you want me to relive your pointless pain? What good would that do? No one wants to hear any more tales of futile deaths in equally futile wars.

TOM: They would if you made someat of it.

JOHN *walks away, towards* HELEN *who studies her Plan.*

She turns, seeing him. He smiles at her.

JOHN: It's so difficult to imagine what it was like, isn't it?

She nods.

HELEN: This was the temple of Athena, where they kept Helen.

JOHN: Oh, was it?

She looks at him for a moment, then turns away. He sits near her. The DOCTOR *smiles at* EILEEN. *She is clearly embarrassed by this particular attention.*

DOCTOR: Did you buy that guide book in Istanbul?

She shakes her head and moves away.

EILEEN: It's so hot here. It must've been lovely when they had all the pillars up.

PAUL *crosses to* CASS. TOM *turns to watch him.*

PAUL (*nervous*): Excuse me, but I see you are wearing a crucifix . . .

She looks up so alarmed that PAUL *backs away.*

TOM (*angry*): Can't you see she wants her privacy?

He crosses back to her. JOHN *turns to him.*

JOHN: Don't you get tired with all this deceit of caring?

TOM: Are you so different? You never take your eyes off that lass.

JOHN: It's only a game, Grandfather. They say 'The challenge of lust diverts the heroes.'

TOM: Don't talk fancy wi' me. It's all pretend wi' you.

JOHN: Do you possess reality?

TOM: Only for fishes but they know nought of fantasy.

DORIS: Where's the bus? It must be time to eat soon.

DOCTOR: And then set sail for the isles of Greece: Lesbos, Samos, Patmos. Away from the mad Turks to the heirs of a Great Empire. (*To* EILEEN:) Oh, I'm sorry. I forget. You are, I believe, married to a Turkish Cypriot?

HELEN *smiles at her.*

EILEEN (*uncertain, to* HELEN): We run a hotel, well a large guest house really, but —

DOCTOR: If I know my Turks, you run and he sits in the shade.

EILEEN: Actually, he is not really at all like —

DOCTOR: A vicious race. Dividing an island. A forced military occupation.

EILEEN *looks around, distraught.*

EILEEN: Excuse me.

She leaves. The DOCTOR *realises* HELEN *is looking at him.*

Silence.

HELEN (*softly*): Was Troy destroyed for a lover's lust? They wrote a great deal of Paris's passion, but what went on in Helen's heart?

She does not wait for the DOCTOR*'s reply. She turns away and follows after* EILEEN. CASS *leans forward, hand outstretched towards the dog.*

JOHN *faces* TOM.

JOHN: What would you do to stay?

TOM: Anything.

JOHN: Get me that girl.

TOM: How can I?

JOHN: Find out her darkest thoughts. I need the key to her.

Silence.

TOM: Half a min . . . I've got standards. There were plenty of painted women hangin' round the theatre, but I were never a pandar. I allers respected women whatever their powder.

CASS *calls softly to the dog. The* DOCTOR *notices* CASS.

DOCTOR (*shouts*): Don't touch the dog!

She draws back in terror, staring at her hand. Almost in tears, she runs out.

DORIS: You frighten the poor child.

DOCTOR: Better a fright than rabies. A dog's bite here can cost your sanity and life.

JOHN (*to* TOM): Your girl is in need of a guardian angel.

TOM: It's no way to treat your grand-father.

JOHN: We all have to sing for our supper.
Get me her.

PAUL *moves down to the dog.*

PAUL: Get away! Shoo!

TOM *stiffens and salutes his grandson.*

TOM: Sir!

He exits after HELEN.

JOHN: To see how easily even the finest
are compromised by passion gives me
no satisfaction. Troy. The challenge
of lust diverts the heroes. They place
it at the centre of their walled city.
They hollow out the bellies of horses
for it.

PAUL: Shoo!

Blackout.

Scene Three

The cabins.
    HELEN *dries herself after a shower* —
TOM *wipes the brow of his hat, and
attempts to respect her modesty.*

TOM: It's bloody hot down here in the
bowels of the ship. Were a place like
this where I lay naked and a woman
gazed on me. (*Groans.*) Why an't sixty
years of water doused me desire? I'm
sweating like a squaddie in a Turkish
brothel.

*She drags a small pile of underclothing
from her rucksack.* TOM *studies a
pair as she dresses.*

Well, some things change, don't they?
When I was your age, it were like
fighting through sails of flannel to
gain satisfaction. I'm not complaining.
I always found the fumbling gave me
time to adjust to feelings. But now wi'
only that between me and a skin,
Christ, a man'd have to have a swift
confidence to touch your thigh.

She sits, and begins a letter.

Hope you don't mind me chatting to
you like this but it gi's a feel of a

relationship, one I woun't wish to take
advantage of. Like just now. After the
first shock of seeing you without . . . I
mean I turned straight away when you
. . . It was the same wi' me wife. I
allers respected her desire with regard
to the absence of light.

DORIS *struggles to drag a trunk to
block her door. She sees* PAUL *pass.
He is now in shorts.*

DORIS: Stop! What are you, an angel?
All in white.

PAUL: Sorry?

DORIS: The lock is broken. It does not
lock. No time to wake before men
drag you away. I try to block this side
but . . . at best, a few seconds. No time
to dress. You see my predicament.

PAUL: I'll have a look at it for you.

DORIS: English?

PAUL: Yes.

DORIS: I am English, too. I think.

HELEN *addresses an envelope.* TOM
reads it over her shoulder.

TOM: Ah, Ireland. Oh, pardon me.
I don't like to pry. I believe
in folk's right to privacy. The faith of
my Irish forefathers lingers on in me
socialism. I woun't be here if I weren't
on duty.

He begins to search the room. HELEN
sits, staring at the letter. PAUL *works
on the door.*

DORIS: Do I know you?

PAUL: No.

DORIS: Then why do you do this?

PAUL: Jesus tells us to help one another.

DORIS: I was Jewish, I think. Perhaps
my husband. I cannot remember. I
remember my husband, but they say
that was years ago. No, I say, the first
time, when they took him, yes, years
ago, but he came back. Yes, they say,
but now he has gone. Years. A week,
I say, because I'm silly, I should be

dead. (*Smiles.*) The first few days he was away, fine, peace, very good. We'd lived too much in each others' pocket. First two days' fresh change, smell like clean linen on the line. But . . . (*Pauses.*) English angel. In Hebrew, angel is mal'ak means messenger. Mal'ak Yehovah, messenger from God. You bring me a message?

PAUL (*smiling*): Perhaps.

DORIS: From my husband? he tells me where to meet him?

PAUL: Never trust messages from spirits.

DORIS (*disappointed*): Is this the message?

PAUL: Except from the Holy Ghost.

CASS *cries out in her sleep.*

CASS: God! God help me!

PAUL *registers only a faint cry. HELEN hears it and stands listening. TOM jumps up alarmed, and steps through the wall.*

TOM: In't it fantastic what you can do wi'out a body? Daft to yearn for one so much.

CASS (*apparently delirious*): Tell him to leave me, God. I don't encourage him. I sleep with my clothes on. It doesn't stop him. Stop him. Stop him following me.

TOM: Oh, if only I could help you. I'd spend my time here, nursing the gash some bloke has made.

HELEN *puts down the letter.*

HELEN (*softly*): You were right. Yes. 'The need to confess in letters can betray the others.'

She burns the letter.

TOM: Bloody hell. I can't be in two places at once.

CASS (*cries out*): He's there!

TOM: Me?

CASS: I know your face, even though you only come in the dark.

TOM: No not me. Some other shadow. Not me.

PAUL *knocks at the door. CASS shakes herself and wakes up.*

PAUL: Are you all right?

CASS: Yes.

PAUL: Only I —

CASS: I'm fine. Fine thank you.

TOM: I'm sorry. I have other duties. Private letter to read, underwear to rifle. But if it buys me time with you.

CASS *nods to herself and climbs out of bed. She is dressed. TOM re-enters HELEN's room. HELEN puts on her jeans and begins to hum a tune. EILEEN in her room picks up her guidebook. PAUL turns back to DORIS.*

DORIS: All I want is to feel the hand of my husband on me. Is that wrong?

PAUL: Put away these thoughts of the flesh.

DORIS (*laughing*): See, messages come like Union Express.

TOM (*studies the ashes*): Give me a clue. I daren't go back to my master, empty handed.

PAUL: The lock is fixed.

DORIS: Mal'ak.

TOM (*softly*): Please, God.

HELEN *sings. The women move forward, listening to her. PAUL moves away. TOM follows. The tune has an echo of an Irish folk song in its lyricism. The sound of cicadas.*

Scene Four

The cliff edge at Lesbos.

HELEN (*sings*):
Whenever I spy your face
fire steals through my every limb
leaving only ash as a trace
and all my words betray me

Chorus. .

Paler than the grass of summer
I shudder with the caress of death
Must I always suffer
being merely
poor poverty's mother
can the unwanted lover
never be the one to recover?

My eyes are dead to all light
and the wave of sweat overwhelms me
my ears beat out with fright
why won't my desire set me free?

Chorus.

TOM: I'll tell my lad you sing a lovely song.

Silence.

DORIS *nods.* EILEEN *smiles.* CASS *stares out over the edge of the cliff.* TOM *watches her nervously.* *Sunset.*

That's my serenade for you, my love. That song says it all.

DORIS: Is this your song?

HELEN: The tune is mine, but the words are translated from Sappho.

DORIS: Good.

EILEEN (*tentatively*): Was Sappho really a . . .

HELEN (*gently*): What, a lesbian?

DORIS: Even the men are Lesbians, here on Lesbos.

TOM: Lesbian? That won't written by a lesbian. That's by a man like me.

EILEEN: Only my book says that's a myth about her. And that she threw herself off this cliff, because of unrequited love for a young man.

TOM: Much more likely.

HELEN: Or perhaps she jumped, not because she failed to catch her man, but because she refused to be a quarry?

CASS (*turning*): Quarry?

TOM: It's a cliff, not a quarry. Stand back my love.

EILEEN (*noticing* CASS): Had we better be getting back? The men will be waiting.

HELEN: Just a few more moments without the male voice.

TOM: Away from the edge, Cass. Come on.

She stares over. Silence. EILEEN *is the first to break it.*

EILEEN (*to* HELEN): Where are you heading?

HELEN (*pauses*): I don't know.

EILEEN: Extended holiday, is it?

HELEN: Sort of.

EILEEN: It must be nice to have a job with such long holidays.

HELEN: Your husband's Turkish, isn't he?

EILEEN: Cypriot. Turkish Cypriot. But we live on our side. Not on . . .

HELEN: Do you have children?

EILEEN: They both live in England now. We paid for their school there. A divided land is no place for education. Not that I wish to talk of partition. Cyprus is a holiday centre, not a battlefront.

HELEN: Do women meet up there to talk to each other?

EILEEN (*pauses*): The local women do, in each other's houses.

DORIS (*smiling*): We met in what we called cells. And sometimes in what they called cells. It was all the same. Meetings went on. In solitary confinement one composed amendments to amendments in song.

She looks up at the two women and smiles, apparently unconscious of the effect she's caused. Silence.

CASS, *oblivious, takes a step nearer the edge of the cliff.*

EILEEN: Cass!

She steps back, startled.

It is Cass, isn't it?

She nods.

(*Smiling.*) You're so quiet.

CASS: I was listening.

EILEEN: I wasn't criticisng. (*Pause.*) Where are you going?

CASS: Israel.

HELEN: Why?

CASS (*smiling*): To pick oranges.

DORIS: They say I go home to Israel. No. The land I was born in does not exist. This they also told me. But the mountains, have they moved the mountains? They change the name to fool the liberal — but where have they hid the mountains and the sea?

HELEN: Where was this?

DORIS: So many names. And now I must for my dinner, although why I know not. When I was a girl, I was as thin as a cleaner from my father's pipe, and just as white from lack of food. Now I have no future, I could eat a horse for breakfast. (*Laughs.*) It pleases me to know God has a sense of humour as well as occasional amnesia.

HELEN: I'll come with you. It's steep.

CASS (*suddenly*): She was haunted by a man you say?

HELEN: Hunted. Yes.

CASS *stares back over the water.* HELEN *and* DORIS *exit.*

EILEEN: Are you coming? It's getting very dark.

CASS: I'll stay for a second. It's good to feel the breeze after so much heat.

EILEEN (*uncertain*): Too many exams, I suppose? My son was exactly the same.

CASS: Did he get through them?

EILEEN: Almost.

CASS *smiles.* EILEEN *reaches out to touch her face, then stops. She grins nervously, and moves off.* CASS *turns back to the edge.*

TOM: Turn to me, my love. Let me serenade my lady now I've found my song.

TOM *begins humming the tune of his serenade.*

CASS: If I go down, his shadow will be above me, scraping my skin, as I lie back.

TOM: 'When I spy your face, fire steals through my every limb —'

CASS: His heat burns my belly, scorches my hair into ashes. Its stench cremates my faith.

TOM: Forget this lad, my love. Listen to the wind. 'My eyes are dead to all light —'

CASS: He cries, 'Don't put on the light.' As if I would, as if I would, as if I ever dared to see the face I know.

TOM: 'The wave of sweat overwhelms me My ears beat out with fright —'

CASS: His sweat pours down over me, mingling with my own salt tears, so I can't even tell my sorrow from his satisfaction.

TOM: Don't take the boy to heart so much. First love is —

CASS: Not to be able to find your own in among your father's sweat. To hear whispered that the love of family must possess all one's being.

TOM: Families? What's all this of families and fathers?

CASS (*cries out*): Father, father . . . what kind of love is this?

TOM *backs away.*

TOM: Father? Your father? I thought you talked of young love, crudely performed perhaps but —

CASS: Father, your face stains my pillow. Like my first blood on the sheets you made me hide. No more dark blood for me, father, I've run dry, not even marking the months and moons. My blood's as white as the foam on the rocks.

TOM: This is a father's love? I had daughters, daughters I'll never see. Perhaps that's for the best if we men take only the shapes of monsters from our passion.

CASS (*sings*):
No one told me they'd poisoned the air
But all of my friends knew
We never confided our secret fear
Not to one another
And certainly not to you

TOM: Don't mistake me. I'm a man but not of the same mould. I don't force or betray secrets on any gal.

She begins an almost imperceptible dance.

CASS (*sings*):
I could tell by its tasteless taste
I could tell by its sightless sight
I could tell by its smell in the storm
and by the edge of its shape in the night

TOM: Step back, love, please. Heed me. If she could only hear me. I know the waters here.

CASS: Sea air will clear the lungs
The salt will spray the poison.

You'll stop at the edge of the cliff, won't you, father?

TOM: If only I could speak, touch, I would . . . More bones of angels down there are no comfort to me. Please God.

CASS: When men leave you little choice, the little choice is all. One moment of flight with a poetess, above the shadows and the white birds.

TOM: Oh, God, no! Don't bring me back to be a witness only of death. My tongue breaks uselessly against my teeth.

CASS: I am paler than the grass of summer

I shudder with the caress of death

TOM: God! Please. Let me make a move into the real world. What's a spirit for if not to help the living. I demand. I will. The dead. The past. I WILL INTO THE FUTURE!

CASS: Must I always suffer
Being merely
Poor poverty's mother?

As she apparently, in the dark, seems to fall forward, TOM *howls and pulls her back and down by the leg. On all fours he bounds away into the seclusion of the dark.*

TOM (*amazed*): She felt it. (*Triumphant.*) She felt the pain I caused her. Felt my bite.

CASS: What's there? Come on boy, let me see. It's all right. Don't be frightened.

TOM: Is she talking to me?

He growls nervously.

CASS: Did I frighten you? Did you think I was going to jump? And you saved me. Good boy. Good boy.

She crawls over to stroke him.

There you are. Oh, you're just like my dog I had at home.

He rolls over, whimpering, onto his back.

TOM: Oh, to be touched. Even as a dog. To be touched. Oh, God.

She rubs his belly.

CASS: You like that, do you? (*Laughs.*) The doctor was wrong. Turkish dogs are just the same as English ones. They love being stroked.

He licks her face.

Are you lonely? I couldn't leave you, could I? I did that once before and the bad master . . . But not this time. Not again.

TOM *is almost ecstatic.*

TOM: Ah, to be touched. To be touched

by the one I love is better than fish tickling me ribs, even if I do have to be a mongrel with fleas feeding off me.

CASS: I'll smuggle you aboard, dog of the night, and you can feed from my hand and sleep under my bed. And we'll be friends and talk to each other of lost families.

TOM *barks wildly in agreement, and rolls her over, pinning her down gently.*

TOM: Listen, I'm sorry, I'm not trying to force anything on you, but it's been a very long time and . . . I have to make clear what kind of love I'm talking about.

He howls. Silence.

CASS (*softly*): Once I thought I had a man's monster inside my belly. My blood turned white with fright. Now the red of a woman's sea is as dry as a desert for me. A man did that to me. In such circumstances, to turn to the love of a true beast is perhaps only human.

She embraces him.

Scene Five

The sundeck at Izmir.
Early evening. The boat lies silent in Izmir harbour. A table, around which sits EILEEN, *avoiding the eye of the* DOCTOR, *who sits with her, drinking. She studies her guide book.*
DORIS sits, patiently waiting. PAUL *reads his Bible and occasionally looks up at the candles on the table.*
HELEN stands apart, holding her wine glass. JOHN *approaches her.*

JOHN: More wine?

HELEN: No, thank you. Why do you think we're waiting?

JOHN: Some game of the doctors.

HELEN: Why does he insist on trying to keep all us English together?

JOHN: I think it's a religion with him.

HELEN: If he tells us this is the birth-place of Homer once more.

JOHN *smiles. She seems to relax for a moment.*

JOHN: Have you been down this coast before?

HELEN: No. Have you?

JOHN: A long time ago.

HELEN: Brings back memories for you then?

JOHN (*pauses*): It was with my wife. When our daughter was very young. She loved it here. The Turks spoilt her. They treat blonde, blue-eyed girls like goddesses here.

HELEN (*mildly*): That wasn't my experience of Istanbul.

JOHN: What's cherished in the child is often challenged in the adult.

HELEN: Yes.

JOHN: Are you . . . do you have children?

HELEN: No. I taught for a time.

JOHN: Where?

HELEN: But I gave it up.

JOHN: Why?

HELEN: The lies you are expected to teach them.

JOHN: Perhaps we should only tell them fairy stories, and leave them to work out life for themselves.

HELEN: Is that what you do with your child?

JOHN: I don't see her very often now.

HELEN: But did you tell her such stories?

JOHN: Once upon a time. I made up quite a lot when we were on holiday here.

HELEN: What were they about?

JOHN: There was one about a doll she

carried around with her, called Jeni, who she was always losing on the beach. Jeni wanted more than anything to come alive and go for a ride on a sea horse.

HELEN: And did she?

JOHN (*shrugs*): I can't remember.

HELEN: Perhaps your daughter might.

JOHN: I doubt it. All she can remember is the name of pop stars. That's not really my field. Were you a music teacher?

HELEN (*smiling*): No.

JOHN: But you write songs, don't you?

HELEN: Who told you that?

JOHN: I don't know. I — somebody must've —

HELEN: I don't sing.

She turns away from the rails.

JOHN: I must be —

HELEN (*to the* DOCTOR): What's causing the delay?

PAUL *lights the candles on a table ready for dinner. The others, with the exception of* CASS *and* TOM, *have clearly been waiting for food for some time. Early evening. Silence.*

DORIS: I could eat a horse.

DOCTOR: Unfortunately, this being an English vessel, no such delicacy is on offer. Nothing but the finest Aegean sea foods.

JOHN: What's the problem?

DOCTOR: We had to take Turks on board to cater with the crabs. Always a mistake. Never stay in a Turkish hotel.

HELEN *smiles at* EILEEN. *Silence.*

HELEN: Why the celebration?

DORIS: Look at him. The big grin. Secret, eh?

DOCTOR (*smiling*): All in good time.

CASS *enters, running.*

CASS: I'm very sorry I'm late.

She notices the empty table.

CASS: Oh, you haven't started. You weren't waiting for me?

Oh, you haven't started. You weren't waiting for me?

CASS: Sorry?

PAUL (*confused*): The Turks have got the crabs.

EILEEN: You look radiant.

CASS: It was the cliff at Lesbos. So bracing.

EILEEN: Beware chapped skin. Not that I should give advice.

CASS *is uncertain where to sit.* PAUL *moves up for her. She sits.*
Silence.

CASS: Aren't the candles lovely?

DOCTOR: They're our young friend's contribution.

CASS: What are they for?

PAUL (*eagerly*): They're the seven candles of the seven churches in Asia Minor. Ephesus, where we go next, Smyrna, or Izmir, where we are now, Pergamos, where some of us have been, Thyatira, Laodicea and Sardis, where I hope to go, and Philadelphia, which I can't find.

DOCTOR: Utopia.

HELEN: So is this some kind of religious occasion?

PAUL: Agape.

HELEN: What?

DOCTOR: One of four Greek words denoting love, of which the most disappointing is Eros.

PAUL: It's more than just love. It means love feast, an ecstatic union of sharing as the Holy Ghost passed among the early Christians.

DOCTOR: I fear our chef hasn't got anything quite like that in mind for us.

JOHN: What does he have in mind?

HELEN: I'd like to get ashore before dark.

JOHN: So would I.

EILEEN: You'll enjoy it. It may look like an industrial town, but there's plenty of history. My husband's family come from here.

HELEN: Will you visit them?

EILEEN: I had enough of relatives in England.

DORIS: But that was a funeral.

EILEEN (*surprised*): Did I say that?

DORIS: The English give so little to eat at funerals.

EILEEN (*nervous*): It was my father's funeral. It wasn't a surprise. He wasn't young, obviously. (*Smiles.*) In some ways it was a welcome break before the season — Oh, does that sound callous? It wasn't meant to be.

HELEN: No.

DORIS: In some countries, funerals are the only time the poor get to eat. Then they are a feast of real rejoicing.

PAUL: Where?

DORIS: They keep changing the names.

EILEEN: Izmir was originally called Smyrna.

DOCTOR: The birth place of the world's greatest author.

JOHN: Kipling?

HELEN *smiles.*

DOCTOR: Homer!

He pours himself another drink.

EILEEN: It used to be famous as a gun running centre.

DOCTOR: Still is. Now it supplies the PLO.

HELEN (*quickly*): Why did they alter all the names?

EILEEN: Attaturk ordered it after he had got rid of the Greek invaders, in 1926. He fought the last battle here.

DOCTOR: Greek invaders? Do you mean the sons of Homer? It was by this very harbour, that the greatest Greek of them all had dreamed of his heroes setting out on their Odyssey. Ullyses. Achilles. Ajax. And the ghost of this blind old man had to suffer the screams of his heirs, as, on their return, the Turks drowned them in the safety of their own port.

CASS: What? What are you saying?

DOCTOR: The Turks refused the Greeks' surrender. They just kept pushing, pushing, pushing them back into the water. This is the deepest harbour in the Aegean, did you know that?

CASS *shakes her head.*

Alas, there was no Dunkirk of gallant boats to pick them up. None were allowed to land again, not alive.

TOM *enters, in his army uniform, humming 'Lily of Laguna'. CASS stares out towards him. She stops uncertain of whether she can see him.*

And our Paul's Christ could have walked the water here, on the backs of the drowned soldiers.

CASS (*standing, trembling*): No!

TOM: Can you see me? No. I'm only part of your dark dream, surely?

CASS *holds onto the edge of the table, unable to speak, she shakes her head. EILEEN rises to comfort her. The DOCTOR seizes her wrist.*

DOCTOR: Leave her be!

EILEEN: You've terrified the girl.

DOCTOR: The young have to face war.

TOM: The young always face war.

CASS *runs out.*

EILEEN: Let me go.

DOCTOR: You're distressed. Let me help you.

She breaks free.

EILEEN: Don't wait dinner for me.

She exits.

DORIS: What dinner? Crabs are notoriously slow creatures. Possibly they are not even here yet.

JOHN: What is the meaning of all this?

DOCTOR: It's quite cléar.

JOHN: Not to me.

DOCTOR: If we can still weep at a defeat, can we not equally rejoice at the thought of victory?

HELEN: Victory? What victory?

DOCTOR: Early this afternoon we sank a ship that was endangering our exclusion zone.

Silence. HELEN and JOHN look at one another, disbelieving. DORIS seems unaffected. PAUL does not know how to respond.

JOHN: You brought us together to celebrate that?

DOCTOR: Is the fight for freedom not a cause for rejoicing?

HELEN: Freedom? What freedom are you talking about?

DOCTOR: The freedom that our nation has always cherished, that makes us ready to fight for those Human Rights that —

HELEN: Human rights? Freedom? What right do we have to these words? You sound as though we own them. How do we know we are right? How can you be so certain?

She stands, shaking with rage, almost unable to speak. JOHN holds her wrist.

JOHN: Don't let him get to you.

HELEN: He's out to kill us all.

DOCTOR: I gain no satisfaction from a lost patient.

HELEN: We are not your patients!

She stares down at JOHN's hand. He takes it away.

JOHN: I'm with you.

HELEN: I'll eat ashore.

JOHN: May I come?

She pauses for a second, shakes her head, and leaves.

DORIS: Not stay even for the starter?

Silence.

DOCTOR: Isn't it important that we show solidarity whilst we are strangers in a strange land?

JOHN *turns away and leaves the table. The* DOCTOR *looks at* PAUL *for support.*

PAUL (*nervous*): That's a Christian quote.

DOCTOR (*savagely*): Is that all you can do? Quote chapter and verse? Don't you ever feel the urge to take some real decision leading to real action? There were lads your age, floating in this water, but at least they died, fighting for something. Their lives possessed a meaning.

TOM: How the old love to feed their goldfish with their children's seed.

PAUL: I can take decisions. I can take actions.

DOCTOR stares at him. PAUL *rises, not without dignity.*

PAUL: St Paul spoke of the need for purification of mind and body in times of trial. If our country is in a crisis then I'll undergo a fast. I will not eat until I reach Philadelphia.

He turns to go.

DOCTOR: We don't go to Philadelphia. It doesn't exist.

DORIS: Change the name, the place still remains.

DOCTOR (*firmly*): No!

DORIS: I think so, yes.

The DOCTOR *pours himself another drink.*

DOCTOR: Well, so much for his Agape.

TOM (*to* JOHN): The fish that feasted on me fed on those Greeks. Our flesh met in the belly of octopus and squid. Now maybe their appetite for soldier makes them swim the Atlantic. We are all one brotherhood under the waves, comrade.

JOHN *turns aside.*

Stop turning away from my death.

JOHN: Why? You think that my facing it might serve some use?

TOM (*defiant*): Yes.

JOHN: What?

TOM *is unable to answer.*

You're talking mysticism, grandfather. When idealists can no longer face the savage edge of the world, they turn to the ultimate. The mystic. The eternals. Last refuge of the immature. It should be banned to all poets by law. At least spare me that degradation.

DORIS: Even a crab would not be this late for dinner.

DOCTOR: I eat little. (*He rises.*) It was the ritual I had been anticipating. My services are needed elsewhere. One can only help those who request it.

He makes a slightly unsteady exit.

TOM: You shouldn't have given up.

JOHN: Kids always disappoint their parents. You were spared that.

TOM (*angry*): Don't tell me what I was spared.

JOHN *gets a drink from the table.*

DORIS: I am quite prepared to sing for my supper.

JOHN (*smiling*): I don't think that will be necessary.

DORIS: I only need to be asked.

TOM: Don't you dream at all?

JOHN *sighs and looks at him. Silence.*

JOHN: Do you?

TOM (*pauses*): Ye'.

JOHN: Of what?

TOM: When you're dead, your dreams are dead ordinary. (*Smiles.*) You know, pictures of a decent world for your kids to play in. For ordinary folk. They've paid for it. They deserve it.

JOHN (*sharply*): Deserve? Folk don't get what they deserve. They get what they desire. And right now they desire the tremor of distant drums and the sacrifice of somebody else's son. They embrace the dark just as keenly as your girl embraces her demon lover.

TOM: What . . . what do you know about that?

JOHN: I can imagine.

TOM: What do you imagine?

JOHN: Only what I desire. Right now, I desire fire, the burning of a letter, and freedom from the past.

He makes to leave.

TOM (*desperate*): No, don't. Please. Her, she, she burns letters.

JOHN: What?

TOM: I'll find out, find out what they are, who they're to. Just gi' me a bit more time. Please. Don't you desire her more than a burning? I'm not used to begging off me own children. Gi' me one night more. Please.

JOHN: Curiosity makes its endless battle with destruction.

TOM: Curiosity? You love her, like I do mine.

JOHN: Romantic. I'll leave her memory on the quay with the smell of the spray. (*Pause.*) You have until the morning.

He exits.

TOM (*to himself*): Now he lies to himself instead of others. Perhaps that's an improvement.

As he passes DORIS, she reacts as if being served the hors d'oevre.

DORIS: Ah! Red mullet. Are you Turkish? Turkiye? Delicious the . . . barbanua? Barbanya. Exquisite.

She mimes eating.

TOM: We used to play that game in the trenches, only for fags and bottles of brown ale.

He exits.

DORIS: For my main course, not kebab. Aubergines, of course, with rice, pine nuts. Patlican salatasi. Then, why not something I've never eaten before, kilich baligi. (*Pause.*) Swordfish.

She's surprised as 'food' appears.

DORIS: Oh, what quick service. I will tip you later.

She settles down to eat.

Scene Six

The cabins.
    HELEN *sits writing.* CASS *lies in her bed, in the dark.* TOM *whimpers mournfully.*

CASS: Don't hide under there, boy. Come back to bed. It doesn't matter.

TOM *howls.*

Don't desert me. My father would always leave immediately. He slid out of the door, slid out of me, leaving the seed that made me slipping down my thigh. I'd lie there, too terrified to breathe, as it dried, gripping my flesh under its scab. He'd left his own skin over me as a bridge for my shame to flow under. (*Pause.*) Dog, black dog, if my father came you'd guard me, wouldn't you?

TOM *growls.*

(*Sleepily:*) If only I could walk cliffs

with you, throw sticks into the sea. (*Pause.*) We missed out on courtship.

TOM *wearily slides out from under the bed.*

TOM: Are you asleep? Oh, my love, I'd dive back in the sea for you, but how can I love you when a burning letter may rip me from your breast? Excuse me. I love you. I'm a man. I've got me work to do.

He enters HELEN's room.

TOM (*wearily*): I've been through this room half a dozen times. Nothing. It's as though she expected blokes to come prying. (*Sits.*) Come on, Helen, there must be some ragged edges you carry that cause you pain or pleasure. It in't natural, this emptiness. (*Pause.*) Oh God, make her speak. It in't much to ask. Next door miracles occur, we play out Beauty and the Beast. Surely a few words in a dark cell can't be impossible.

HELEN *puts down her letter, and looks up.*

HELEN: I have no address to find you anyway.

TOM: Don't stop now.

HELEN: Where are you, Sean? With your death, the beauty of the cause withered for me. United Ireland was where we would be, not where others might scatter petals of remembrance on our heroes' graves.

TOM: United Ireland? Don't tell me they are still taking the corpses of young lads for that cause.

HELEN: Your friends were right. I would have talked. I'm no Trappist, no nun. The silence of the grave is difficult for me to live with.

TOM: There in't no silence. The bones chatter constantly. They just don't listen to each other.

HELEN (*smiles*): My faith has all been in words. Even now I write a letter to a dead lover. And I have to bite my

tongue not to talk to someone here,
a man I feel might be in sympathy.
(*Pause.*)

TOM: No, don't bite your tongue, lass.
Let my lad do that for you. Oh, you
and he are a perfect pair. You might
even resurrect the freedom fighter
in him.

HELEN: Sean, I can no longer travel with
you. I saw you drawn for a dream
into a violence my words of love could
not prevent. I would not betray you,
or your friends, but forgive me, I can
no longer search for you. We must
both wash the blood from off our
dream in separate seas.

*She strikes a match. DORIS in her
room begins to hum a song.*

Don't think me superstitious, Sean.
It's not a pyre. Only the destruction
of the evidence in case the hunters
trap me.

She lights the letter.

TOM (*gleeful*): Now I've the key to the
door, says the man who walks through
walls. And I can give my love my love
for evermore. John, all you do is talk
of Ireland, lost love and revolution.
You only have to echo your own past
to gain an entry.

HELEN *extinguishes the flames.*
DORIS *stands up and sings:*

Scene Seven

The theatre at Ephesus.

DORIS: Pel putschiet ken
mut mut milka
sol penidir tama
kil kil kolien
takin enmakin
sakinta pakarma

Em achaka kun
chin chit chanka
benidnanta udarma
pel takep mitep
kapin el dramina
sakinta los kavina.

ykiccka em
inta collisrevoluta
ova fent
anakem
fan inda minuta
ve bisil canila
O sol los
Sak pakar ov pucandas
apep delantos

En mur a tanka chin
O sodas ki
Atta do ve peant
O dromos ki
Tapin ik sankinta
Di em os
Kee.

*She finishes the song. A moment's
silence. Then applause. Lights up
to reveal the others, minus TOM,
standing around her, applauding.*

PAUL: Bravo! Bravo!

EILEEN: It was beautiful.

PAUL: Encore.

DORIS: No. No more. I normally get
money when I sing.

DOCTOR: Applause is the true reward of
the artist.

DORIS: What rubbish you talk.

HELEN: What is the song about?

DORIS: It is in my real tongue.

JOHN: Is it translated?

DORIS: My husband wrote it.

CASS: Is it a love song?

DORIS: Perhaps. Perhaps it is political.

CASS (*to* PAUL): Wasn't it beautiful?

PAUL: Oh, yes. Very.

DOCTOR: You should put Ephesus on
your regular tour.

DORIS: This theatre no women were
allowed to play. I sing here once. Only
once.

EILEEN: Mark your map with the red
cross.

JOHN *and* HELEN *walk a little apart.*

JOHN: I heard songs like that in Ireland.

HELEN: Were they in Gaelic?

JOHN: I didn't understand a word of them. But the feeling was clear.

HELEN: What's wonderful is how the people know them off by heart. Even my schoolchildren would —

PAUL: John! How many would it have sat?

JOHN: I'm not sure. Ten, fifteen thousand.

DORIS: Small first house. Maybe better second.

JOHN: Don't take it personally. Armed guards tend to keep the audience away.

EILEEN: He was quite polite though.

HELEN: Tyrants love tourists.

CASS: It's so strange having the place entirely to ourselves.

PAUL: Pity we can't watch a play.

DOCTOR: Perhaps John would give us an excerpt from one of his.

HELEN: What are they like?

JOHN *shakes his head.*

DOCTOR: Po-liti-cal plays.

CASS: Not love stories.

DOCTOR: Drab, grey communist plays, set in slums, and tower blocks and car parks. We don't want any of that. What we want is song and dance.

HELEN (*following* JOHN): Are they political?

JOHN (*grins*): That's a subject of some debate.

DOCTOR: Who will divert us first? Helen?

HELEN (*firmly*): I don't perform.

DOCTOR: Not even a teeny weeny protest song?

She looks at him for a moment, before

joining JOHN. *They talk softly, delicately, together.*

Eileen, you must know a thing or two about keeping up the old holiday spirit.

EILEEN: I don't do anything.

DOCTOR (*conspiratorially*): You could always dance.

EILEEN: I can't.

DOCTOR: You could at one time.

EILEEN (*unnerved*): How do you know so much about me?

CASS: Dance for us.

EILEEN: I want to know how he knows my secrets.

DORIS: This is a good spot for dancing.

CASS: Can you teach us how to dance?

DORIS: The mazurka? Or is that a meal. Food and art are so close of course. Only the Philistine thinks otherwise.

EILEEN: Ah! It was crossed out on my passport!

DOCTOR: Just pulling your leg. Your dancer's leg.

PAUL: What sort of dancer were you?

EILEEN: It should have said nurse. I was really more a nurse.

CASS: Please, dance for us.

EILEEN: My dancing days are over.

DOCTOR (*sings*):
I won't dance, don't ask me
I won't dance madame with you —

DORIS: Good. You do it.

DOCTOR: I'm the director.

EILEEN: I prefer to be an audience now.

DOCTOR: We'll end with a tableau of Rule Britannia, Britannia rules the Waves.

He salutes. EILEEN *moves away with her guidebook.* CASS *begins to hum* DORIS's *tune.* HELEN *and* JOHN *sit apart.*

JOHN (*mildly*): 'Rule, Britannia.' If I ended a play with that I could make a fortune. .

HELEN: Then why don't you?

JOHN: Can you imagine a country so insane, that it can believe it could catch a wave, never mind rule it? One day the government will rewrite history and make Canute a saint. They've already turned the nineteenth century into a myth of self help and benign philanthropy. They're well on their way.

HELEN: What happens if they do rewrite it all?

JOHN: They won't. They won't get away with it. We'll fight them for every last word.

The DOCTOR *surveys the scene.*

DOCTOR: The show must go on, even when the professionals desert us. The English are masters of improvisation. Now come on, Cass, it's up to you. This is your chance to become a star.

CASS: No. (*To* DORIS:) Will you teach me the tune. It's almost as though I know it already.

PAUL: I'll learn the accompaniment.

DORIS: Have you brought your drums with you?

PAUL: I could learn. I will remember.

DORIS (*smiles*): Yes.

She hums the song to them. The DOCTOR *crosses over to* EILEEN *who sits reading.*

HELEN: Do you believe in the power of words to change things?

JOHN: They're keys to open or close doors. To let others in, or keep them out. My job is to find the right one.

HELEN: And then what?

JOHN: Sorry?

HELEN: Do you open or lock the door?

JOHN: That I don't know about my craft. They want to keep us apart.

He looks down. She watches him. The DOCTOR *kneels by* EILEEN.

DOCTOR (*quietly*): We have so much in common, you and I. Believe me.

She does not look up. JOHN *glances across at them.*

JOHN: How do strangers communicate? How do they cross the empty space? Must you always be like Doris, with that rare courage to step bravely forward? What about those of us who resort to tiny signals, half gestures, like spies in a crowded bar, never really admitting the desire for intercourse for fear of rejection?

HELEN: What makes you speak of spies?

JOHN (*looking at her*): It's merely an image of loneliness.

HELEN *looks away.*

DOCTOR (*softly*): Why do you resist me all the time? Don't you find that curious? When we've so much in common. Take your island, Cyprus, that eye watching over the mouth of Suez. I know it well. I arrived there on my first boat bound for the East, like all the tales of my youth, Kipling, Conrad. And there that mouth snapped shut in front of me on the day our whole nation lost its voice. But now on other distant shores, we are finding it again, and those of us who can remember can hear the echo in its rising whisper. You hear it as well, don't you?

EILEEN: No, I don't. Quite the opposite. I hear only the cry from a mouth with my son's hand across it.

She begins to cry softly. The DOCTOR *moves away.*

HELEN: I want to trust you, but . . .

JOHN: It could be a mistake. Yes, I know, I know. But —

DOCTOR: John! If the women won't perform, what shall we men do?

JOHN: Nothing. Our male theatre turned into a zoo where lions were fed with Christians. I want no more of it.

DOCTOR: Brilliant. Androcles. Paul!

PAUL: Yes?

CASS *remains absorbed within her song.*

JOHN: I don't ask you to trust me.

HELEN: There is no other way.

The DOCTOR *puts his arm around* PAUL.

DOCTOR: You want to be like St Paul, don't you? You want to imitate him?

PAUL (*smiling*): Well, that's what saints are for.

DOCTOR: So here is a place of imitation. Go ahead, imitate.

PAUL: It's not quite that sort of imitation.

DOCTOR: Is it not? Think of it. Treading the same boards as the great man himself. What exactly did he do here, in order to get arrested?

PAUL: He argued with the silversmiths, who worshipped Artemis.

DOCTOR: And was he victorious?

PAUL: Yes.

DOCTOR: Except he got arrested?

PAUL: Yes, but he made many converts. They became possessed by the Holy Ghost. They spoke in tongues.

DOCTOR: Well, you never know, you might convert us. Stranger things have happened. The Holy Ghost may descend again.

PAUL: Is this some sort of game?

DOCTOR: Of course, but can you resist the challenge? Would St Paul have walked away? (*Pause.*) Good. Are you ready?

PAUL *nods.*

Ladies and gentlemen, for your delectation and delight one of the most distinguished stars of the Olde Tyme Music Hall, I bring to you none other than an artist whose last performance here was one of all the time peaks of magic and mystery.

PAUL: Not magic. Reason.

DOCTOR: Give us reason then!

PAUL (*nervous*): I only know his letter to the Ephesians. Not the actual speech he made.

DOCTOR: Anything. Anything. I'm positive they'll love you.

PAUL (*eventually*): 'Paul by the will of God, to the saints which are at Ephesus, and the faithful in Jesus Christ. Let no man deceive you with vain words; for because of these things cometh the wrath of God upon the children of disobedience.

Be ye not therefore partakers with them.

For ye were sometimes darkness, but are ye light in the Lord: walk as children of the light.

For the fruit of the Spirit is in all goodness and righteousness and truth.

Proving what is acceptable unto the Lord.

And have no fellowship with the unfruitful works of darkness but rather reprove them.

For it is a shame even to speak of those things which are done in them in secret.

But all things that are reproved are made manifest by the light: for whatsoever doth make manifest is light.

Wherefore he saith, Awake thou that sleepest, and arise from the dead, and Christ shall give thee light.

See then that ye walk circumspectly, not as fools, but as the wise.'

DOCTOR: Walk circumspectly, yes.

He begins to circle the apprehensive Paul.

PAUL: 'Redeeming the time, because the days are evil.

Wherefore be ye not unwise, but understanding what the will of the Lord is. And be not drunk with wine, wherein is excess, but be filled with the Spirit.'

DOCTOR: Of gin.

JOHN: Stop it!

HELEN: Leave him alone.

PAUL: No. No.

DOCTOR: See? It's his choice.
Martyrdom demands a little suffering.

PAUL: 'Speaking to yourselves in psalms and hymns, in spiritual songs, singing, and making melody in your heart to the —'

The DOCTOR *begins to roar.*

DOCTOR: Where there are Christians in the theatre, there are bound to be lions.

PAUL *stands, confused.*

PAUL: What am I supposed to do now?

DOCTOR: Pray!

Roaring, he leaps on him and they fall to the ground.

PAUL: I'm not fighting. I'm not fighting.

The others move in to assist him, apart from CASS *who suddenly cries out in surprise.*

Silence. They turn towards her.

CASS (*to herself*): I remember. I knew I knew it. It's Love's Corridor.

She sings the song, gently, to herself, hardly aware the others are there.

(*Sings:*)
They the plainclothed men came
bang bang bashing

with their boots against the door
smash smash smashing
kicking and laughing
into love's corridor

We who were naked came
writhing and twisting
sliding in sweat across the floor
they kick us, slap us
slicing one breath
into their separate corridor

Putting us
in the van of revolution
only the memory
of one breath between us
filtering pollution

and still in the tongue of dog
you caress me
in the curve of a wet leaf
you undress me
walking this corridor
will make us
free.

JOHN (*softly, urgently*): Is that it?
Is that the translation?

DORIS: What?

HELEN: Is that what the song means?

She looks at them both. Silence. CASS turns, noticing them. DORIS nods, smiling. CASS grins. PAUL rises from the dust and approaches CASS, and then stops. JOHN reaches out and touches HELEN's arm lightly.

HELEN (*pauses*): I will. I'll take the risk. I want to.

He takes her hand.

ACT TWO

Scene One

The sundeck at Patmos.
    *JOHN and HELEN asleep on adjacent
loungers. She is in bathing costume. His
hand rests on her arm. Between them
TOM. He watches as JOHN moves in his
sleep. He sighs.*

TOM: The fear of waitin's someat I know
    someat about. I've watched 'em in the
    wings, doubled over wi' stage fright,
    then up and dancing swans on tiptoe.
    I've waited hours for a cue meself,
    though the only satisfaction I got was
    dodging shrapnel. I've never done no
    waiting that paid wi' a round of
    applause. P'raps that's my lot. So I'm
    waiting for my grandkid to gi' me
    marching orders or demob now he's
    won a war. Never disturb a man too
    quick after loving. They always turn
    nasty. And this lad has me destiny
    in his hands.

He gazes up at the sun.

And I wait for the black of night, shit
scared of this sun in case Cass caught
a glimpse of me and knew her lover for
a drowned soldier. That'd make her
lock her door and throw away the key.
And I'm no father to force an entry.
So I wait the frenzy of the night.
Like some French tart in a wooden
caravan. No, I'm not a prisoner of
passion like that. I've queued for such
gals, as alabaster as madonnas, kept
from sun and shame by satin curtains.
Like miners dig for coal, them lasses
dug for gold in the fold of trousers.

Pause.

Our love's not like that. It's not
just my future I'm shoring up. But
where lies our future and the freeing
of our souls?

*Silence. He wipes his sweating face.
He moves to the rails.*

It's too bloody hot for me. I wish I
dare risk a swim.

Pause.

I'm not unhappy. Just desiring more,
like all men.

*The ship's horn. JOHN moves his arm
and checks his watch. He sits up
confused and turns to look at HELEN.
He very gently touches her arm.*

HELEN (*softly*): Am I burning?

*He moves forward as if to kiss her.
The ship's horn. They move apart.
She sits up.*

Why are we leaving so early?

He shakes his head.

(*Smiling:*) It's very different from
the Heysham ferry. There all you get
are soldiers backing you up against
the rails.

JOHN: Well, if you miss that sort of
    thing . . .

*He reaches towards her. She stops his
hand and kisses it. She smells it, then
checks it against her own smell.*

HELEN: I can smell you on me.

*He smiles. He leans over to smell her.
They kiss.*

(*Softly:*) It doesn't have to be the way
it was with your wife. The same
pattern isn't set for ever, is it? Things
can change, can't they?

JOHN: Yes.

HELEN: Do you believe that?

JOHN (*pauses*): Yes.

HELEN: I'm not trying to —

JOHN: No, I know.

HELEN: Only for me, too, there was a
    silence, a . . . Of course, that was after
    Sean's death, but I thought that's the
    end, a death is the end of course but —

JOHN: Yes, I understand.

HELEN: Do you?

Silence.

(*Smiling:*) They'll be coming back
soon. They'll all be wondering how we

came to miss the trip.

JOHN: Perhaps we should let them sniff us. It would save a lot of embarrassing explanations.

HELEN: Or we could just pretend nothing had happened.

JOHN (*pauses*): I'd rather not do that. I don't want to do that. I want us to stay together.

HELEN: I didn't mean to force you . . . to put any pressure . . .

He takes her wrist.

JOHN (*intensely*): Listen. I want to tell the world. I want to write a love story.

HELEN (*smiling*): You're not giving up politics, John?

JOHN: I meant what I said last night. I'm not going back on anything.

She puts her hand to stop his mouth.

HELEN: 'Nuff said. If we're planning to go back . . . home, I'd better work on my tan now.

She lies back and closes her eyes. He sits on the edge of his lounger watching her.

TOM *moves to stand patiently behind him.* JOHN *does not turn to him.*

JOHN: I love her, Tom. You were right. I won't leave her on the quayside.

Silence.

TOM (*softly*): But where does that leave me, John?

JOHN: When I was a kid, your daughter used to go on and on how much I took after you.

TOM: She hardly knew me, 'cept as fantasy.

JOHN: She taught me how to pray to you. To the brightest star in the sky, to my Guardian Angel. 'Our father'.

Pause.

When I got older, she told me how you'd been killed.

TOM: She won't there.

JOHN: It weighed on my mind for years, 'til like most lads, I stopped praying, and my kneeling at the edge of the bed was in worship of the girls from the *News of the World*. But always, always at the moment of coming, my eyes framed on the woman, at that split second that should be joy I'd feel you standing behind me, full of sorrow and sympathy. Feel the weight on my shoulders of your disappointment.

Pause.

That has to end now. I can't take the weight of your future. You're linked in my life with shame.

He turns to him.

I want to start again, Tom. Afresh.

TOM: I was never there, John. I've allers respected privacy. (*Pause.*) What you goin' to do wi' me?

EILEEN *enters.*
TOM *backs away.*
JOHN *stands.*

EILEEN: There you are, stick in the muds.

JOHN: Welcome home, pilgrim.

HELEN (*waking up*): Did you get to the monastery?

EILEEN (*laughing*): No. I was so relieved to find you know who wasn't around, that I just lazed on the beach all day.

JOHN: Where was Herr Doktor?

EILEEN: Oh, he won't set foot on Patmos. Says the Christians have desecrated it!

JOHN: Thank Heaven for small mercies.

EILEEN *puts a hand to her forehead.*

HELEN (*moving to her*): You should have had some protection.

EILEEN: Nobody bothered me.

HELEN: No, I meant, sitting out in the sun. Mad dogs and Englishmen. Come on. Sit down.

She steers her towards the lounger.

EILEEN: No, really. There's no need.

HELEN: You're on fire.

EILEEN: Well, I suppose I'm a —

HELEN: I've got some calomine.

She roots around in her rucksack.

EILEEN: Oh, please. I didn't mean to disturb you both. I'm fine. If I just get ten minutes with my eyes closed. (*Groans.*) Oh, I do feel just a little queasy.

JOHN *props up the cushions for her.* HELEN *applies the lotion.*

Oh, oh that's heaven.

HELEN: Lie back and enjoy it.

EILEEN: I'm not used to treats like this. I'll probably fall asleep.

Moaning gently, she closes her eyes. HELEN *and* JOHN *keep exchanging smiles, glances, as she treats* EILEEN.

TOM: What do you plan to do with me?

JOHN: You kept your part of the bargain. You brought me to Helen, and she's brought me to out of some of the dark.

TOM: But what about me?

JOHN: You're free. You can do what you like. Just leave me in peace. That's a fair deal, isn't it? What more could two generations offer each other than freedom and peace?

TOM (*confused*): No, that's not right. That don't give me peace. I've got some other work to do. I won't just summoned here to pimp for you, John.

Silence. JOHN *turns to him.*

JOHN: Grandfather, you weren't summoned.

TOM: How did I get here then?

JOHN: You wanted to return. To haunt us.

TOM: For what? Why would I want to do that?

Silence.

(*Suddenly, desperately:*) You've got to listen to my story.

JOHN *turns away to look over the rails.*

JOHN: I have my own choice. No.

TOM: It's important.

JOHN: The last moments of a drowning man in a war that wasted millions. It's not important. It just causes useless pain that's all. I don't want the details. I can't deal with them. Take your freedom and run, grandfather. Throw your uniform in the water and have done. Don't anger me.

TOM: You have to tell my story!

JOHN: Don't hand me your cross to carry. I've told enough stories I thought would make some change, only to find the storm of hate throwing them back in my face like spit in the wind. If you believe in your tale take responsibility. You tell it to them you think it'll free.

TOM: How can I do that?

JOHN: Tell Cass. She should be the first to hear it. It would free her from the deception of a dog.

TOM: How can I tell her? If she knows who I am she'll bolt the door against me.

JOHN: You want to offload it on me, so you can breathe easy in your lover's arms. Tales don't always open up to love. There's no virtue in it anymore. The truth can just as easy lock the door.

TOM: That's not right.

JOHN *points at the boarding party.*

JOHN: She'll be up any second. Tell her. Tell your demon lover. Wait here. Tell her the truth.

TOM *shakes his head.*

(*Gently*:) Tom. We're father and son. It's not easy for either of us to learn idealism only leads to isolation.

TOM *backs away and hides in the shadows.* JOHN *lights a cigarette and begins to relax.*

EILEEN (*drowsily*): You two decided to give it a miss then?

HELEN: We . . . er . . . I . . . (*Pauses.*) We overslept.

EILEEN: Hm.

She nods. HELEN *grins.*

HELEN: Those walls are so thin. Did we keep you awake?

EILEEN: No. Only one cry, that suddenly stopped.

HELEN: I was trying to be quiet.

EILEEN: Those sort always wake a mother. You panic when a cry stops midflight.

EILEEN *is almost asleep as she talks.* HELEN *looks at* JOHN *as she very gently continues the massage.*

I heard a cry like that on my last night at my son's. You know how you wake, and you're not sure if you heard something or not, because it's all so quiet. I thought it's from next door, although I hadn't a clue who was there, or where I was, or even when it was. My son's twenty now. He could have been a child or not even born for all I knew.

Pause.

I found myself outside this door. I could hear gasps, no clear cry, I thought my child, somebody's child, choking. I pushed open the door, and there, in the light of the lamp, lay my child my son pressed against the back of another boy, my son's hand across his mouth to stop him crying out, and waking me. (*Softly.*) I said, Let him breath. He let go his hand, the boy cried out, his head dropped forward in a sort of . . . swoon. My mouth

opened wide in a yawn almost anyway no sound. I put my hand over it politely. I left quietly.

Pause.

In the morning it was as though nothing had happened. The friend had disappeared — we didn't mention it. That poor lad, he could have suffocated him, for me. So as not to disturb me. Men have often treated me in this way.

Silence. EILEEN *seems to have fallen asleep. The pulse into life of the ship's engines. She comes round slowly, and looks around.* HELEN *kneels and hugs her.*

EILEEN (*laughing: in pain*): Steady!

CASS *runs on, carrying a bag of presents, and wearing a new straw hat.* DORIS *follows.*

CASS: There you are. Where were you two?

JOHN: Did we miss much?

DORIS: Cass kissed a dead man.

HELEN: What?

CASS (*laughing*): Through glass. Not . . . (*She shivers.*)

DORIS: He was a saint, so they say.

CASS: I got trapped in this long line of women, in a tiny chapel, and so I just kept following them. The woman in front of me went down on one knee, and so I did the same. And lo and behold!

HELEN: How did it feel?

CASS *pulls a face.*

JOHN: Was that in the monastery?

DORIS: You couldn't get in. You need pants to turn a corner there.

CASS: She wanted me to run down and get her a pair.

HELEN: Are you that keen to enter a man's world?

DORIS: Certainly.

HELEN: Why?

DORIS: Good to know what they're planning. (*To* EILEEN:) Eh, look at you. Lobster. We have you for tea. No need for the boiling water.

EILEEN (*laughing*): I can hardly move. I'm paying for my sins.

DORIS: Captive partner. Perfect for backgammon.

She digs into her bag for her pocket set. The DOCTOR *enters.* EILEEN *sits up.*

DOCTOR: All aboard me hearties?

JOHN: Why are we leaving so early?

DOCTOR: Where's our wandering pilgrim?

HELEN: Anybody seen Paul?

DOCTOR: Nobody see him come aboard?

Silence. Sirens. The boat begins to move off from port.

CASS: Has he missed the boat?

JOHN: He can always catch the hydrofoil and pick us up at Kos.

DOCTOR: I wouldn't bet on that.

DORIS: Kos I look forward to. The home of the lettuce. Perhaps that will tempt the boy to break his fast.

JOHN: Speak of the devil.

PAUL *runs in.*

DORIS: Mal'ak.

He stands in front of the DOCTOR, *fighting for breath, attempting to control the tears of frustration.*

PAUL: Why . . .

DOCTOR (*shaking his head*): Running in this climate.

PAUL: Why . . .

DOCTOR: It's most inadvisable.

HELEN: Let him speak.

DOCTOR: Of course. Take your time.

PAUL: Why . . .

DOCTOR: Is the boat?

PAUL: Is the boat . . .

DOCTOR: Leaving . . .

PAUL: Leaving . . .

DOCTOR: So early?

PAUL: So early?

DOCTOR: Good. Well done.

PAUL (*desperate*): Well?

DOCTOR: I'm sorry.

PAUL: I . . . demand . . . to know.

DOCTOR: I'm afraid I can't —

PAUL (*still breathless*): Listen! St John's Grotto. You can . . . see the shelf where he laid . . . his head. See the shelf . . . where he dictated . . . Revelations.

DOCTOR: Oh, I'm delighted you didn't miss it.

PAUL: I did miss it!

DOCTOR: But you have such a clear image?

PAUL: I've seen a photo.

DOCTOR: So?

PAUL: That's not the same as seeing the real thing.

DOCTOR: It's often much better. Reality can be so disappointing.

JOHN: He wants an explanation, not a philosophy lecture.

DOCTOR: I am unable to supply that at present.

DORIS: A secret! Look at him. Like the cat that lapped the cheese. Cheddar. The Cheddar Cat.

EILEEN: Cheshire. Cheshire cat. It's Lewis Carrol.

DORIS: What?

JOHN: Look, what's going on here?

The DOCTOR *shakes his head.*

DOCTOR: I'm not allowed to say.

HELEN: Are you deliberately trying to panic us?

DOCTOR: There'll be an official statement later.

JOHN: About what?

He remains silent.

HELEN: As a doctor, you should allay fears not create them.

DOCTOR (*pause*): Well, I personally feel you should be told before the other passengers and now we are actually at sea —

JOHN: Told what?

DOCTOR: Our next port of call is not to be Kos.

EILEEN: What?

JOHN: Then where is?

DOCTOR: Malta. You are all to disembark at Malta.

EILEEN: Malta. But I'm almost home. Why would I want to go to Malta?

JOHN: There's something wrong with the ship?

DOCTOR: On the contrary.

HELEN: What is it then?

DOCTOR (*pauses*): We're on route back to Gibraltar to refit for possible active service, in the Atlantic.

Silence.

CASS: But this isn't a cruiser, I mean this is a cruise ship, it's not a . . .

DOCTOR: We won't be transforming it into a destroyer. It's medical back-up ships they need. That's why I'll be there with it.

EILEEN: But what about us?

DOCTOR: You'll have first class accommodation courtesy of Her Majesty's Government until you successfully re-route out for your seperate destinations.

EILEEN: From Malta?

JOHN: Where the media will no doubt record us singing 'Rule Britannia' as we march down the gangplank.

DOCTOR: We're not planning a spontaneous demonstration. We leave that sort of thing to our Iron Curtain colleagues.

EILEEN: Why didn't you tell us at Patmos? Then we could have gone on from there?

DOCTOR: I'm sure you appreciate the need for security.

Pause.

The captain requests you all to share his table tonight. That might be a good place to continue this discussion.

HELEN: I'm not going to any dinner. (*Pause.*) And I'm not going to Malta.

DOCTOR: Oh, you're going to swim for it, are you?

HELEN: I can't swim.

DOCTOR: Then you'll have to go with the tide like the rest of us.

Pause.

Look, no one wants reminding we live in a time where soldiers are necessary. But the world is no utopia, and we have to protect our own. There's a significant difference between jingoism and patriotism. I'd ask you to remember that when we reach the media.

He exits. HELEN *stares at the others, who are attempting to absorb the shock. She catches* CASS's *eye. She nervously makes to go.*

HELEN: Where are you going?

CASS (*hesitant*): I thought I'd go and get ready.

HELEN *is clearly furious.*

CASS: Well . . . it just doesn't seem right my making a fuss over my arrangements, when there's a . . . I mean, it's not even an inconvenience for me. (*Smiles.*) Just a few less oranges to pick.

HELEN: What are you saying?

EILEEN: Don't pick on the child.

HELEN: There are boys her age being blown into the sea.

CASS (*desperate*): Yes, but . . . what can I do? It's all so far away.

HELEN: It was. Now we are standing in the middle of it. On the burning deck. We step aside, and we let some boy take our place under the bombs.

EILEEN: But it's going to be a medical ship. You can't condemn that. It'll be out there saving lives.

HELEN: Red Cross ships don't save lives. They only comfort us at home into thinking we're doing all we can. Florence Nightingale kept the Crimea ablaze. War will go on as long as there are lovely girls like her to kiss the heads of corpses.

CASS *puts her hand to her mouth and runs out.* TOM *appears from the shadows.* EILEEN *stares angrily at* HELEN. PAUL, *uncertain, starts to follow* CASS.

JOHN: Leave her, Paul. It's best she has some privacy.

PAUL: Oh, yes. Right.

JOHN (*to* TOM): Go to her. She needs you.

JOHN *turns to watch* HELEN.

EILEEN: What good does that do?

Silence.

You have to admit that soldiers sometimes save lives.

HELEN: Is that true of Cyprus?

EILEEN (*turning away*): I don't want to get drawn into a political discussion.

HELEN: Have you heard this sort of talk before, Doris?

DORIS (*mildly*): I have heard many people talk in many languages. Whether they live by the moral of the tales they tell, that is another story. Sometimes they settle for the heat from anger at the folly of their friends.

HELEN (*quietly*): Yes. That's true. Thank you.

She moves to the railings. EILEEN *sits exhausted.*

EILEEN: I can't play any more, Doris. I must close my eyes.

DORIS: I win, anyway.

EILEEN *lies down.* PAUL *moves towards them.* DORIS *looks up at him.*

PAUL: Will you play me?

DORIS: Of course.

As JOHN *moves towards* HELEN, TOM *steps in his path.*

TOM: Could you go to her? I daren't. Not while she has the ghost of dead soldiers in her eyes.

JOHN: I would, Tom, but I have my own lover to tend to.

He crosses to HELEN *who turns to him. He holds her.*

HELEN: I didn't mean to hurt Cass.

TOM: No, I know.

HELEN: But we can't walk down that gangplank singing, can we? We can't make our return under the shade of the Union Jack?

JOHN: We can't talk here. Let's go —

HELEN: We have to make them hear us. Make them know someone's against this crazy war.

TOM: I'm with you. I didn't come back meself to be trapped on another deathship.

HELEN: They have to listen to us.

JOHN: They won't listen.

HELEN: They've got to.

JOHN (*gently*): What do we do? Mutiny? Run up the skull and crossbones?

HELEN: If we talked to the engineers

maybe they'll stop the boat.

JOHN: Helen, they'll have been the first to sign on for the noble sacrifice.

HELEN: We've got to stop it, John.

JOHN: How can we? The only thing that would stop this war is more violence. That's the only language they understand.

HELEN: No, if you believed that you'd never do anything. It'd be just a nightmare. We can stop it. I know we can.

JOHN: Look, even if we could, what good would that do? Do you think they'd let us get away with it? Listen, they've just launched the entire fucking armada including nuclear submarines on a Holy War against a country of Spam makers, and you think, you think for one moment that that bloody thirsty bunch of flag-waving maniacs is going to let a single woman rock their boat? They'll swat you like a fly.

HELEN: But isn't this what we talked about last night? Didn't you say we had to stand against the tide? Didn't you —

JOHN: Last night? Yes, I know what I said last night. Look, we all lie in our lovers' arms. If every man had to live by what he said in bed there'd be no survivors.

HELEN: You were lying to me?

JOHN (*furious*): What are you . . . you're like a little girl, what do you mean, 'You were lying to me?' Listen! What you plan against this futile war is an equally futile gesture. The tide is against us. Canute might have seemed a hero when he walked across the sand, but he looked a bloody idiot half an hour later.

HELEN (*quietly*): So you think we should remain silent?

JOHN: At least it will keep us alive.

HELEN: Alive?

JOHN: You. Me. Alive. That happens to be very important to me. What good is a dead lover to anyone?

HELEN: Who's talking about a dead lover?

JOHN: You are.

HELEN: What?

Silence.

JOHN: You're not doing this for peace, or . . . you're doing it to expiate some guilt you feel for failing Sean, for not preventing him from walking into violence. But Sean is dead. You can't save him. Look at me. I'm alive. Don't leave me for him.

HELEN: How do we live then, John?

JOHN: We live inside our love. We build a raft from it to ride out the storm. We survive. Isn't our love worth living for?

HELEN: And of the others who die? What will we say when they come for our children? Or do we still remain silent?

She turns away. He grabs her arm.

JOHN: You're doing this because I lied to you. You'll risk your life to spite me.

HELEN: Do you believe that, John?

JOHN: No, you'll do it because you're mad. Because you want to embrace your dead lover.

HELEN: You'd like to believe that, wouldn't you?

JOHN: Don't, please. Don't be a martyr for nothing. I want to help you. Please.

HELEN: Then make sure they know my story.

JOHN: Oh, yes. I'll tell your story. I'll save you. I'll tell the doctor first if you try anything. I'll tell him you're mad, and then they'll lock you in your cell and leave you for a lunatic.

HELEN: You're hurting me.

She pulls away and exits. TOM faces him. It is almost night. JOHN is shaking.

TOM: It's important what she's trying to do. I shoun't have let meself be talked into war by me children, thinking revolution would hold on, and we'd sort it out later.

JOHN: I'll smash her door down myself and drag her back to her senses.

TOM: You'd betray her would you?

JOHN: Betray? What're you talking about? She's mad. What am I supposed to do, just stand back and let her jump to her death? Did you step back from Cass at the cliff's edge? Or was that, in some way, different? Don't be a hypocrite with me, grandfather. Love for you is just the same. Don't say it should be noble sacrifice for me, when you cling on like grim death to what you desire.

TOM (*uncertain*): I din't betray her. I saved her.

JOHN: Betrayal and lies. Just like the rest of us. You daren't even let your lover see you in the light, in case then she has the truth to make a real choice. Is that an act of freedom and equality?

CASS enters distressed.

TOM (*uncertain*): What I've done, I've done to save her pain.

JOHN: Exactly the same.

TOM stares at him.

TOM: No, it in't. I'm sure it in't.

JOHN: You're lying to yourself, Grandfather. I'm not blaming you. Just don't sit in judgement on me. Unless you want to tell her now.

TOM turns to see CASS enter. He automatically moves away.

CASS: She won't talk to me. She's locked her door.

JOHN puts out his cigarette.

I don't want people to die. But I don't know what to do about war.

JOHN: Don't cry.

CASS: Something terrible's going to happen.

He reaches out towards her. She puts her face in her hand, and begins to weep silently. TOM moves behind her, and puts his arms around her. Slowly, she looks up, takes his hand and holds it over her mouth.

CASS (*softly*): Can I see you? Can I see you in the light?

Silence. TOM releases her. She turns to him.

TOM (*surprised*): You knew. You knew I was a soldier. How?

CASS: From the wounds at the tip of my fingers. But I'll nurse you.

He steps back from her.

TOM: My wounds are past hope, Cass. Those scars were long since doors for fish into my cold heart. I'm dead, my love. I only play a part in your dream as a black dog.

CASS: But my love has freed you from that spell.

TOM (*shakes his head*): No. My love must free you from it.

CASS: Free me! How can you free me?

He makes to turn away.

Please. Let's go back into the dark. I'll pretend I've never seen you. Let's pull the curtains and forget the world.

TOM: Love is not a private affair, no matter what your father taught you.

CASS: You're leaving me?

TOM: Yes.

CASS: You want to go to war again. You want to leave your love on the shore. I won't have that. I won't have it.

TOM: I'm dead. I go back to the sea.

CASS: Then I come with you. You kept

me alive. If you leave me, I'll die. I'd
rather come with you, and let the sea
horses drive me to church.

TOM: If only death were . . . it's not like
that. When I was killed . . .

She puts her hands over her ears.

CASS: I don't want to hear. Will you
stay with me?

He shakes his head.

Then I'll haunt you with my unrequited
love.

She turns to the rails. PAUL *looks up
and sees her.*

Neither JOHN *nor* TOM *move.*

Once your love saved me from the fall.
Let the waters take me this time.

JOHN: Tom, what do you want me to
do?

TOM *backs away.* CASS *prepares to
jump.*

PAUL: John!

He rushes forward to seize CASS,
who fights frantically. JOHN *and*
EILEEN *move in to help.* CASS *falls
to the ground.*

EILEEN: Don't hold her. It's some form
of fit. Give her air.

DORIS: What is it?

EILEEN: I don't know. John, get the
doctor.

He moves off for a moment facing
TOM.

TOM: At the very least don't tell the
doctor what you know.

EILEEN: Quickly!

He exits.

PAUL: Will she be all right?

EILEEN: How do I know?

The fit gradually subsides.

Scene Two

The sundeck.
   *Later that night. The ship's engines
are silent. Decoration lights illuminate
the area. The distant strains of a small
dance band, playing Greek music.*
   The DOCTOR *gazes up into the sky.*
TOM *stands behind him on watch.*
   JOHN *enters, but seeing the* DOCTOR
turns to go.

DOCTOR: John. Have you been to see
your friend, Helen?

JOHN: She won't open the door.

DOCTOR: Migraine attacks are like that.
It's better she is left alone.

JOHN: Why has the ship turned back
towards Kos?

Silence.

DOCTOR: Let's not play games with one
another, John. You know what's
going on, don't you? What is she
planning? We have to take her
seriously. It is a critical time. We can
hardly be seen to lose a boat through
the treachery of one of our own
people.

Pause.

Did she tell you about her boyfriend?

Silence.

The IRA send their recruits to the
Lebanon to train with the Palestinians.
Did you know that? It is the custom in
the east to take your friends a gift.
Izmir is an excellent centre for suitable
presents.

JOHN: What are you suggesting?

DOCTOR: If, and I say if, she has
explosives did she give you any idea
where they were hidden?

JOHN: Explosives? She hasn't got
any . . . did she say she had explosives?

DOCTOR: She's said nothing other than
the ship must stop, or she would
stop it, and that her protest should be

broadcast over the World Service.

JOHN: She's mad. Leave her there. Just ignore her.

DOCTOR: We can hardly do that.

JOHN: She hasn't got any explosives.

DOCTOR: I'm afraid we can't be that confident with the lives of the other passengers in our hands.

JOHN: I'll get her out. Help me break down the door.

DOCTOR: Did she give you any idea if she had explosives where they might be?

JOHN: She hasn't any. Your notion is as crazy as hers, if you think that —

DOCTOR: Our notion is a reasonable deduction from the known facts.

JOHN: So what will you do?

DOCTOR: We'll give her the night to think it through. But I beg you. Don't tell the other passengers. There's no need to cause a general panic. They all have quite enough to cope with with Cass's rabies, without —

The sound of an approaching helicopter. He wipes his hands and neck. DORIS *and* EILEEN *enter.*

DOCTOR: The helicopter's here.

DORIS: Will it land?

DOCTOR: A ladder.

DORIS: Jacob's ladder.

EILEEN: Why don't you fly Cass out?

DOCTOR: Let me ask you again, please stay away from the cabin area, while her father visits. It's enough to see your daughter near the end, without having to bump into concerned strangers.

EILEEN: Are you sure of your diagnosis?

DOCTOR: The scar on her ankle confirms it. Probably that blasted dog back at Troy. John, please get Paul from her bedside, before I have another patient on my hands.

He nods. JOHN *exits.*

DORIS: Will she live?

DOCTOR: Not with the onset of hydrophobia.

DORIS: What is that?

DOCTOR: It's literally a dread of water, but with rabies, the patient's dementia takes the form of pleading for it.

DORIS: Then give her the water.

DOCTOR: The slightest sip would start a spasm in the throat causing asphyxiation.

DORIS: What about a vaccine?

EILEEN: It's too late for that.

DOCTOR: You've treated this disease?

EILEEN: I've watched someone die of it. (*Pause.*) Why are we going on to Kos, instead of on our way to Malta?

The DOCTOR *points at the helicopter as though he can't hear. It is now overhead. Its lights cut across the deck. They struggle against the wind from it. Although* TOM *is unmoved by it. He raises his fist against it, and shouts, above the noise —*

TOM: Father! Traitor! Betrayer of your own seed! I curse you!

He stands, almost heroic, statuesque against it.

Scene Three

The cabins.
   HELEN *sits, immobile, in her room. She holds a portable radio in her hand. The yellow rucksack lies by the bed.* PAUL *leans over* CASS, *taking down her faint mumblings in his notebook.* JOHN *enters.* CASS *cries out.*

CASS: Water!

He picks up a damp flannel.

JOHN: Don't let the water touch her lips.

PAUL (*surprised*): I only wash her body.

He wipes her.

JOHN: Her father's here. You must leave her.

PAUL: She needs me.

JOHN: She doesn't know who you are.

PAUL: Yes, she does.

JOHN: She's delirious, Paul.

PAUL: No. She's not ill. She's possessed by the Holy Spirit.

JOHN: What?

PAUL (*pauses*): She speaks in tongues. I should have realised that with the song at Ephesus. I have to record what she says.

JOHN: What's the point? It's the ravings of madness. It's meaningless what she says. Leave her. Leave her alone. There is nothing you can do. Let the doctor look after her.

Silence.

PAUL (*near to tears*): When my folks were killed, I went through the house from top to bottom, searching for a letter or postcard, something with a bit of message on it, that they might have left me. But we'd never been apart. We were a close family. There won't even a will with words on it to me.

Pause.

I don't know what she means, but I do know she wants me to hear, and I want to listen.

JOHN: You're possessed. She possesses you.

PAUL: Does listening mean she's taken me over?

JOHN (*suddenly*): If you want to listen to somebody, listen to me.

PAUL: What do you have to say?

Silence. The DOCTOR *enters.*

PAUL: It's all right. We're leaving.

DOCTOR: The ladies are in the lounge.

They exit. The DOCTOR *opens his case, checks a syringe, then signals through the door.*

I'm sorry. I wish it could be otherwise. But peace and security always cost lives.

The DOCTOR *shakes* CASS *violently, and, as she comes round, slaps her across the face. She screams out.*

HELEN *stands listening. The* DOCTOR *blocks the scream with his hand.*

Sudden silence.

Blackout.

The deafening roar of the helicopter, as it hovers, turns, and moves off.

An hour later.

The cabins.
DORIS *sits, apparently asleep, in the chair in her room.* HELEN*'s room is empty.*

CASS (*delirious*): Free me . . . free me . . .

PAUL: Why is there no light?

He switches on the lamp. TOM *stands behind the door.*

CASS: Free me . . . please . . .

PAUL *loosens the bedding.* CASS *suddenly sits up, and clutches hold of him. She sees* TOM.

I knew. I knew you'd never desert me.

PAUL: No, never.

CASS: You'll not leave me on the quayside.

PAUL: I'll look after you, I promise.

CASS: Give me the water. Please.

TOM: Don't ask me.

CASS: Don't you see, you can't leave me. I am you. I am on your ship, my arms and legs strapped down like yours. I'll go through death with you.

TOM: What do you know . . . I never spoke of that. Forget, please.

CASS: Water . . . water . . .

PAUL: No, my love, it's not possible.

CASS: Please.

TOM: No.

She begins to choke, fighting for breath, speech. JOHN *enters.*

JOHN: Where's the doctor? What's going —

PAUL (*urgent*): Quick. Nurse her. Keep her head up. Before she chokes.

JOHN *takes her.* TOM *steps back into the shadows.* PAUL *reaches for his notepad, and kneels on the floor to write them.*

JOHN: Why did her father leave?

PAUL: Please. Listen. Please.

Silence.

When CASS *fights for speech, it is with a tone and accent akin to* TOM*'s.*

CASS: They've . . . strapped me down. Me a swimmer. (*Laughs.*) To stop me rolling on a glass sea. Oh! Wha's that? Can't be an iceberg in the Med. Hardly the Titanic. (*Laughs.*) Scuse me, nurse. Excuse me. Can I ask —

JOHN: What's happening? What is she doing? She's talking to someone is she?

PAUL: Please, just hold her.

CASS: Plane? Bomb? No, I'm not worried. She explains it to me. All I'm thinkin' is me hand on her knee.

PAUL: She's possessed by the spirit of a man. Perhaps a sailor who was trapped in this —

JOHN: Stop her! I don't want to hear this.

CASS: Who'd sink a Red Cross? We keep the convention. Red Cross she says is a Greek cross. I din't know that. Learn someat every day. Anyway she says we can't be hit. The Cross protects us.

JOHN (*terrified*): Look it's crazy sitting here. Get the doctor.

CASS: Who's that screaming? The boat tilts her into my arms, if my arms were free. She holds on to me. Free me. Free me. Let me swim in my own sweat.

She becomes inaudible.

PAUL: What's she saying? It's important. Please.

JOHN: It's just . . . the ship, his ship's sinking.

PAUL: Her words. Her words!

JOHN (*reluctant*): Speaks of a fishbowl, on a mantlepiece. It's just raving. It's not . . . in my home. I'm in its home. Different worlds above the fire. No, I can't. I can't go on with this.

PAUL: You must!

JOHN: My soul . . . no my sole thought is . . . (*Shakes his head.*) Dirty the water is I can't make out dirty the ship is filthy the bandages shit of dying men floating the water dirty with the dirt of men . . . I want . . .

He continues listening, apparently exhausted, but will not give her words.

PAUL: What does she say?

JOHN *shakes his head.* TOM *steps forward for the first time.*

TOM: You bastard! You still won't tell my story.

JOHN *stares up at him.*

CASS: Water . . . a sip of clear water.

TOM: If that's what you want, my love.

TOM *takes up a handful of water, and gently wipes her lips with it. She smiles at him. She quietly puts her head against* JOHN*'s chest.*

Silence. PAUL *looks up.*

JOHN (*quietly*): Get the doctor.

PAUL: What? She's not dead.

JOHN: Get the doctor.

PAUL *rushes out.*

JOHN: I've never held death in my arms before.

TOM: All your love embraces turns to corpses. Take your hands off her.

JOHN *looks up at him. He lays her down.*

JOHN: I never wanted this. I only wanted what you dreamt of, of a world where people could live without fear of —

TOM: You want a world of sleepwalkers, of sunbathers, that's not what I dreamt of. How near does the water have to lap before you'll heed its anger?

JOHN: Please. Go to Helen. Bring me back a message.

TOM *wipes his hands with a flannel.*

TOM: You misuse the imagination. It in't for what you call masturbation at the edge of your bed, replacing prayer. It's a call to action. Use your legs.

JOHN: Please. Just tell me she's still all right.

TOM: The seance is over. You've no more power over me. I'm me own master. I'll come and go as I please.

He steps through into DORIS's *room. She speaks without opening her eyes.*

DORIS: They were not for me this time? Which woman did they take? I'm so tired. The dead understand enough to wait 'til morning for me to grieve.

JOHN *rises and leaves the room.*

I don't sleep in the bed anymore. They won't catch me undressed, not a second time.

TOM *stretches out on her bed.* JOHN *knocks on* HELEN's *door. He opens it and enters. He puts on the light, sees her clothes are gone, sits on the edge of the bed.* PAUL *and* EILEEN *enter* CASS's *room.*

PAUL: I couldn't find the doctor but —

He looks around.

PAUL: Everybody keeps vanishing.

EILEEN: Out of my way!

She checks on CASS.

PAUL: Please God please, let her be alive.

Silence.

EILEEN: She's still breathing.

PAUL: I knew. I knew.

EILEEN: Her fever seems to have dropped.

CASS *mumbles something.*

PAUL: What's she saying?

EILEEN: It can't just have disappeared like that. It's not possible.

She attempts to move her.

EILEEN: Come on, my love. Just let me check your pulse.

EILEEN *takes her wrist.* CASS *screams.*

CASS: NO!

JOHN *stands listening.* TOM *sits up, and remains in that position.* CASS *puts her hand across her mouth, and begins to weep.*

EILEEN: It's all right, my love. It's all right. Nobody's going to hurt you.

CASS *stares as though trying to make them out.* PAUL *grins at her.*

EILEEN: Lie down. Rest. Sleep. You'll feel a lot better.

CASS *lies back.* EILEEN *takes her pulse.* JOHN *kneels by* HELEN's *bed. He puts his hands over his face.* EILEEN *shakes her head.*

PAUL: What?

EILEEN: It couldn't have been rabies . . . The symptoms could never vanish this quickly. It must have been some form of hysteria, or fit.

PAUL: Possession.

EILEEN (*pauses*): Leave her now. Let her get a good night's sleep.

PAUL: I'd like to stay.

EILEEN: I'm sure she'll sleep right through. All right. She might need someone.

She moves to the door.

PAUL: I knew it wasn't rabies.

She smiles at him, and exits. He switches off the light, and kneels in prayer. EILEEN *enters her room, switches on her light, and startled, backs away. The* DOCTOR, *stripped to the waist, rises from her chair.*

EILEEN: How did you get in here?

DOCTOR: Pass key.

EILEEN: Get out!

DOCTOR: I startled you. I apologise. It came out of a genuine desire.

EILEEN: What?

DOCTOR: To avoid a general panic. (*Holds up his hand.*) My patient bit me. You appreciate immediate precautions in such circumstances.

EILEEN: You're trembling.

He opens his medical case.

DOCTOR: It's not the possibility of death I fear, but the preceding loss of my faculties. If one is to face death, it should be at least with the clarity of thought.

He holds out the needle.

DOCTOR: The needle has to be directly injected into the stomach. Hence the impossibility of healing myself. And the lack of attire.

EILEEN: There's no need.

DOCTOR: What?

EILEEN: Cass hasn't got rabies.

DOCTOR: Let's not argue diagnosis. That's really my speciality.

EILEEN (*pauses*): Of course, doctor. You know best. Better safe than sorry.

DOCTOR: I knew we understood one another.

She takes the needle.

EILEEN: Please, lie back.

PAUL *pulls a blanket over himself, and curls up by the side of the bed.*

DOCTOR (*lying down*): Are you this caring to your husband?

EILEEN: I was a nurse when I first met him.

DOCTOR: Not a . . . dancer?

EILEEN: No. A nurse. Undo the top of your trousers.

EILEEN *injects him.*
As they move into the next scene –

Scene Four

The beach at Kos
DORIS *quietly sings her song. The sound of cicadas.*
Upstage on a sunbed, the DOCTOR, *stripped to the waist, dark sunglasses make it impossible to tell if he is awake.* EILEEN *stands watching him.*
JOHN *lies curled up, in a foetal position, by another empty sunbed.*
PAUL *attempts to put up a sunshade over* CASS *on her sunbed.* DORIS *stands looking out to sea.*

DORIS: Is that our ship?

EILEEN *turns away from the* DOCTOR.

EILEEN: I think so. It's so small you could put it in your pocket.

She moves down towards DORIS *stopping by* JOHN.

DORIS: You won't go back on it?

EILEEN (*shakes her head*): I'll catch a boat to Rhodes, and then home. Will you?

DORIS: I have played Malta. Not a place for an encore.

EILEEN: What will you do?

DORIS: I don't know. I might stay on this beach for ever. The world is my . . . is it . . . oyster?

She takes out her map.
EILEEN turns to watch JOHN.
PAUL drops the parasol on CASS.
She covers her face.

PAUL: Oh, sorry.

She is clearly still on edge.

What . . . what will you do? (*Pause.*) Will you go on to Israel? (*Pause.*) I thought of going back to Patmos, but I could . . . I could do anything. Jerusalem must be very interesting. What will you do?

CASS: My father is coming to collect me.

PAUL, *disappointed, digs into his rucksack. He takes out the notebooks.*

PAUL: Then you'd better have these.

She stares at him.

They belong to you really.

CASS: No.

PAUL: Not the notebooks, but what's in them. (*Pause.*) When you were . . . when they all thought you were ill, you talked, all the time. I wrote most of it down.

CASS: Why?

PAUL: I thought you might not remember.

CASS: Why would I want to remember? I was ill.

Silence.

PAUL: Well, they're yours anyway.

He places them by her, and moves unintentionally towards JOHN. JOHN looks at him. PAUL stands rooted with embarrassment. EILEEN notices.

DORIS: Should we make a last trip together?

EILEEN: We could visit the ancient hospital.

JOHN: The holiday's over. There's been a death. She's dead. What does it take to make you understand?

He covers his face. He is crying silently. EILEEN kneels by him. Eventually –

EILEEN (*quietly*): Why did she try to leave the ship, John?

He does not reply.

(*She pauses.*) John, I have to know. She spoke to me. Through the wall. I could hardly hear her. I shut off listening. I covered my head with the blankets. I didn't want to listen I was so angry the way she'd treated Cass.

Pause.

It wasn't true, was it?

DORIS: What was not true?

EILEEN (*looking at JOHN*): I'm not sure I heard her properly. Perhaps it is all best forgotten.

DORIS: What did she say to you?

EILEEN: I'm sure it wasn't –

DORIS: What did she say?

EILEEN: She was hysterical. Why else would she try to swim off the ship?

DORIS: What did she say?

EILEEN: She said she was going to stop it.

CASS: Stop what?

EILEEN: Stop the ship. Make it turn round and stop it heading towards the war.

PAUL: But the ship did turn round.

EILEEN: Yes, but that was because of Cass, wasn't it?

Silence.

DORIS: What did she say to you, John?

JOHN: I thought there'd be a note, a message for me. This was all there was. (*He holds out a scrap of paper.*) I can't understand it. I . . .

DORIS: Read it.

JOHN (*reads*):
Paler than the grass of summer
I shudder with the caress of death
leaving only ash as a —

CASS *gasps.*

What is it?

CASS: It's not a letter. It's a song.

JOHN: One she wrote?

DORIS: She put the tune to it.

JOHN (*to* CASS): Can you sing it?

CASS: I don't know it.

JOHN: Doris? Or don't you sing at English funerals?

DORIS: Is this a funeral? You want a song to say farewell? No, I do not sing for this.

JOHN: What else is there but to forget? She speaks only of ashes, and death.

DORIS *shakes her head, and turns away.*

DORIS: Let him have his ritual. He knows only the sea and the albatross, but the phoenix rises from the ashes.

JOHN *strikes the match and sets the paper alight.* CASS *shudders, as behind them* TOM *appears, dressed in his army uniform.* PAUL *moves forward to put a blanket around her.* EILEEN *moves towards them.*

PAUL: Are you all right?

EILEEN *feels her forehead.* JOHN *looks up to see* TOM. *He stiffens and puts his hand in the fire.* TOM *shakes his head.* JOHN *stands, but dare not turn round.* HELEN, *in her swimsuit, stands behind him. She puts her hand across his mouth.*

TOM: If the desire can't be satisfied, destroy it. Do you still think that, John? No. You're not free to make such a choice. We won't let you.

She slowly takes her hand away.

JOHN: What can I do? What do you want of me?

HELEN: I come from the sea, with salt to rub into your wounds.

JOHN: You've every right to torment me.

HELEN: Do the dead only return for revenge, John? Can't they possibly return for peace and freedom?

JOHN: What do I have to do to set you free? I want to give you peace.

HELEN: To give me peace? (*Laughs.*) Oh, John. You have such a strange idea of death.

JOHN: Help me then. Please.

HELEN: I'm not here to comfort you, John. As soon as I see I'm easing your pain, I'll disappear again. I'm not a symbol for you to finger. I'm here to make you tell my story.

JOHN: Why did you try to escape?

She laughs.

HELEN: Work it out for yourself.

JOHN: How can I when I wasn't there?

HELEN: There's a limit you can learn from your own imagination. Try listening to others.

JOHN *looks around. She moves to sit in the sunbed, and begins to dry herself.*

CASS: I'm fine. Please believe me, I'm fine.

EILEEN: Of course.

EILEEN *moves away, but* PAUL *still hovers.* TOM *crosses to* CASS, *who does not notice him.*

TOM (*smiling*): You never were going to jump off that cliff, were you? It wasn't my passion that pulled you back, but yours that shaped a dog to bite your ankle.

PAUL: Do you want anything?

She shakes her head.

TOM: Love is an endless surprise. It brings a strange delight. I can bear my isolation, knowing you're alive.

CASS: Please, stop staring at me. I don't need any more help.

Both TOM *and* PAUL *turn away.*

TOM: It's nice to make the beach for once.

He turns round to catch JOHN *staring at him.*

Oh, son. We all have to sing for our supper. Remember.

JOHN *turns away back to* HELEN. *She drags out the suntan lotion from her yellow rucksack and pours some on the back of her neck. He, almost mechanically, puts his hand towards her.*

HELEN: Don't touch me!

JOHN: I want you very badly.

HELEN: How quickly you try to bend the fantasy to your use. With all your dreams of demon lovers. And now you want to bury your soul between my thighs.

JOHN (*softly*): Yes.

She turns to him, smiling.

HELEN: No. Your desire for me will bring no solace. And when you come close enough to kiss, I'll tear away the skin and leave the maggots on your tongue.

She turns away.

It's lovely to paddle in the sea. But what I can't bear is when the sea bed vanishes from under me.

She lies back.

(*Suddenly.*) You can't swim!

The others, except TOM, *turn to look at him.*

JOHN: She couldn't swim!

Silence.

JOHN: She said so herself. She couldn't have tried to swim from the boat.

EILEEN: You mean, she fell in? It was an accident?

PAUL: That's not right. I'm sorry, but . . . (*Pause.*) John, you said there was nothing in her room?

JOHN: Only the song.

PAUL: Why would she have taken her rucksack? It could only have weighed her down in the water.

Silence.

JOHN: Suicide.

CASS: Her song is of Sappho and suicide. Being pushed to the cliff edge and . . .

EILEEN: Why would she commit suicide?

JOHN: She did try to stop the ship. She locked herself away, and attempted to hold it to some crazy ransom. Her nerve must have given way. (*Pause.*) And she was totally alone.

DORIS: Not correct. No. The will does not break after such decisions.

JOHN: What other explanation can there be?

DORIS: I went early to my room last night. I don't take doctors' orders. They are not good for me.

Pause.

This rucksack. Is it yellow with brown straps?

JOHN: Yes, it was. Why?

DORIS: Have you such a rucksack, Cass?

CASS *shakes her head.*

EILEEN: What is it?

DORIS: I bumped into a man with such a rucksack last night.

JOHN: Who? Who was it?

DORIS: The man from the helicopter. It was your father, Cass.

CASS (*cries out*): No!

She puts her hand over her mouth. For a moment, it seems she might have another fit. They move towards her. TOM *sits quietly nearby.*

PAUL: What is it? Are you all right?

She puts her hand out to stop him. She nods her head.

JOHN: Cass, why would your father have Helen's rucksack?

CASS: I don't know. How would I know?

JOHN: What happened last night when your father arrived?

CASS (*desperate*): I don't remember. I don't remember anything. I was ill.

DORIS: You remember something.

CASS: Leave me alone. I want to forget all that, and get well. I don't want to have to go home and . . .

JOHN: Do you remember your father being there at all?

CASS: I don't remember anything.

JOHN: You remember me being there? Listening to your story.

CASS: What story?

JOHN: Do you remember me giving you a sip of water?

CASS (*sharply*): That wasn't you!

TOM *sits up.*

JOHN: Well, who the hell was it then?

CASS *buries her face in her hands.*

CASS: No. It was a nightmare, that's all. Please don't make me live through that again. Please.

PAUL *sits by her, not quite daring to put his arm around her.* JOHN *turns to* TOM.

TOM (*mildly*): Does she remember my story? Is that just another futile thought?

JOHN *moves suddenly forward to the notebooks.*

JOHN: Which one of these is last night's?

PAUL: Is there any reason to distress her further?

JOHN: It was you who said they were important.

PAUL: I didn't keep them to cause her pain.

JOHN: She has to remember. (*To* CASS:) Last night you talked of drowning. Do you remember that?

CASS: Leave me alone, please.

JOHN: Look, only you survived the water. Only you can give us the truth. I have to know. We have to know what happened.

He finds the page.

(*Reading wildly:*) This is it. 'The boat tilts her into my arms . . . if my arms were free. Free me. Let me swim in my sweat.' Where's the rest of it?

PAUL: You said you didn't hear any more.

CASS: Please stop. It means nothing to me.

JOHN: It means something to me.

He looks up at TOM *who lies down stretched out on the sand.* JOHN *turns back to* CASS, *who does not take her eyes from his face.*

Eventually –

JOHN (*softly, as though telling a children's story*): My grandfather was injured by a horse that ran wild at the landing at Gallipoli. Its belly had been ripped open by the barbed wire hidden under the surface of the water. Somehow, in all that carnage, his comrades got him on a Red Cross ship. He thought he was lucky, on his way back to Devon to recuperate. Heaven. But the ship was bombed, not far from here. It sank in a clear glass sea. It was not one of those stormy days that Ullysses beat his way through. Ideal holiday weather. Of course a Red Cross should not have been attacked. Geneva conventions. But both sides by this time had been running arms and fresh troops under its flag. His ship, however, was the real thing, not sailing under false colours, but he, and many others, had to pay the price for the deceit of generals as always. This much is known history.

He wipes his hands and face.

As the water poured into his ward, a nurse tried to calm him, although she must have been terrified herself. She wiped his sweat away, and gave him a sip of clear water. He thought this gesture absurd as the water rose around their feet. Absurd but . . . fine. He loved her so much in that moment that it hurt him more than his injury. She didn't try to escape, perhaps there was no escape, perhaps it never crossed her mind. That he'd never know, just as he would never know if anyone survived.

Pause.

As the first wave of water hit them, she'd freed his arms but not his legs. The screams of the dying men were deafening, echoing against the broken skin of the ship. He hung around her neck, holding on. The second wave covered them. They held their bursting breath, but that last air does not last into eternity. And so they gulped in the water, as though they'd wandered in from out a desert. And he thought, in that torrent that so suddenly became a silent pool, he thought he could see tears trickling down her face. He knew this to be crazy, how could you see such a thing? With all that water around you?

He smiles.

And even if you could, even if there were tears, what did it matter to either of them, or to anybody else. They were dead, anyway.

Silence.

CASS *touches the notebook in front of her.* TOM *sings very gently.*

TOM (*sings*):
She's my lady love
She is my one and only love
She's no one for sitting down to read
She's the only one Laguna knows

CASS (*softly*): How do you know about that?

JOHN: You told me.

She nods.

(*Gently:*) Tell me the rest. Tell us what you saw. Don't try to seperate fact from fantasy. Not for the moment. Just tell us what you see.

CASS: I was asleep. Someone hit me. I screamed. He put his hand over my face. I tasted his blood.

JOHN: Was it your father?

CASS: A man in white.

EILEEN: The doctor. He came to me for an injection against the bite.

CASS: It's true then. It happened.

JOHN: Go on.

CASS: There was a woman in the room, she came towards me, to help me. I thought it was a nurse. Then I thought she was me. My father stepped out from behind her. Behind me. I wanted to scream. Put his hand over my mouth. I couldn't breathe. The other man, white like a ghost, took my arm, and pricked me. I thought they're going to rape me. I could see them both with me, with my body in their arms. With their hands across my mouth. I closed my eyes, thinking I'm dead. I want to die. I want to be free.

Silence.

It wasn't me, was it? It wasn't a nightmare. It was Helen. The doctor. The man wasn't my father. It was another man. But it might as well have been.

Silence.

JOHN: Helen must have heard your cry and come to help you.

DORIS: Live bait. Very clever.

PAUL: They killed her? (*Pause.*) But why?

DORIS: They are very greedy. And our silence is the gold for rich men.

JOHN *turns to move towards the* DOCTOR. DORIS *blocks his path.*

What are you going to do? Kill him? Is that what Helen would have wanted?

JOHN: I have to do something.

DORIS: What good will that do?

JOHN: Good? What are you talking about, good?

DORIS: Good. Is this not a word in your language? Wait. Together we know the story. He should not be the first to hear it.

Pause.

Stay silent. Pretend to be asleep if you can't hide your feelings. When there is a group there is more than one way to skin a rat.

JOHN *refuses.*

JOHN: I can't just sit by and —

DORIS: We are both of the theatre. Do you learn nothing?

JOHN: What?

DORIS: Timing. The art of timing is everything.

JOHN *turns back to* HELEN *who is apparently sleeping.*

PAUL: He could have heard every word we said.

DORIS: He's here to watch Cass. They must be panicking on what she might know.

EILEEN: Did he ask you questions this morning?

She nods.

CASS: I said I remembered nothing. He seemed very strange.

EILEEN: It could be the reaction to the vaccine.

DORIS: Good. Offer him a drink of water. It could be the end of him.

EILEEN: See if he's asleep.

PAUL *crosses to the* DOCTOR *and shakes him. The* DOCTOR *wakes up. He tries to stand somewhat shakily.*

DOCTOR: Too much midday sun.

EILEEN: Mad dogs and Englishmen.

DOCTOR (*sings*):
'Go out in the midday sun,
The Chinese would not dare to . . .
The Japanese . . .'

He cannot recall the rest of it. He stands, he is shaking. He puts on his shirt. The others watch him apart from CASS *who stares out.*

DOCTOR: How is my patient?

EILEEN: Alive, and well.

Silence.

DOCTOR: What are you all planning to do now?

DORIS: We're staying here.

DOCTOR: What? All of you? Aren't you all ready for your separate destinations?

EILEEN: We need some time to think, to reflect, after the —

DOCTOR: The tragedy. Yes. Such a highly strung girl. What could have possessed her?

Silence.

But you'll be going back, won't you, Cass?

She shakes her head.

You have to stay under medical care. It might seem like a miracle cure, but nothing works like that really. We need to keep you under observation.

EILEEN: I'll look after her.

DOCTOR: Your father might have something to say about that.

EILEEN: She's over eighteen.

CASS: Have you spoken to my father?

DOCTOR: Of course we've spoken to him. He was with you last night. Don't you remember?

Silence.

Well, if you are all feeling so fit and well, why don't you come with me on a guided tour of the Aesculapion? Hippocrates formulated his famous oath there.

DORIS: Never trust a doctor. They even have to swear an oath to make them honest, but it does no good.

DOCTOR: It's really not to be missed.

EILEEN: We'll stay here.

DOCTOR: What will you do here?

DORIS: Wait. We'll have a picnic.

DOCTOR: With what?

PAUL: I've got my food for breaking my fast.

DOCTOR: Why are you breaking your fast? We haven't reached Philadelphia yet. Or have you given up that crazy idea?

Silence.

PAUL *takes out his food.*

DOCTOR: A few paltry olives and cheese. Not even a Kos lettuce.

DORIS: Well, bring us one on your way back.

They begin to share it around.

DOCTOR: Well, I suppose you won't come to any harm here.

The DOCTOR *leaves.*

JOHN: I wanted to believe in your suicide. — Why?

HELEN: Go for a swim. Graze your foot on a rock. I'm the eternal salt in the sore. I insist you love me. I insist you tell my story.

TOM *stands by him.*

TOM: And thank you for telling mine, John. Much appreciated. Course it won't exactly like that, but . . .

PAUL (*offering* JOHN *an olive*): John.

TOM *turns to* HELEN.

TOM: Will you teach me your song, Helen?

She smiles, and softly hums the tune.

DORIS *looks to where the* DOCTOR *has gone off.*

DORIS: Is that man with the doctor, the man who was your father?

CASS *stands.*
She shades her eyes.

CASS: It could be my father.

She rises.

I'm frightened. I'm scared of meeting him alone.

EILEEN: We will meet him together.

EILEEN *stands.*

DORIS: Now we have eaten.

JOHN *turns to* HELEN.

JOHN: I will. I will risk it.

HELEN: You have no other real choice, John.

They all slowly rise as —

TOM (*sings*):
My eyes are dark to the light
Waves of sweat overwhelm me
My ears beat out with fright
Why don't our desires set us free?

Paler than the grass of summer
I shudder with the caress of death
Must we always suffer
being poverty's mother
can the unwanted lover
never be the one to recover?

STARS

KITTY (*to* VIVIAN LEIGH): There are two sorts of people, Myra; those who get the breaks, and those who don't.

ROBERT TAYLOR (*to* VIVIAN): It isn't real, is it? Shall we wake up suddenly to find it isn't true?

Waterloo Bridge, 1940

Stars was first presented at Scarborough Library Theatre in 1976, with the following cast:

DICK	Malcolm Hebden
GIRL	Diane Bull
JANE	Elaine Strickland
BOY	Robin Herford

Directed by Alan Ayckburn

Nottingham. Early June, 1944.

ACT ONE

Film Fun

Nottingham. Early June 1944.
A Projection: Dick Powell and Ruby
Keeler, dancing 'I Only Have Eyes For
You'. Music: 'Dames'.
DICK's office. An old desk, filing
cabinet, two chairs, a swivel for the boss,
and a straight back. There is not a smell
of money in the air. DICK sits, studying
his face in a small mirror. He's small,
fast-moving, dark, with slightly receding,
wavy hair. A bit of a dapper, he is dressed
in dinner jacket, white shirt, bow-tie. He's
just the wrong side of forty. His accent
moves continually across the Atlantic
from his basic middle accent to his
attempt at an all purpose American.

DICK (*singing softly*): What do you go
   for,
   to see the show for
   tell the truth
   you go to see those —

(*Carefully examining his image.*) Sod.
Why do they grow there?

(*He rummages through his drawers.*)
Course, some people don't care. This is
me, they say, the way nature intended.

(*He finds large scissors.*) Christ.
(*Gingerly cuts off hair protruding*
from nostril.) There. Only takes a
second to weed the garden. Or you get
hair growing out of everywhere. Like
Joe. He's got 'em sprouting out of his
ears, like spring onions. Him a
barber — woun't you think he'd care?
It's like looking up into an armpit.

(*He stands up and brushes down his*
jacket.) Going round like King Kong.
Well, King Kong never won fair lady.
You've got to take a bit of pride in
yourself. See yourself as others see
you. Put on the best show you can.

A knock at the door. Outside a young
girl, tall, slim, nervously straightens
her dress.

(*Nervous.*) Just a sec! (*Takes up a*
cigar; does not light it.) Wait! (*More*

expansively:) In my business, you
know, image is everything. Creating
stars. Finding faces to fit those
yearnings in all our breasts. Well, I
wouldn't have risen to where I am now
if I didn't have an intuitive feel for
face. Pick 'em out of a crowd. Those
stars that make you happy. And if
you're happy, I'm happy. (*He practises*
some beautiful smiles into the mirror.)
If you're happy, I'm happy. (*Well*
content, he rises, all youth, charm,
energy, and tap-dances to the door,
singing.)
What do you go for
To see the show for
Tell the truth
You go to see
Those beautiful dames.

(*He opens the door.*) Wheel the
next one in, please.

The GIRL looks up and down the
hall.

GIRL: There's only me 'ere.

DICK *returns to his side of the desk.*

DICK: Welcome.

GIRL: If you're busy, I'll —

DICK: Goodness gracious no. Step into
   the light, Miss —?

GIRL: Leicester.

DICK: Just walk about.

GIRL: Pardon?

DICK: Turn around.

GIRL: What for?

DICK: I have to picture you.

GIRL: Oh. (*She turns.*)

DICK: Good. Good.

GIRL: Can I stop now?

DICK: Fine. Fine.

GIRL: Only I've just 'ad carrot flan.

DICK *offers her a chair.*

DICK: Please.

GIRL: Thank you. I've come about the —

DICK: I know why you've come.

GIRL: You do?

DICK: You want to break into pictures.

GIRL: Well —

DICK: You want to make it in the mad world of movies.

GIRL: I —

DICK: If I had a penny, well — perhaps it's for the best that you've no idea how many hopes I've seen dashed against that slithery pole.

GIRL: Pole?

DICK: But for some they exist, kid; those bright lights exist somewhere, over that rainbow. For those prepared to sacrifice. But to get there you've got to work and sweat and work some more. You've got to work day and night, and between times. And if you don't think you're going to like that, you'd better quit right now. Listen, kid, I want you to close the door, but I want you to think carefully which side of it you're going to be on. 'Cos if you stay, and don't let me sway you either way, but if you stay the next time you go through that door, oh, you'll still go through it a youngster all right — but you've gotta come back a star!

GIRL: It's —

DICK: Take your time, kid.

GIRL: I —

DICK: You don't make decisions like this every day.

DICK *rises and crosses to the open door.*

Well?

GIRL: It's about the part-time usherette job. It were in the evening paper.

DICK (*thrown*): Ye', that's right.

GIRL: Oh. Only I wondered.

DICK (*desperate*): They all had to start somewhere. Ruby, Ginger, Joan,

Winnie . . .

GIRL: Really?

DICK: Hell of a draught in here, in't there? (*He closes the door. Crossing to his desk.*) Just à propos, have you ever done any dancing?

GIRL: Not to speak of. Not proper.

DICK: You should. It's in your walk.

GIRL: You think so?

DICK: I know so. Sing?

GIRL: Not —

DICK: Not that it matters. What does matter is the chemistry.

GIRL: Chemistry?

DICK: The magic of that moment when the lights come up, and you're standing there, alone, in front of a packed house. Silence. A moment's uncertainty. And then, then you can feel them, feel them coming towards you. You've got them. They want your Kiaora. They want you. You make them happy, you make me happy. That's all that matters, kid.

GIRL: I'll —

DICK: And I think you will make them happy.

GIRL: Thank you, Mr Milles.

DICK: Dick. Now, tell me all about yourself.

GIRL: Well, I —

DICK: Country girl? Bit of a tomboy, when you were a kid? Raiding the orchards, swimming the river, climbing the biggest trees with the best of them, eh? Until suddenly, one day, POW! Everything's changed, and you don't know why, but you get the feeling there's more to life than milkshakes and playing sax in Mickey Rooney's band. Time to move on. Into the big city. Have I got the right picture?

GIRL: It's —

DICK: You've made a brave choice, kid.

I like a girl with spunk.

GIRL: Wha'?

DICK: I'm going to do what I can to help you.

GIRL: Thank you.

DICK (*leaning earnestly forward*): A couple of small points.

GIRL: Pardon?

DICK: Maybe crop the hair a little. Darker lipstick to accentuate the bow. Capture that moment of sensual innocence of the girl on the verge of womanhood. Innocent sensuality.

(*Suddenly*:) Ruby Keeler. The girl-next-door. We can do it. Ruby and Dick. Get a good routine going. Work together.

GIRL: Excuse me?

DICK: I can see it now.

GIRL: The wages.

DICK: The wages?

GIRL: Are they fixed at what it says in the paper?

She pauses, coughs.

DICK. Well, that's where you start, kid, but for a girl with talent, the sky's the limit.

She looks at him, quietly, with almost a sensual innocence.

Within reason, you understand. I mean, after all, it is only an usherette's job. Part-time. Tuesdays, Thursdays, Saturdays. Another girl does Mondays, Wednesdays and Fridays.

She continues to stare at him.

We're only a small cinema, you see.

She rises slowly from her chair.

But there's a lot of perks. Working in a cinema.

GIRL: Yes?

DICK: Yes.

She sits.

You get to see the films free.

There is a long pause.

GIRL (*helpfully*): Ice cream?

DICK: Ah, ice cream. No. Rationing.

GIRL: Free uniform?

DICK *bounds across to the filing cabinet.*

DICK: Costume! Uniform sounds so military, doesn't it? Costume. Neatly folded away. Down here somewhere. Oh, got it. Here, look at this. (*He takes out a dress.*) None of your blackout curtaining here. Had it made up out of spare on the cinema curtains. Just like *Gone With The Wind*.

GIRL: Pardon?

DICK: Vivian Leigh. Velvet. Look lovely when the lights hit them. Feel that.

GIRL: Nice.

DICK: Take it in if it's too large.

GIRL: Easy enough.

DICK: One snag, though. If it's too small. I doubt it will be, but — well, the curtain hardly covers the screen as it is. I don't know how we'd manage. A bit like Cinderella. If the dress fits you can be Queen of the Ball.

GIRL: Ye'.

DICK: Would you like to try it on?

GIRL: All right.

DICK: There's a powder room down the hall, Ruby.

GIRL: Oh ye'. Just one more thing.

DICK: Yes.

GIRL: Who the hell's Ruby Keeler?

Blackout. Spot on JANE, *a small, dark, attractive woman of around forty. She is in a slip. She picks out a few desultory tap steps.*

JANE (*singing flatly*):
Are there stars out tonight
I don't know if it's cloudy or bright
For I only have eyes for you, dear.

She stands, quietly, head to one side.
Spot on DICK.

The moon may be high,
But I can't see a thing in the sky,
For I only have eyes for you, dear.

DICK *crosses to centre-stage to* JANE
– they dance. Orchestra. It builds
towards a fine routine.

DICK: I don't know if we're in a garden
Or on a crowded avenue
You are here, so am I
Maybe millions of people go by
But they all disappear from view

DICK *returns towards the* GIRL.

For I only have eyes for you.

Lights up as before, plus low lights on
JANE*'s room. Dressing-table, sofa,*
coffee table. JANE *stands as before.*

The GIRL *has taken her dress off. She*
steps out of it.

GIRL: Who the hell's Ruby Keeler?

DICK: Who's Ruby Keeler?

GIRL: Ye', who is she? (*Embarrassed.*)

DICK: There's a ladies down the . . .
She's a star. She danced. Sang 'I only
have eyes for you'. Dozens of movies.
42nd Street. Dames. Footlight Parade.
Gold Diggers of 1933.

GIRL: 1933! Eleven years ago. Christ,
she must be knocking on a bit.

JANE *coughs, lights a cigarette, and*
returns to her dressing mirror, getting
dressed during this scene.

DICK: Used to partner Dick Powell.

GIRL: Who?

DICK *sighs.*

Can't stand musicals anyway.
(*Rummaging in her bag.*) Must have
lost them.

DICK: Can I help?

GIRL: Lost me fags.

DICK: Have one of mine. (*He gives her a*
small Woodbine from his top pocket.)

GIRL: Ta. (*She sits on the edge of the*
desk.)

DICK (*by way of conversation*): What
sort of films do you like then?

GIRL: I like someat wi' a bit of action.
Thrillers. Private dicks. Alan Ladd.
That sort of thing.

DICK (*holding out the dress*): Would you
care to –

GIRL: I used to have long hair down one
side, like Veronica Lake. But they
made me cut it off in the factory.

DICK: Shame. There's a ladies down
the –

GIRL: You're a gent, aren't you?

DICK: Well, you mustn't tempt us too
far, you know.

GIRL (*taking the dress*): Why not?

DICK (*embarrassed*): Dick Powell,
actually, he's just . . . he's just made a
private dick film. *Farewell My Lovely.*
He's Philip Marlowe. And he's got this
crummy office in L.A. and – (*He*
loosens his bow-tie.)

GIRL (*putting the dress over her head*):
Nearly there.

DICK: Yes. (*He opens the filing cabinet,*
and takes out a bottle and glass.) And
all these fast-talking living women
keep dropping by, and –

GIRL: Do us up.

DICK: Sure. (*He takes the glass he's*
poured with him. She takes it and
knocks it back.) Oh yes, that was for
you. Yes. You know, you can really
feel the heat of L.A. in here. You
know, the hot, the heat.

GIRL: It's round the back.

DICK: Of course.

GIRL: Out of practice?

DICK: A guy like me don't get out of
practice.

GIRL: Oh yeah?

DICK: Oh yeah. (*He eventually manages the zip. She turns to face him.*)

GIRL: How does it look?

DICK: Swell. Swell.

GIRL: Two swells. Well, well.

DICK: Another shot?

GIRL: Just put the bottle on the table.

DICK: Sure.

She takes another slug.

OK sister, lay it on me. What do you figure?

GIRL: I'll level with you, Dick. There don't seem no ice in it for me.

DICK: Ice? Oh ye', ice, I'm with you.

GIRL: So?

DICK: Hold on. I have something here for you.

He freezes. A frantic search of drawers, filing cabinets. The BOY, *an American G.I. enters the (now dressed)* JANE's *parlour.*

Projection: Dick Powell/Ruby Keeler. Rehearsing dance. 42nd Street.

BOY: A fine place you have here, ma'am. Really fine.

JANE: It suits me.

BOY: Ye', well I can appreciate that.

JANE: It doesn't get a lot of light in the daytime.

BOY: Oh?

JANE: Faces north, you see.

BOY: Ah. Shame.

DICK: Look at this. (*He brings out a large torch.*) You can keep it for your own personal use. But watch out for the batteries, aren't easy to come by.

GIRL: Seems like nothing is easy to come by.

DICK: Everything's on rations.

GIRL: You sure look that way.

DICK: Might just have some spare.

JANE: May I take your coat?

BOY: Sure. (*He hands his coat to* JANE.)

JANE (*hardly able to lift it*): Goodness.

BOY: Oh, 'scuse me, ma'am. I almost forgot. (*He takes his coat back.*) I bought you a few — well, I hope you won't think I'm being forward, but I — well, there's some coffee, cornbeef, chocolate, dried eggs, oranges, bananas, I don't know if they're any use to you, ma'am — (*He unloads them onto the coffee table.*) I hope you won't think me forward, ma'am.

JANE: Goodness. You shouldn't have, really, you shouldn't. I mean it was I who invited you for tea, but — bananas, goodness, I don't recall how long it is since I've seen a banana —

BOY (*offering*): Would you like one now, ma'am?

JANE: May I . . . save it for later?

BOY: Oh, ye', and there's this.

He hands her a small present, wrapped in tissue.

JANE: It's just like a birthday. I must save the tissues.

DICK: No. Sorry.

GIRL: Is this all? Just a dress and a torch?

DICK: Well, yes.

GIRL: Nothing else?

DICK: No. I don't think so.

GIRL: Nylons? No nylons?

JANE: Nylons! Nylons. Well, I'm not all together sure that it isn't just a little bit forward of you to bring a lady nylons on your first meeting, but they're more than welcome.

DICK: Nylons are very hard to come by.

BOY: Sarge down at PX said the ladies here go a bundle on them.

JANE: Go a bundle?

BOY: That's what Sarge said.

JANE: He sounds like a man of some experience. (*She puts the stockings on the table. Occasionally, she is drawn to touch them; to check on them.*) Well, thank you, thank you again.

BOY: My privilege, ma'am. Just a small token of appreciation for all you kind ladies who make us so welcome in their homes.

JANE: You've been to others?

BOY: Oh, no, ma'am. You're the first.

JANE: I see. A spot of tea?

Lights down on JANE's room. In the office, DICK is still sitting, holding the torch.

DICK: I know a man who knows a man . . . I'll see what I can do.

GIRL: Tonight?

DICK: I'll do my best.

GIRL (*standing and taking torch*): OK. I'll stick around.

DICK: Fine.

GIRL (*going to the door*): And when you want me . . . just whistle. You know how to whistle, don't you, Dick? You just put your lips together and blow.

She exits, fade down on DICK trying to whistle. JANE and the BOY are sitting, somewhat rigidly, on the couch, having just had tea.

JANE: More tea?

BOY: Three is ample, thank you.

JANE: I'd offer you a can of beer, but, alas —

BOY: Tea is fine.

JANE: Do smoke if you wish.

BOY (*he takes out a pack of Camels, offers JANE, she refuses, he lights one for himself*): Thank you. Yes, well —

JANE: Yes?

BOY: I was just going to say how nice it is, to get off-base and find yourself in a nice place like this. We don't get much time off-base. It makes a real

nice change.

JANE: I would have imagined a young man like yourself would have preferred to spend his free time painting the town red, jitterbugging to Glen Miller.

BOY: Well to be honest, ma'am —

JANE: Jane.

BOY: Jane, to be honest, jitterbugging isn't really my —

JANE: Cup of tea?

BOY: No, thanks. Oh, right. I get you. No, it's not my cup of tea.

JANE: You don't care much for dancing?

BOY: Well, you know, everyone crammed together like that — I don't call that dancing.

JANE: You prefer something with a little more class?

BOY: Well, I wouldn't say that exactly.

JANE: No, you wouldn't say that. Because you're far too modest. But I can see you have an innate dancer's grace about you. The way you smoke your cigarette, the way you sip your tea.

BOY (*coughing*): No, Jane. I've never been any good.

JANE: Have you ever tried?

BOY: Not really. You see, where I come from there's a straight choice. Between dancing and baseball. Girls do dancing, and boys do baseball. I did baseball.

JANE: It's time you expanded your horizons. We can't afford to let our talents go to waste.

BOY: Pardon?

JANE (*rising*): I'll teach you a few steps.

BOY: I'll sit this one out.

JANE: Wall-flower. Now come along. If I can't teach you a few steps, then I'll give up. Come on.

BOY: I'll only break something.

JANE: No, you won't. And I won't take no for an answer. On your feet, soldier.

BOY: OK, but it's your funeral.

JANE: Now, I'm going to do a simple shuffle-hop-step. (*She demonstrates.*) Now you try.

BOY: Well, it looks easy enough, but how do you do it with two left feet?

JANE: After me. (*He does it.*) Good. See, I told you. In no time at all we'll have you dancing on Broadway. Get yourself a good partner, young, light on her feet, and you're in business. (*She begins to tap slowly, walking in front of him.*) Want me to show you? (*She gets faster.*)

BOY: Great. That's great. Go, go.

On a turn, she trips, and cries out. He catches her as she falls.

BOY: You OK?

JANE: I think so.

BOY: Sure you haven't twisted it? Put some weight on it.

JANE: Ouch! I think I have. May be just a sprain. Could you help me to the couch?

He picks her up in his arms.

My, you are strong.

BOY: Don't want to take no chance of putting any weight on it, ma'am.

JANE: Me, Jane.

BOY: Jane.

JANE: You Tarzan. (*Pause; softly.*) Isn't this frightfully silly?

They come close to a kiss, initiated by JANE.
However:
a siren. Blackout.

A match is struck. DICK *lights the cigarette in the corner of his mouth. He's wearing a grey double-breasted raincoat, with the belt knotted across, and a trilby hat. He partakes of*

something of the image of The Private Eye, which he aspires to, and something of the image of the Dirty Raincoat Brigade, which he may end up as.

DICK (*American*): An air-raid warning has just been sounded. If you wish to leave the cinema, please do so as quietly as possible. Those who wish to remain do so at their own risk. (*He grinds out the cigarette.*) Anybody? (*Sudden torchlight.*) OK you wise guys, cool it at the back there. (*Dark again.*) Miss Leicester to the manager's office. The film now continues.

Projection: Vivian Leigh embraces Leslie Howard after his return from the war. Gone With The Wind.

The sound comes back first. Soft moans. Lights. JANE *is lying on the couch; the* BOY *is massaging her ankle.*

JANE (*moaning softly*): Is it swelling?

BOY: Yes, I think it is. A little bit. Yes.

JANE: Soft hands for a soldier.

BOY: Well, I've always tried to keep them er —

JANE: For such a strong man.

BOY: I can easily pop out and get a doctor.

JANE: It's often that way though, isn't it?

BOY: It wouldn't take me a second. One-two-three and here I am again, with a doctor.

JANE: Shall we wait and see if it goes down first?

BOY: Well, that's fine. That's fine. I mean, that's fine with me but you, these things, well you never know do you?

JANE: That's true. Don't stop. But I prefer to wait and see what develops. Could I have a cigarette?

BOY: Fine. Sure (*He drops a few. Picking*

them up.) I'll leave you a few, for the morning. Or the afternoon. (*He lights her cigarette.*) If you're out. Well, even if you're not out. I mean, I got plenty. Packs.

JANE: Ah, that throbbing. Throbbing.

BOY: And gum. I have plenty of packs of gum as well.

JANE: The light in my eyes — would you . . . the lamp?

BOY: Switch on the lamp. Sure. That's fine. (*He does so.*)

JANE: And switch off the main light.

BOY: Ah, you want the main . . . well, yes, I can do that. That's easy enough. (*Switches it off.*) Not too dark for you?

JANE: I'll just close my eyes. Ease the pain behind them. It always comes with my body's pain. But it is not of my body. You understand?

BOY: Oh yes, of course.

JANE: The pain of one who's known love, and borne the loss of it.

BOY: Yes, indeed. You're wanting to go to sleep? I can always come back another time. Any time. Well, I say any time, we're expecting to be posted on the big push overseas any day now, but, apart from that, I can come round almost any time.

JANE: I saw it in your face, the moment we met. The mark of the same suffering. A man who has looked into the heart of beauty and seen the worm of the world. It leaves its scar. Where is your scar?

BOY: I could easily go out and get any-body. Somebody. A doctor.

JANE: Was she beautiful?

BOY: Who? Oh, yes. Yes. She was. Yes. I think it's really wonderful how you get those ducks flying up the wall like that. I think that's a really wonderful effect.

JANE: And rich?

BOY: Rich? Oh ye', was she rich. Well, she could have bought dozens of those ducks. Is it one duck with a family, baby up to father, or is it one duck just growing up in stages? What do you think?

JANE: And was she wild?

BOY: Wild. Geese. I mean geese. I can't think why I said ducks.

JANE: It hurts you to talk about it. I can tell by the way you're pacing about.

BOY: No. No. I'm fine.

JANE: Best to get it out, you know.

BOY: Is it?

JANE: Sit down. Please. (*He sits.*) She loved you.

BOY: Well, I s'pose —

JANE: And you loved her?

BOY: Well, she was rich and wild and beautiful and she loved me. I mean, it would have been stupid and ill-mannered not to have done. (*He laughs almost hysterically.*) Well, there you are. Can I get you something? A cold compost, or —

JANE: And you were the tough kid from the other side of the track. Just a poor kid, with his shirt hanging out who believed that love and freedom were the great truths, and that all one needed was a woman and a song to set down the dusty roads to your dreams.

BOY: Ye', that sounds like me.

JANE: But she was spoilt. She wanted both love and luxury. Even you, with the touch of an angel, even you were not all softness with her. You could be mean to her, when the mood came —

BOY: Well, now you come to mention it, I guess maybe I was, looked at in that light I guess I could be pretty rough, you know, when I wanted to be. When I was in the mood.

JANE: But not half as rough as the rich men who had other plans for her —

BOY: No? I was pretty rough.

JANE: They gave you a rough time, but it didn't stop you.

BOY: It wouldn't. It didn't.

JANE: But now there were men between you and the woman you desired, and those men gave you a rough time —

BOY: Scarred me —

JANE: But they weren't half as rough as you were with them. You tracked them down one by one, ruthlessly, remorselessly, a boy born in hate into a man, and you drove on towards the body you craved for —

BOY: Yes. That's me. (*Half-engrossed, half-nervous wreck, he has taken to mindlessly toying with the fruit.*)

JANE: And then, that evening, finally, after so much blood, you came —

BOY: Yes. Yes.

JANE: Through the French windows. Up the stairs.

BOY: I remember.

JANE: To the very door of her room. You didn't knock.

BOY: Hell, no.

JANE: Straight in. And there she lay. She never spoke.

BOY: Not a word. (*He unpeels a banana.*)

JANE: But you saw, you saw, in her eyes, something new. That had not been there in the summerdays of dust and corn. Something that touched the winter in your blood. A look in her eyes — a look of many men before you, of many men between you, and your love went cold.

BOY (*unbuttoning his jacket*): Cold.

JANE: But, strangely, your passion was fed anew. You knew now, and would never forget, the terrible attraction of the tarnished woman, and you knew you could not resist. Stroke my brow.

The pain. The pain,

BOY: The pain. The pain. (*He sees the banana.*) Oh.

JANE: Come.

BOY: I think I'm losing my senses.

JANE: Yes. Yes.

BOY: I've peeled a —

JANE: Yes. Yes.

BOY: And the crazy thing is —

JANE: Yes. Yes.

BOY: I don't even like them. Would you care for it?

JANE (*shouting*): Yes! (*She opens her eyes, like one awaking from a nightmare; then, with considerable restraint.*) No. No. No, thank you. Not right this minute. Put it down. I'll pop it in water later.

BOY: Sorry. Hate to see waste.

JANE: Yes. Oh yes.

BOY: How's the swelling?

JANE: Better, thank you.

BOY: Oh, I am pleased.

JANE: But I feel my legs deserve a treat.

BOY: I can get you a bowl of salt water.

JANE: To feel nylons on my legs again. It's been so long. Would you be so kind as to help me?

BOY: Put . . . put . . . put . . . put . . .

JANE: No. Just help me up.

Projection: Vivian Leigh visits Gable in prison. She wears her velvet dress. Gone With The Wind.

He helps her. Lights up on DICK's office. Trench coat, hat and all, DICK sits slumped in his chair. He looks up as the GIRL enters the room. He takes a shot of rye.

DICK: Here's looking at you, kid.

GIRL: What you got your coat on for?

DICK: Pardon?

GIRL: Have you sprung a leak?

DICK: Gets kind of cold back here. Long December nights. Sleet stabbing at the windows.

GIRL: It's the first of June.

DICK (*confused*): Never mind the details.

GIRL: No.

DICK: Si' down.

She does so. He slowly, laboriously, takes a small parcel out of his inside pocket, and slides it across the table.

Open it.

JANE *is now standing.*

JANE: Such stuff as dreams are made of.

GIRL: Nylons! Nylons! Oh, Dick, aren't they wonderful? Look at them. Aren't they beautiful? Where on earth did you get them?

DICK: You ask too many questions.

GIRL: Oh, thank you. Thank you. (*She runs round to kiss him.*)

DICK: Easy, baby, easy.

BOY: Would you like me to leave the room?

JANE: You just sit there, and be a gentleman.

BOY: How?

JANE: Hands over your eyes.

DICK: Put 'em on!

GIRL (*surprised*): Put them on? Here?

DICK (*taking another shot*): You don't like them?

GIRL: Of course. I love them. Only I —

DICK: So — (*He coughs.*) Put 'em on. Please.

GIRL: Whatever you say, boss.

DICK (*slurred*): Here's looking at you, kid.

His head drops the last few inches to his chest. The GIRL begins to put on the nylons, resting her leg on the chair. The BOY sits, tensely, on the edge of

the couch, eyes covered.

JANE: No peeking, mind.

BOY: No, ma'am.

GIRL (*ecstatic.* JANE *puts on her stockings*): Oh! You can't guess what this means to me, after all these years of dreary, dreary stockings. And everybody saying you're lucky to have a pair of them for best. And now — lovely things to wear. That's what's so awful about this war. A pretty girl forced to wear flannelettes, and utility suits. No make-up. No nylons. No nothing. It in't fair. You've got nothing to look back on. You can't say to yourself, well I did look nice then. Even if you get the top half decent, underneath you're wearing summat'd make a Bevin-lad blush. If you got knocked down, or hit by a bomb, honest, you'd be ashamed. But being put in an ambulance wi' nylons on, well then they know they're dealing with somebody wi' a bit of class. Class. When I went straight out o' school into lace market, in '40, I remember me mam bringing home little snippets of Nottingham lace, black, white, blue, all colours, too small for you to do ought wi' but hoard them like precious jewels, but I thought, I'll soon be old enough to buy some underskirts laced round with this. There, aren't they lovely?

JANE: Are you sure you're not peeking?

BOY: Yes, ma'am. Jane.

She sits opposite him, and passes a hand in front of his face. Gaining no reaction, she sighs. She studies him.

GIRL (*walking about looking at them*): And what happened? They'd stopped making lace. Stopped making all that beauty. Put me to work on mosquito nets. I din't even get to go on parachutes, where at least you could nick a bit of silk for your undies. Mosquito nets! And I was earning the money, but you coun't buy ought wi' it. You had to have coupons, and even they'd hardly get ought any more. (*She sits, quietly.*) Feel that. That's lovely. Touch of nylon. The lads out there, they think they're making all the sacrifices, so they come home and think they can play us like muck, cos they're paying the whole price. But I'm paying as well. I'm paying wi' knowing that the best years of my life are being spent, and I'll have nought wi' a bit of class to remember them by. 'Cept for this touch of nylon, and what I can get wheeling and dealing, in coupons. Do you know I hardly eat, so's I can do deals. There in't enough to start wi' and I eat less than that. It takes the years away from you. All this running about. Still –

She strokes her legs. JANE *slowly reaches out a hand, as if to caress the* BOY'*s face. A certain tenderness. Silence.*

BOY: Have you nearly finished?

A siren. The all clear. It seems to rouse them out of their reveries.

JANE: All clear.

GIRL: Dick? (*She shakes him.*) Can I get back to Waterloo Bridge?

DICK (*shocked*): Trent Bridge? Not for the likes of you, kid. You're too good to tout for trade on Trent Bridge. I'll get you what you want. Trust me.

GIRL: I won't saying ought about Trent Bridge. *Waterloo Bridge.*

DICK: What?

GIRL: The film. They've just got engaged, and they're waltzing, with 'Auld Lang Syne' playing, and candles all around 'em.

DICK: Candles. Roman candles. Fireworks if you stick wi' me, kid.

BOY (*rising*): I'd best be getting back to base.

JANE (*showing off her stockings*): You like them?

BOY: Ye', they look real nice, ma'am.

You've got nice legs. Betty Grable had better watch out.

JANE: Well, I do declare, if you ain't the perfect gentleman. Thank you, kind sir.

BOY (*recognising her imitation*): Scarlett O'Hara. Gee, I love Vivian Leigh. That was the first really great movie I ever saw. Fire-red hair against the burning city. She's a real Great Briton, eh?

JANE: You should see her in *Waterloo Bridge.* With Robert Taylor.

GIRL: It's such a sad film. Her thinking him killed in the war, and her so poor but proud, having to go on the game to keep body and soul together.

DICK: Who's on the game? I keep telling you I'll keep you. And when I want you, I'll just whistle. (*He attempts it.*)

JANE: It's on at the Essoldo this week. Why don't you go tomorrow, Saturday? It's a lovely film.

BOY (*evasively*): Tomorrow's another day.

JANE (*not comprehending*): Yes, I know it is.

BOY: Vivian Leigh.

JANE: Oh, you don't look a bit like Vivian Leigh.

BOY: That's more your cup of tea.

JANE: Silver-tongued, aren't you? Just like Robert Taylor, in your uniform. (*She pauses.*) Come tomorrow?

BOY: Oh, I don't think I can make Saturday.

JANE: I'm working Saturday as well. Have you never seen it?

BOY: No.

GIRL: And then he comes back from the war and bumps into her on Waterloo Station. Her with her French beret on, and still he dun't twig it.

DICK: I'll get you a French beret. Resistance. (*Grinning:*) No, no resistance.

GIRL (*suddenly*): What will you get me?

DICK: Well, you want to look nice, don't you?

JANE: Taylor's a captain in it. Are you a captain?

BOY: Navigator.

GIRL: Course he dun't realise what she's had to suffer.

JANE: Is there someone waiting for you back home?

BOY: No.

JANE: I had someone once. He went on a mission, and . . .

BOY: I'm sorry.

JANE: We all have to make sacrifices.

BOY: I guess.

JANE: You should catch it if you can. Shame I'm working. I would have liked to have seen it again.

BOY: Well, now I think, I figure I can make it Saturday. Where did you say it was on?

JANE: The Essoldo.

GIRL: What will you get me?

DICK: What's a handful of clothing coupons worth?

JANE: Good. I know you'll enjoy it.

BOY: I'm only sorry you couldn't make it.

JANE: Well, perhaps you could walk me home afterwards.

BOY: How's that, ma'am?

JANE: I'm the usherette.

DICK: Stay behind after the film. I might have someat for you, Vivian.

GIRL (*pauses*): When? Tonight?

BOY: Well, I guess I'll see you there then.

DICK: Saturday night.

JANE: At the movies.

Fade. Music 'Auld Lang Syne'.

ACT TWO

Saturday Night at the Movies

Projection: Leigh and Taylor meet on Waterloo Bridge.
The foyer and 'powder room'. The BOY *stands patiently waiting in the foyer.*
Climax of 'God Save the King'.
Lighting. The Powder Room. The two women sit, facing the 'mirrors'. As much as is possible they both aspire to the Vivian Leigh look. The GIRL *applies lipstick, with the aid of a match and an almost empty lipstick case. They occasionally take a sly glance at each other. Eventually:*

GIRL: Mr Milles din't say ought about anyone else being on as well on Saturdays.

JANE: Did he not? It no doubt slipped his mind. Always two on Saturdays. The clientele get a little boisterous on Saturdays. Especially the Allies.

GIRL: I wouldn't know.

JANE: Really? (*She turns to her.*) I wouldn't overplay the bow of the lips if I were you, my dear. It can, on the one hand, bring a certain child-like — I was tempted to say Minnie Mouse — quality to the features, but it can all too easily also leave a tang of the . . . tartish. If you know what I mean.

The GIRL *throws her lipstick into the bin, and picks up the mascara.*

JANE: I believe that mascara is mine.

GIRL: Is it?

JANE: Does it have a name on it?

GIRL: No.

JANE: That's right. Made by a friend of mine.

GIRL: Where?

JANE: I think she's stopped now. Just one batch. May I?

The GIRL *passes the treasure over.*

What I miss most, I think, are those

marvellous perfumes. The sheer luxury of Bourjois' Ashes of Roses. Those pre-war days are haunted with the hint of it. Do you remember it?

GIRL: I was only a kid then.

JANE: How sad.

GIRL: I'd love a good scent.

DICK *enters the foyer, whistling. He is dressed in ARP uniform. He sees the* BOY. DICK *is attempting to grow a Robert Taylor moustache – however, the* BOY *has the advantage of youth and a better uniform.*

DICK: Who the hell are you?

The BOY *puts on his cap. So does* DICK.

BOY: I'm waiting for someone.

DICK: Well, you can't wait here. It in't Slab Square, you know. Hop it.

BOY: Well, I would, sir, but –

DICK: Do I know you?

BOY: I don't think so.

DICK: No. Well, go on. On your way. You've had two and a half rounds of 'God Save The King'. You can't say we don't give you value for money.

BOY: If I could just –

DICK (*in whining tone*): 'Any gum, chum?'

BOY: Well, ye' sure –

DICK: I'm up to here with hearing that. Everywhere you go. 'Any gum, chum?' What nobody seems to care about is that all the gum our kind allies dish out ends up stuck on my seats. I spend hours scraping it off. It's typical of the Yanks, it really is. Inventing someat you chew but can't swallow, I ask you.

BOY: I don't want to get into all that scene with you, pal. I mean, I can see your point. Personally, I never touch gum, so if you can just spare me a minute or two while I wait for my girl to come out of the can.

DICK: Powder room!

BOY: She's just getting herself ready.

DICK: And what may I ask, is she doing unready? I don't know what sort of place you people think a cinema is. I can only imagine that in the States they run a close second to a New Orleans whore-house. It just makes me sick. You bring a decent English girl supposedly to see a film, and, by the end of it, they're what you call broads, and they have to spend half an hour in the lav before they can present an even half-decent picture to the world. And, on top of that calm as a cucumber, you expect us to stay up all night while all this is going on.

BOY: It's not that way at all. Honest. She's not that type of –

DICK: Listen, let me ask you something. I'll give you the benefit of the doubt. Maybe, at worst, you're just thoughtless. It's a thing with youth, I know. I'm not saying I was much different. But let me put it to you. Have you ever thought that this girl you've made unready, this English Rose – ever thought that perhaps she has a boyfriend, or even a husband out there somewhere. Some local lad, been away maybe five years, as a desert rat, or fighting the jungles in the Far East. He's not fresh and smiling to the war like a knight in shining armour. He's dusty, hungry, aged before his due, and all that this ally of yours has to sustain him, as he stands alone against Rommel, or struggles on with malaria, is the picture of his girl back home, the girl-next-door, the girl of his dreams. And here she is, innocent that she is, suddenly swept away by some GI Valentino with time and money on his hands. Some Valentino who'll disappear, like the blown bubble of his gum, leaving behind a woman perhaps unready ever to receive honourably the valiant hero. (*He takes out a hankie and blows his nose.*) Is that nice? I ask you? Is that nice?

BOY: That's terrible.

DICK: You're not a bad lad.

BOY: But she . . . she's got no one.

DICK: What?

BOY: She lost her . . . loved one. He's never coming back. She's alone now. Lonely.

DICK: Sit down, pal. I've got to wait for my girl, anyway. There's no rush.

They sit.

BOY: Cigarette?

DICK: Woun't say no.

They light up. The girls are nearly ready. JANE *stands.*

JANE (*indicating her nylon seams*): Am I straight?

GIRL: Nylons? How did you get those?

JANE: From a friend.

GIRL: Aren't you lucky?

JANE: Being lucky had very little to do with it.

GIRL: You've kept your legs well.

JANE: Thank you.

GIRL: No, I mean it.

JANE: Thank you.

GIRL (*standing*): Are mine?

JANE (*without looking*): They're all right.

GIRL: The seams?

JANE (*seeing they're nylons*): Yes, well I might have guessed that you had an admirer. Haven't I seen you outside of Yates Wine Lodge?

GIRL: I don't know. What nights do you trade?

A silence you could use for sharpening razors.

DICK: It's lovely in here, when it's all quiet. Feels like a church sometimes. Just put a confessional over there.

Woun't half do some business on a Saturday with the backrow boys. Present company excepted.

BOY: Peace, eh?

DICK: Well, that's what we're all after, in't it?

BOY: Gum?

DICK: When you're smoking?

BOY: Ye'.

DICK: Fair enough then.

They smoke, chew, and blow bubbles through the next sections. JANE *and the* GIRL *face each other.*

JANE: Lace market girl, eh?

GIRL: That's the ticket. (*She sits down.*)

JANE: I should have guessed.

GIRL: We don't smell, you know. Maybe we can't get the best scents, but we've heard of soap.

JANE: Ye'.

GIRL: Suit yourself. But we've got to work together.

Silence.

JANE (*relenting*): I used to work at Cooper's.

GIRL: Get away.

JANE: Mind you, it was a fair bit ago. (*She sits.*) You need a bit of mascara on, duck.

She passes the mascara over.

GIRL: Ta. Fancy that, eh? Coopers? Next door to my place.

She continues her make up. JANE *watches her.*

DICK: In the Air Force?

BOY: Ye'. Getting ready for the big push.

DICK: Any day now, eh? Mind you, we've been saying that for years. Done many missions?

BOY: Not a lot. No. Well, none actually. I've just flown in from Stateside. But we'll see some action soon.

DICK: Soon enough. What do you fly?

BOY: Bombers. Lancasters. Sometimes Dakotas.

DICK: I wish I was with you, kid. Out there, where the action is, doing something that makes a difference.

BOY: You're out of it now, are you?

DICK: War wound. 'Course I still do me bit. ARP Warden. (*He takes out an air pistol.*) Any of them bastards land on my patch, and they'll regret it. Mind you, most of the time it's just checking everybody's maintaining blackout. Sometimes it's so black out there, just seems there's me and the stars left. I get some funny thoughts out there at night. Sometimes think of you chaps as well — up there. Just a frail skin separating you from — sorry, it's not the sort of thought you want to take with you.

BOY: Where did you get it?

DICK: In the back.

BOY: No, I meant, what campaign?

DICK: Well, it was very early on in the war. Before conscription. I'd got things sorted out here — well that took a bit of time — and I was actually on my way down to sign up. It was the first air-raid we'd had round here and I dived for cover in some woman's Anderson, and as I bent over the bomb hit the house and shrapnel got me.

BOY: Hell, that's really tough.

DICK: The woman in the shelter was very nice. She picked out a lot for me. But, well, a lot stayed in. You can imagine.

BOY: I can imagine.

DICK: So . . .

BOY: Sure.

DICK: That's the way —

BOY: The cookie crumbles.

DICK: As you say.

JANE: What's he like? Is he nice?

GIRL: He's . . . what's your's like?

JANE: He's young, and tall, and good-mannered.

GIRL: Who does he look like?

JANE: Well, if he grew a little moustache he'd look like Robert Taylor.

GIRL: No? Really?

JANE: Honestly.

They laugh. The GIRL *suddenly stops, and lays down her lipstick.*

GIRL: I don't know why I bother.

JANE: What's the matter, kid?

GIRL: Nothing.

JANE: Well, I'm almost ready.

DICK: Are you a captain?

BOY: Naviga — no, I'm ground staff.

DICK: Pardon?

BOY: I'm ground staff. I don't fly.

DICK: How's that?

BOY (*sadly*): Television.

DICK: Pardon?

BOY: It's my pa, you see. He thinks television is the coming thing.

DICK *snorts.*

DICK: No chance. If pigs could fly, eh?

BOY: Pardon?

DICK: Sorry. Go on, pal.

BOY: Well, so I specialised in technology at High School and went to evening classes. I was pretty good. When the draft came they put me down as specialised ground crew, and that's all there was to it.

DICK: The cookie sure crumbles sometimes.

BOY: It sure as hell does.

JANE *stands, puts on a beret, and shoulder bag. The* GIRL *has similar.*

JANE: Are you coming?

The GIRL *rummages through her bag.*

What have you lost?

GIRL: I need a fag.

JANE: He must be some guy. Here. (*She gives her a 'Camel'.*)

GIRL: Ta.

JANE: I know what it's like to be without.

GIRL: The war means sacrifice, I suppose.

JANE: What's up?

GIRL: I'm fine. Fine.

JANE: Come on, then.

GIRL: No, I'll sit here and finish this off first.

JANE: Your young man will be waiting.

GIRL: I believe in keeping 'em waiting.

JANE *stands, undecided.*

DICK: She's taking her time, that lass of yours.

BOY: Well, she has to change out of her uniform.

DICK: What is she? (*Laughing.*) A sergeant in the Home Guard?

BOY: No, she's the usher here.

DICK: Usher?

BOY: Ye', the dark haired usher.

JANE: You do look white.

GIRL: It's me powder. Only sort I could get.

JANE: Suit yourself, then.

She leaves the room, and enters the foyer, just as DICK *leaps to his feet.*

DICK (*to the* BOY): Out! Out this instant! I don't allow my staff, young girls in my care, to consort with the customers. This is a cinema you know, not a house of sin. Now get out, and take your stinking gum with you!

He sees JANE, *who is quietly putting on her gloves.*

And what the hell are you doing still here?

JANE: I was about to ask you the same question. Isn't it your night for star-gazing?

DICK: It would be if my cinema wasn't choc-a-block with Yanks trying to seduce the younger staff.

JANE: Younger staff?

DICK: Kindly show this gentleman out as you go, will you?

JANE: My pleasure. (*She crosses over to him.*)

BOY: Evening, Jane.

JANE (*quickly*): This way, sir.

DICK: Jane?

JANE: Let's go.

DICK: Wait a minute. The penny drops. You were waiting for Jane.

BOY: Yes, sir.

DICK: Well, if that doesn't take the biscuit. (*He begins to laugh, it increases to an almost uncontrollable mixture of laughs, wheezes, etc.* JANE *stands patiently by.*)

JANE: When you have quite finished, Mr Milles.

DICK (*laughing*): Now I done seen everything. Now I've seen an elephant fly.

BOY: What's the big joke around here?

JANE: Mr Milles has a rather pathetic sense of humour. We'd better wait for him to finish. He's an ageing man. He might have an attack. I wouldn't like to miss it if he did.

BOY: Should I pat him on the back?

JANE: Not unless you have a bayonet handy.

DICK: Oh, Jane, you'll be the death of me.

JANE: You give me hope.

DICK: But I'll live this time.

JANE: You can't win them all, Dick.

DICK: Why don't you two love-birds hop along and enjoy yourself? While the night is still young.

JANE: You don't care at all, do you?

DICK: Why should I care?

JANE (*quietly*): You bugger.

DICK: It's better than being a bitch on heat.

BOY (*stepping forward*): Sir, that's no way to speak to a lady.

DICK: Sir, that's no lady. That's my wife. (*Sets off fresh paroxysms of laughter.*) I've always wanted to say that.

The BOY *stands confused between them.*

JANE: We have an arrangement. Not that it works. Not for me, anyway. You'd best be off.

BOY: I don't know what to say.

JANE: That's an honest reaction.

BOY: Well, I guess I'd best be off then.

JANE: Goodnight.

DICK: Just a sec . . . Where do you think you're going?

BOY: I think you should perhaps talk to your wife, Mr Milles.

DICK: Well, that's a lovely idea, lad. Lovely. But right this minute it's a little bit tricky. So, if you'd be so kind, Galahad, as to walk my little lady home for me.

BOY: I think you should do that.

DICK: Believe me, nothing would give me greater pleasure, but unfortunately, you may not have heard, but there's a war on, and old Jerry won't wait while I get my little marital problems sorted out. It's my job tonight to sit on the roof of this cinema, and watch out for fires. I have to stay awake, so that others can sleep. So if you'd just see her home. She's a fragile bit of

Dresden is my little missis, and it's a wicked city. I'd be most grateful.

JANE: I can walk meself home.

BOY: It would be my pleasure, ma'am.

DICK: Spoken like a gentleman, sir. Now if you'll excuse me. I have a war to be going on with.

The GIRL *enters.*

DICK: Ah, Miss Leicester. Are you still here as well?

GIRL: I'm ready now, Dick.

JANE: Dick?

DICK: Good. Thank you, Miss Leicester. That means I can finally get the place locked up. Good. Good show.

GIRL: I've put them on.

DICK: Good, good. Good show.

GIRL: Shall I go to the office?

A long pause.

JANE (*mimicking*): 'Shall I go to the office, Dicky Sugardad?'

DICK: I was waiting for that.

JANE: 'I have a war to be going on with.' Mister High and Mighty.

DICK: Yes, go up to the office, Miss Leicester. I'm just showing these people out.

JANE: You dirty little man.

DICK: That's the pot calling the kettle black, isn't it?

GIRL: What are you doing still here?

JANE: Whatever he promised you, you're going to be sadly disappointed, duck.

DICK: You have a sick mind, Jane.

JANE: Sick! You talk to me about sick!

GIRL: I'll wait upstairs.

BOY: Should I wait outside?

There is a sudden lighting change. 'Romantic Spots' on the GIRL *and* BOY, *on either side of the stage, as they see each other for the first time. The* BOY *smiles, and puts his hand*

*uncertainly out. Creep in a few bars of
'The Dying Swan' theme from* Swan
Lake. JANE *and* DICK *freeze in the
shadows. Equally sudden change back
again.*

DICK: Tried to maintain this cinema as a
centre for all the family. A place
where Ruby and Dick and Ginger —
but you, you had to bring your
innuendos, and your smiling, over-
weening ways into it. Pawing over
ticket-stubs. Giggling and joking.

JANE: You're so pure. What's this
after-hours session with pasty-face,
then? Not that I care. Your body has
about as much attraction for me as
a gasmask.

DICK: Miss Leicester was going in for
after-hours training.

JANE: How to handle a torch. Lesson
four.

DICK: Your mind has the distinction
of being even uglier than your body.

JANE: Thank you for the Oscar. And
while we're giving out awards, what's
that growing under your nose?

DICK: That's nothing to do with you.

JANE: Don't tell me. No, it can't be.
Yes, it is. It's your attempt at a
moustache, isn't it? It's very nice,
well done. 'Course if Hitler ever
gets over here, it's going to cause
some confusion. Meanwhile, it's bound
to get a laugh.

DICK: That's the way it's always
been — ever since the war began.

JANE: It was you and your blackouts —

DICK: Goering!

JANE: Short arse!

*Lights again. The Lovers, having been
moving slowly during the above, have
both now covered one-quarter of the
traverse carpet.*

BOY: Hi.

Swan Lake *definitely swelling.*

GIRL: Hi.

Lighting as before.

JANE: Don't let's argue, my little friend.
Don't let's spoil the rich tapestry of
silence we have shared since the
blackout.

DICK: So you can get back to your
gigolos.

JANE: And you can creep off on your
ARP, hoping to catch some trollop's
silhouette stripping for bed. They do
it just to get you going. I hear 'em
talking about it. They think it's a great
laugh.

DICK: I look at you, and I can't
think . . . I can't think whatever it
could have been that I saw in you.
How you covered up all this malice
all those years I'll never know.

JANE: You've bitten off a bit more than
you can chew this time, though,
Dicky. This is not your regular dirty
raincoat stuff. This one's alive, or
hadn't you realised. She might bite.

DICK: What I can't forgive is you telling
that lad I was killed overseas. Calling
up the poor kid's sympathy. That
really is awful — taking in vain the
name of them good lads who died out
there.

JANE: Don't bring that up.

DICK: I think that trick is the bottom of
the barrel.

JANE: Don't! (*She hits him.*)

DICK: War!

*Lights. The Lovers have now made the
middle. 'The Dying Swan' louder.
They look into each other's eyes. Sighs.*

BOY: Gum?

GIRL: Ta.

*He reaches into his pocket, never
taking his eyes from hers. He offers
her the gum. Lights.* DICK *crosses
angrily over to the girl, grabbing her
arm.*

DICK: Come on, doll, let's me and you go paint the town.

GIRL: Here! (*She drops her bag.*)

BOY: What's the game?

JANE (*crossing to the* BOY): Take me arm.

DICK bends down to pick up the bag.

GIRL: What you up to?

BOY: Leave her alone, pal.

The GIRL *kicks out, and hits* DICK *on the leg, as he rises holding the bag.*

DICK: Here take it easy.

JANE: Come on. Let's get out of here.

Both girls are now clinging on to the GI.

BOY (*angry*): You shouldn't go pushing people around, mister.

DICK (*nursing his leg*): Let go of my woman.

BOY: Just take it easy, or you'll rile me.

DICK: What the hell has it got to do with you? Nobody asked you to get involved in our fight, so don't make out you're doing us any favours. You're in it for a piece of the action, same as all of us. Well, you can have her. Any action you can get out of that —

BOY: I'm wild when I get riled.

DICK: What you yelling for, Galahad? I know your sort. You wait 'til they've backed you in a corner, and then when we've done all the work, and we've knackered ourself and it's all on a plate, you come charging across the horizon in your smart new cavalry uniform, blowing your bugle.

GIRL: Look, he's ripped me nylons. (*Crying.*)

BOY: Don't fret, honey, I can get you plenty more.

GIRL: You can?

DICK: But it don't wash with me, boy.

Do you hear? It don't wash with me.

BOY: I'll take you away from this madhouse. (*He quietly sets* JANE *to one side.*) Sorry, ma'am, but I figure you can look after yourself.

JANE (*sadly*): Yes. Adios amigo.

BOY (*to* GIRL): Let's get out of here.

DICK: Hold it right there.

He puts his hand to his inside pocket.

BOY: Watch out. He's got a gun.

JANE: Don't be a fool, Dick.

BOY: Take it easy, mister.

The GIRL *screams.* DICK *takes his clenched fist from inside his coat.*

DICK: Look what I got. (*He limps across, clenched hand outstretched.*) I said I would. Look.

GIRL: Don't let him near me.

DICK: Clothing coupons. That's what you wanted. I've kept my word.

BOY: I can get you plenty of clothes, honey.

DICK (*quietly*): I see. You might as well have them. I don't want them.

He makes a small gesture, to move the hair out of the GIRL's *face; as he does so, she kicks out, and gets him on the other leg. The coupons fly into the air. He hops from one foot to the other.*

GIRL: Me bag. He's got me bag.

The GI steps forward to take it. Thinking he's going to strike him DICK *lunges out from his position of precarious balance. He falls to his knees. The* BOY *picks up the bag. The* GIRL *buries her head in his chest.* DICK *sighs.*

He's ripped the other one now.

The BOY *quietly takes the* GIRL *downstage, as if off. 'The Dying Swan' dies.* DICK *is still kneeling.* JANE *stands apart. Long silence.*

DICK: Farewell my lovely.

He checks his moustache, gazes around at the coupons. Manages to move his legs into a more comfortable sitting position.

I may never dance again.

JANE *takes the grips out of her hair, and places them in her bag.*

JANE: I've forgotten what colour my hair really is.

Downstage in the street the BOY *tilts the* GIRL's *face in the moonlight.*

BOY: I want the memory of it. Your eyes in the moonlight. The stars glistening in your tears. (*She smiles.*) That's better. I've never seen a girl so sad, when there's so much to live for.

GIRL: What's the good of it?

BOY: You're a strange girl, aren't you? What's the good of anything? What's the good of living?

GIRL: That's a question too.

BOY: The good of living is that this sort of thing can happen.

They kiss.

JANE: Shouldn't you be manning your post?

DICK: I'm not on tonight.

JANE: Ah.

DICK: 'Sides, you get daft ideas up there.

JANE: You get daft ideas down here.

DICK: Looking up at them stars all night. There they are, millions of them, millions of miles away from us, and each other, and yet they look so close you feel you could reach up and pick one right out of the sky. And we don't know anything about them really. But we give them names.

BOY: I'll write to you. Will you answer?

GIRL: You know I will.

BOY: Do you think we'll ever see each other again?

GIRL: I think it's doubtful, don't you?

BOY: Yes, I suppose it is.

JANE: Would you have slept with her?

DICK: If I could. I was very nervous.

JANE: So was I.

DICK: You know, I can spend the whole night on the top of that roof, and don't feel lonely. Tell you what it does, too, I don't know why. It makes me smile.

JANE *smiles.*

Funny that, isn't it?

Music: to the very end, very softly, 'The Farewell Waltz', a version of 'Auld Lang Syne'.

BOY: Can you imagine that, our never seeing each other again?

GIRL: Yes.

BOY: Nothing to do now but say goodbye.

GIRL: Goodbye.

BOY: Keep well.

GIRL: Yes, keep well.

BOY: Leave me first please.

She turns to go. At the 'door' she stops.

GIRL: Please.

He follows her into the house.

JANE *crosses to* DICK *and holds out her hand.*

JANE: You'd better try your legs.

They waltz.

DICK: You made a good Ruby Keeler.

JANE: You made a passable Dick Powell.

DICK: Do you remember the first time we danced together?

JANE: 1925. I had just heard the news of Valentino's death.

DICK: Pola Negri was in tears.

JANE: I was ye'.

DICK: And then —

JANE: He entered. Hair shiny, and split down the middle. My funny Valentino.

DICK: A tango.

They dance.

BOY: Should I put the lights on?

GIRL: Sssssh.

She lights the candles in her small bedroom. The BOY *takes off his jacket.*

DICK: I know a dark, secluded place —

JANE (*stopping*): No more blackouts. No more dark. No more keeping the light from getting in, like in that cinema. Down with the blackout. Let's go home.

They cross into JANE's 'bedroom'. *The* BOY *offers the* GIRL *a cigarette.*

GIRL: No. It's not good for my dancing.

BOY: You dance?

GIRL: Ballet. I train in the day. No show at the moment, so I help out at the cinema.

DICK: Who were you before Pola Negri?

JANE: Who was I? I don't remember. I must have been someone. (*She sits on the edge of the bed.*) I feel I may cry.

DICK: What's the matter?

The GIRL *turns so the* BOY *can undo her dress.*

GIRL: Please.

JANE: I'm all right. (*She, too, turns for help with her dress.*) Can you?

DICK: Sure.

JANE: The one who went to war, and never came back.

DICK: Forget it. Forget all about it.

JANE: I didn't make it up.

DICK: No.

JANE: No. But it wasn't this war. It was 1917. He was a pal of my brothers. I was thirteen, it was a wet day. I was standing out on the cobbles at the bottom of Bath Street. I saw him say goodbye to his mam and dad, and he strode down the street to join his mates. As he was going past, he just gave me a peck on the cheek, and said ta-ra. It won't more than a couple of weeks before we heard. Well, I won't much affected, din't seem as though I was, anyway but — when he walked off from me, I saw he had his shirt-tail sticking out over the back of his trousers. He looked so comic and so brave. I've loved him all these years, Dick, and there an't been much room for anyone else. Tonight I had to give him up. (*She folds her dress carefully.*) Do you want to make a friend? I think I might be frightened of you, Dick.

DICK: You're an unknown star to me.

BOY: You shivered.

The girls timidly, delicately, begin to unbutton their men's shirts.

GIRL: What's this?

BOY: My dogtag. Gives my name and number.

GIRL: Richard.

BOY: Dick. What's yours?

GIRL: Jane.

DICK: What's your name, duck?

JANE: What's your name, duck?

GIRL: Me Jane. You Tarzan.

He smiles.

DICK: No names.

JANE: Not any more.

Slow fade. Last strains of the waltz.

STRIVE

'tis we, who lost in stormy visions, keep
with phantoms an unprofitable strife'

Shelley

Strive was first presented at the Sheffield Crucible Studio on 13 October 1983, with the following cast:

MAN	Richard Albrecht
WOMAN	Sue Wallace
GIRL	Jenny Bolt
BOY	Ian Targett

Directed by Jonathan Chadwick

Blue Sky. Space.
An enormous Union Jack flaps slowly
in the light breeze.
As the audience enter:
A young soldier stands, waiting, his
kit stashed against the park bench behind
him.
Upstage, a WOMAN *in her forties, sits*
in a deckchair. She is simply, but
elegantly dressed. She wears sunglasses
and is, apparently, asleep.
In the distance, the sounds of ships'
hooters, crowds singing 'Rule Britannia'
to a military brass band.
The soldier sits, loosens his uniform,
and puts his hand up against the sun. He
grins, and lies out on the bench with his
eyes closed.
A GIRL *enters, and, on seeing him,*
stops. She puts down her bags. The music
ends. She moves silently to lean over him,
checking him, concerned.
She snaps round at the sound of a gun
salute. The BOY *reaches out to hold her.*

BOY: Kiss me, Hardy.

She laughs. Any tension passes. They
touch each other's faces, and then
embrace, laughing. The band plays
'76 Trombones.'

An American, in his late fifties,
watches them. Their reunion gives him
evident pleasure. Putting his sunglasses
away in the top pocket of his light-
weight suit, he moves carefully in on
them.

The GIRL *notices him first, and alerts*
the BOY, *with her slight withdrawal.*
He turns to check the intrusion. The
MAN *keeps his distance, smiling at*
them, rather nervously.

The BOY *is amused.*
The MAN *nods.*

MAN: 'Good show.'

BOY (*grinning*): It's not bad to say I'm a
bit out of practice.

The GIRL *laughs and puts her arm*
around him.

MAN (*embarrassed*): Oh, no, I meant . . .

over there. 'Good show, old chap'.
That's what the RAF lads always used
to say.

BOY: I woun't know. I'm an engineer.

He turns back to the GIRL.

MAN (*tentatively*): I was airforce.

The BOY *and* GIRL *exchange amused*
glances.

Ground staff. For the D-Day landing.
(*Pause.*) Nothing especially heroic. Not
like you boys. You must be very proud
of him, miss.

She smiles, pleasantly, and looks away.
Silence.

The end of that war was the last time I
was here in England. Mind you, I took
a piece of the motherland back with me.
My wife.

The BOY *is trying not to laugh.*

BOY: Ye', great. (*He turns to him.*)
Look, I don't want to seem rude, pal,
but —

MAN (*holds up two fingers*): Our
countries were as close as that then.
As one. Indivisible.

BOY: Ye', well, time's change, don't
they?

MAN: Pardon?

BOY: We weren't so close in the South
Atlantic, were we?

MAN: You took us on the hop. You
move fast for such an old country.
But we were right behind you.

BOY (*edgey*): Not what I heard.

The GIRL *touches his arm, restraining.*
The MAN *moves forward.*

MAN: That's bad communication, that's
all. Something we have to straighten
out.

BOY: Fair enough. But not right now,
pal.

MAN: Sorry?

BOY (*pause*): Look, I don't want to

sound . . . but, we an't even had a chance to say hello to each other yet.

MAN: You two haven't spoken?

BOY (*laughing*): Not yet.

He hugs the GIRL.

MAN: Don't.

They both look up.

(*He is clearly excited, moving in front of them*): Don't speak to each other. Please. Not until I can get my crew up here.

BOY: What crew? (*Warily*.) Listen, pal, your mates can go find their own gals.

MAN (*embarrassed*): Oh, no, no, I'm not calling up the marines. It's my film crew.

He holds out a pocket CB radio. Silence.

BOY: Film crew?

MAN (*waving*): They're down there on the quayside.

Silence.

I'd like to film your meeting, if I may.

BOY (*pause*): What sort of film? Is it a war movie?

MAN: Well, in a way.

BOY: *Apocalypse Now,* sort of thing?

MAN (*smiling*): More *Waterloo Bridge.*

BOY: What?

MAN: A classic reunion movie, between a soldier and his girl. Vivian Leigh. (*Mildly*.) That was the film for me and my girl.

BOY: So you want us to star in your movie?

MAN: In a manner of speaking.

BOY: You taking the piss?

MAN: The what?

BOY: No, you're not, are you?

MAN: All I want is to make a good, honest documentary.

BOY: What?

MAN: The return of the hero. The rookie and his girl. And your meeting here will work to bring our two nations together. After all, our history started here in Plymouth. (*He grins.*) It's more than a make of automobile to us, you know. The Pilgrim Fathers set sail for that freedom, that you lads went out to the Falklands to maintain.

BOY: I'm no pilgrim.

MAN: In a way you are. Or at least a Christian soldier.

BOY (*turning back to the* GIRL): I don't know.

MAN: Look, I'm not here to romanticise you. I just want to tell the truth.

BOY: I can't talk about the war, you know.

MAN: Let's deal in peace, and your plans for the future. Both of you. She's been in the war as much as you in her way.

The GIRL *looks quietly at the man.*

BOY (*to her*): What do you reckon?

She frowns, begins to speak.

MAN: Hold it! (*He steps between them.*) Let me have the first words, right, then decide whether we destroy it, or go on. (*To the* BOY.) It's crazy I know, but just travel with me that far.

BOY: Well, another couple of minutes . . .

MAN: Thank you.

He moves away to call up his crew. The GIRL *stares up uncertainly at the soldier.*

MAN (*almost inaudible*): Well, get 'em . . . see the lighthouse? No, not out at sea, you idiot. Top of the hill.

BOY: Not every day we get a chance to become film stars.

He turns to watch the MAN. *The* GIRL *looks away.*

MAN: Just get 'em up here, OK?

He nods at the BOY.

Cavalry on the way.

The GIRL *rises and crosses to her bags. She takes out a packet of cigarettes and lights one. This passes unnoticed.*

(*Mildly*.) You always want to be a a soldier?

BOY: Just dead set to get out the dump we were in.

MAN: So you figured you'd become a soldier of fortune?

BOY: There in't no fortune. Not like being a pirate. But I failed the eye test for that.

MAN (*grins*): Still, they must pay you enough to keep a wife on.

BOY: If I had a wife.

She returns to the bench, clearly preoccupied, hardly listening to their conversation.

MAN: Do you plan to get a wife?

BOY: I was about to do someat about that, when you popped up.

MAN: What?

Both men turn to the GIRL. *She stares at them.*

BOY: Cat's out of the bag now. We're posted straight off out to Germany. Good married accommodation. What do you say?

Silence. She is clearly distressed.

BOY: What is it?

MAN: Shock. My wife was just the same. (*Moves round the bench to her.*) You were a bit abrupt. Should have gone down on one knee. The ritual gives the woman time to compose herself. It's the same in the animal kingdom.

BOY: Wha'?

MAN (*kneeling by her*): Lady, the speech taboo is off, OK? I don't want to delay the one word that'll change your life. I'm more than willing to trade the moment of meeting for the marriage.

Silence.

BOY: Well, say someat.

GIRL (*rises*): Can we go somewhere?

BOY: What?

GIRL: Can we go somewhere and talk?

BOY: About what?

GIRL (*confused*): I might have to go somewhere.

BOY: Go where?

GIRL: It's not definite. I want us to talk —

BOY: You got a job, or someat?

GIRL: No.

BOY: Is somebody sick? You've got to see somebody sick?

GIRL: It's nothing —

BOY: Not another bloke, is it?

She shakes her head. Silence.

GIRL (*restrained*): I can't talk here.

MAN (*gently*): I'll go. I've panicked you. The thought of a film crew running roughshod on your private territory. I don't want to drive you to build a protective wall around your love — that holds no future.

GIRL: It's not that. It's just that —

MAN: I've been young. I know how you believe anyone in a suit and tie could never be sensitive to your love. (*He smiles.*) In my defence, all I want to do is bring our two countries together again. I mean you no harm, I swear it. Sincerely. (*He laughs.*) My wife used to say that no one over here who was sincere would ever dare admit it. But in America, only the fool keeps silent about what they know to be true. Or else those values are swept away. It's a kind of responsibility of democracy to articulate, that may be worth a little embarrassment.

GIRL (*quietly*): I'm not embarrassed.

MAN (*backing away*): Just talk it through. I want to check out the lighthouse.

He leaves. The BOY *and the* GIRL *face each other, uncertainly.*

BOY (*eventually*): How was your journey?

GIRL: All right. (*She smiles.*) How was yours?

BOY: Glad to be back.

GIRL: I bet.

BOY: I were goin' to bring you a present but I coun't get the penguin in me kitbag.

The tension eases.

I did get you someat. Sort of memento. Shall I give it you now?

GIRL: I can wait.

BOY: Right.

Silence.

BOY: How's your mam?

GIRL: She finally got her veins took out. She's a lot more cheerful. (*She grins.*) Well, a bit more.

BOY: You been round my mam's?

GIRL: Most of the time. Looking at photos of you in your cowboy hat, and the cubs.

BOY: That must have been a laugh, any road.

GIRL: Not for her. She thought you won't coming back.

BOY: Well, I did think of opening a fish and chip shop there.

She does not respond.

GIRL: You're not hurt, or ought?

BOY: Not a scratch.

GIRL: It's just they never tell you ought.

(*Silence. Softly.*) Your sister sends her love.

BOY (*not pleased*): Where you see her?

GIRL: She was home.

BOY: She never goes home.

GIRL: She knew your mam was missing you.

BOY: Were you missing me?

GIRL: Yes. Of course. I love you.

BOY (*pauses*): Well, what's all this song and dance about?

He takes her hand.

GIRL: What was it like out there?

BOY: Freezing.

GIRL: No, I meant, what did you feel?

BOY: What, apart from being shit scared?

GIRL: Were you?

He moves away.

BOY: I din't sign up to get shot at.

GIRL: Did you shoot anybody?

BOY: How do I know? The fog's like pea soup out there. You coun't tell the cries of dying men from dying sheep.

GIRL: You saw the dead, did you?

BOY: Ye', I did, course I did. (*He turns to her.*) What's wi' all this? I don't need this. It's a party and a pint I need. No, fuck the party. All I want's you.

GIRL (*persisting*): What did you feel?

BOY: For crying out loud.

GIRL: Did you feel that —

BOY: I can't remember!

GIRL: What did you think?

BOY (*sighs*): I thought it were a bloody stupid way to end an argument, but we din't start it.

GIRL: Din't we?

BOY: Well, I bloody sure as hell din't. I was a big Argie lover, me. Our family always ate their spam.

He grins at her.

GIRL: You din't start it, but you had to mop it up.

BOY: That's what soldiers do.

GIRL: Is it?

BOY: Listen, I'm not falling over myself to talk about it, right? That's the past. It's the future now, innit? You and me. That's what I want to talk about. Germany.

He stares at her. She looks away.

What's up? You were dead keen before I went away. What's wi' all these questions? You frightened I've come back changed or someat? I've not changed. 'Course it got to me, stands to reason, but I an't turned into some mass murderer or —

GIRL: I never thought that.

BOY: Well, then?

GIRL (*pauses*): You still plannin' to go on?

BOY: What, in the army?

She nods.

BOY: Look, I've done the rough now. Time for a share of the smooth for us.

GIRL: You an't thought of buying your way out?

BOY: Out? Out where? What the fuck's out there? That's why I came in. There's fuck all out there. You know that as well as me. Buyin' out. Who yo' bin talkin' to? (*She looks away. Sharply.*) Yo' bin listenin' to my sister!

BOY (*sharply*): Yo' bin listenin' to my sister!

GIRL: I talked to her, ye'.

BOY: Should 'ave guessed. She hated me signing up. But it's all right for her. College. Nice and cushy. She can afford milky coffee whenever she wants one.

GIRL: It won't just her. It was as much talking wi' your mam or Sharon. All of us sat there not knowing what the hell was happenin' with our brave faces pinned on ready for the telegram.

BOY: You think I din't know that? I was more worried about you worrying about me, than I was about myself. But there was bugger all to be done about it.

GIRL: Not by then, no. It was too late.

BOY: It's always too late.

GIRL: No. It shun't be.

BOY: Shun't be? What could we ever have done?

GIRL: We could've stopped you goin'.

BOY: Oh, ye', got me court martialled. Thanks a million.

GIRL: No, I mean, all of you. Stopped all of you. We women could have —

BOY: We women? Just a sec. (*Pause.*) I've heard this before, an't I? This's my sister's favourite record. 'Women of the World unite, you've nought to lose but your men.' Fat lot she cares about men. Did she teach you the chorus? All men are buggers, don't take a killer for a lover, snuggle up wi' me, just undo me dungaree!

GIRL: She din't say ought like that. She was worried sick for you.

BOY: Oh, ye', I believe that, like I believe in prancing fairies at the bottom of our entry. She's a bleedin' traitor to her family.

GIRL: She tried to help.

BOY: I bet. Did she tuck you up in bed, and read you dirty bits out of her body manual?

GIRL: Christ.

BOY: Look, I know her from old with her big hips and baggy pants. Sour grapes that's all she is. Just wants to piss in my wine. Anything she said take wi' a sea of salt.

GIRL: Please, can we talk about —

BOY: I've had her number since she
woun't play squaw in cowboys and
Indians. Allers had to knick my
cowboy hat, and play Calamity Jane.

GIRL (*desperate*): Why we talking about
her? I don't want to talk about her.

BOY: I bet you bloody don't.

He stands, shaking, staring at her.

BOY: Did she touch you? (*Pause.*) Did
she?

GIRL: Mick! (*Softly:*) Listen to what
you're asking me.

BOY: She did, din't she? Was it good?
It should be. I mean she should know
where to touch, shun't she? She
should know the mechanics, being a
woman, it being the same on her.
Whereas us poor men are nowhere
right, just poking around in the dark.
Ignorant fuckers, right?

She turns away.

True. But I'm willing to learn. Tell me
where to touch and I'll learn. That's
what love is between a man and a
woman — learning. She din't touch
you, did she? Oh, God, I could credit
you needing a bloke in a crisis, but
her? She din't touch you, did she?

She turns to face him.

Well, come on, deny it.

Silence.

I think I'm going to be sick.

GIRL: You don't want to understand,
do you?

BOY: I understand. All too well. So I've
changed into a killer, and you've
changed into a —

GIRL: Mick. It's nought like that. That
in't the problem.

BOY: Fucking shit.

He moves away. Silence.

So what you waitin' for? What do you
want, me blessing? What do I call you,
sister-in-law? Fuck off.

GIRL (*simply*): I love you.

BOY: Sounds like it.

*She sits on the bench, and lights up
another cigarette. Her hand is shaking.*

GIRL: I need to talk to you about how
we live.

BOY: How do you mean, live? You
mean, live together?

GIRL: Just live. Stay alive.

BOY: I'm not wi' you.

GIRL: I can't just sit and wait no more.
It don't do no good. I've got to fight
as well.

BOY: Fight who? Me? Who the fuck was
I out there fighting for?

GIRL: I don't know.

BOY: Oh, great. Great. Jesus.

*He walks off, trying to regain some
self control. Eventually:*

(*More quietly*): What you talking
about? You just talking about being
more . . . liberated, is that it?
Liberated from what? I mean, don't
we both need liberating? From the shit
we live in, from having no money, no
bleedin' future?

GIRL: Yes.

BOY: And won't that what I was doing
when I signed up? Tryin' to gi' us a
heave up out of there. I did that for
both of us.

GIRL: I know.

He sits by her.

BOY: So what more do you want? You
think I'm plannin' to chain you to
the kitchen sink? You think that's
how I am?

GIRL: No, but —

BOY: I'll do my share. I've watched my
old man all my life and I'm bloody
ashamed of him. I'll do the washing
and changing the nappies, right?

He looks up at her, almost reaches out to her.

GIRL: I thought I was pregnant.

BOY: What?

GIRL: Don't panic. I'm not.

BOY: I won't panicking.

Silence.

Ye'?

She shakes her head.

GIRL: Just set me off thinking. Sittin' there wi' your mam, watching the telly. Sharon wi' her youngest on her knee, me, keeping me secret, holding me belly seeing if there was ought to feel. Dreaming of Germany. (*Pause.*) The news said nought but talked of bombs that had been dropped, or might be dropped, bombs over you over there, bombs coming here to hang over us, as if we din't have enough wi' threats of telegrams. (*Pause.*) I coun't picture you and me any more. All I could see was my bloke turning to see the sun on an attacking exocet, and us women, sitting in a mist, watching telly as a cloud blew up around us. I felt . . . hopeless. I was dead pleased when I won't pregnant, one less thing to worry about, but . . . that had been my dream. I want kids, I want a house, not in Germany especially but . . . (*Pause.*) It was like I coun't dream, I coun't sleep for dread of nightmares, scared stiff of saying a word for fear of upsetting the others. Your mam sticking pictures of this kid in front of me.

Silence. She notices her cigarette and puts it out.

Then your sister came home. She talked about the bomb. 'Oh, ye', it's bad, ye' ', we all said, and your mam got up to make the tea, and the mist started comin' over me, but she woun't have it. 'No, tea's no good', she said. 'Tea's only good for waiting, and we've done enough of that. It's time we did someat else.'

BOY (*softly*): Who's we? Women?

GIRL (*facing him, quietly, carefully*): They're out to start a nuclear war. Then there'll be no telegrams for us to prove how brave we are. We have to brave it now. You see, they've made us the front line while you were away.

BOY: What you talking about?

GIRL (*eagerly*): I've got some things I want you to read. They explain what's been going on.

She takes leaflets from her bag, and kneels, laying them out towards him on the bench. He picks them up.

BOY: What are these?

GIRL: They're lying to us. They say these new missiles are for our protection, but they're not. It might save them across the sea, but —

BOY: Where did you get these?

GIRL: They're mad, you see. That can be the only answer to it. No one can hate that much without —

BOY: Where did you get these?

GIRL: Does it matter?

BOY: From her? They're from her?

GIRL: That's not the point. The point is —

BOY: You're just parrotting what she told you, are you?

GIRL: They're *my* thoughts! This is what I'm thinking!

BOY: When I get back I'll do for that little bitch.

GIRL: She in't there.

BOY: Bet she bloody in't. Hiding up somewhere 'til I cool down.

GIRL: She in't hidin'.

BOY: Well, she in't here, is she? Welcomin' me home with open arms.

GIRL: She's got more on her mind.

BOY: Oh, ye', what?

GIRL: She's outside an American base that's planned for cruise missiles.

BOY: A women's camp?

GIRL: Ye'.

BOY: Oh, ye', I've read about them. We got the papers out there. I know you think I only read page three, and none of her crowd'd ever get on there, but I read the other bits as well.

GIRL: Will you read these?

BOY: She's just a shit-stirrer, don't you see that?

Pause.

GIRL: No.

BOY: Christ, she's really got to you.

GIRL: That's right.

BOY: So what you goin' to do? You goin' there are you? That's the some-where is it? Some place I can't get at you.

GIRL: I 'an't made up my mind. I said I'd wait. Talk to you. See what we could do.

BOY: So we're talking.

Silence.

GIRL: I din't mean it to come out like this.

BOY: I bet.

GIRL: Please, will you read these?

BOY: Look, you're upset, right. I understand that. But it'll be all right now, I promise.

GIRL: It won't. It won't.

BOY: I could kill her. Preying on you when you're so obviously in a state.

GIRL: She din't. She helped me.

BOY: Oh, ye'. Ye'. Thanks for reminding me. Well you'd better go, an't you, and set up home wi' her. Maybe she'll take you to Germany, instead of me, and you two can sit by the side of that fucking fence.

He turns to go, picking up his kitbag.

GIRL: Mick! I want, I just want you to —

BOY (*turning*): What? What can you want of me? What can I give you, me, a mere man? And a soldier to boot. What could a fuckin' soldier gi' you?

He is near to breaking down.

GIRL: I just want —

BOY: Oh, ye', course. Got it. Stupid of me. No, I see now. Don't know why I din't see it before. You trackin' all the way down here, must be important.

GIRL: It is important.

BOY: Obvious, in't it? Me back from a silly farting little war that did fuck all, and you off on a major campaign. I mean, what else could it be?

GIRL: What?

BOY: You've come for me gear, an't you? Ye', of course, yo' can have it. I won't be needin' it, will I?

He throws his kitbag to the ground, and drags his equipment out of it. The GIRL just stands, unable to enter into the rage.

Let's see what we've got for you then. Mess cans. Flashlight. Medical kit. Some thermal underwear. Sew up the flies and you won't be reminded of us men. The fucking enemy. Full knife and fork number. All good army surplus. That's what I am, in't it? Fucking army surplus.

He kneels, holding onto the sleeping bag.

Sleeping bag. Well tested for sub-zero temperatures. Wi' a bit of a squeeze you could get two in here. Well you don't need the room for bouncing up and down like you do with a bloke, do you? Mind you, wi' her hips . . .

His voice trails away. He shakes his head. He puts his face in his hands. Silence. The GIRL watches him but does not move. A long wait. The American returns from behind the BOY.

MAN (*to the* GIRL): I figured we might film you at the lighthouse. Symbol of light, saving of lives at sea.

She does not look up at him.

(*Realising.*) Oh, I didn't . . . I'll come back later.

He turns to go.

BOY (*head down*): It's off.

MAN: Sorry?

BOY: The wedding, the film . . . it's off.

MAN (*pauses: tentatively*): May I help? I feel kind of responsible.

GIRL: No.

She sits on the bench. The MAN *does not know what to do.*

MAN: Reunions are fraught with the reefs of misunderstanding. (*He smiles.*) Crossed wires are sort of my speciality. I don't want to intrude but I'd like to help.

He crouches by the boy.

You love her, don't you?

Pause. The smallest of nods. He turns to the GIRL.

Do you love him?

Silence.

(*Softly.*) You do, don't you?

She looks at him, and nods.

(*He stands, sighs.*) Well, the rest should be a piece of pie, but it never is of course. It's always blood, sweat and tears, as old Churchill used to say. But at least we know we're all on the same side. (*He sits on the bench. To the* GIRL:) Something happened while you've been apart? (*Pause.*) Is it another guy?

BOY (*suddenly*): A woman.

Pause.

MAN: What? Ah. And how do you feel

towards this woman?

BOY: I hate her.

MAN: Good. Good. (*He turns to the* GIRL.) Look, I'm not into condoning infidelity, but you have to understand how it is for soldiers, seeking a crude solace in the absence of their dream girls. But he won't be seeing her again, I'm sure of that. Will you?

BOY: We're talking about my sister!

MAN: Your sister. (*Shocked.*) Well, that's way out of my line. I never had a sister, and if I had, I'd never have laid a finger on her.

BOY: It's my sister with her! Not with me! My sister and her. Together.

MAN: You're talking about . . . (*Pause.*) Oh, well, that's more what you expect to hear in L.A. than in England. I don't know what they'd recommend on the West Coast. I dread to think. I'm from Boston.

GIRL: It's not the way it sounds. His sister and me . . . we're, well, sisters. In a way, not . . . It's not like the way he . . .

MAN: You mean, there's nothing, . . . er . . . going on between you?

GIRL: Oh, God.

She stands up and moves away. The MAN *turns eagerly to the* BOY.

MAN: Listen, can you buy that? It's just like schoolgirls, right? They hold hands and . . . but it doesn't amount to —

BOY: That bitch has taken her over. Body and soul.

GIRL: No.

BOY (*looking up*): Why you going to this camp, then?

MAN: What camp?

GIRL: I've been trying to —

BOY: I can't go, can I?

GIRL: I an't definitely made me mind up that —

MAN: Maybe she needs a holiday. Seperate holidays aren't the end of the world.

BOY (*rising*): It in't a holiday camp. It's a fuckin' US Air Force base.

MAN (*rising*): Slow down. Somebody just give me this in one. You're off to a GI base, right?

GIRL: Yes, but —

MAN (*closing his eyes*): Hold it! Hold it!

The BOY turns away, angry, from her look.

(*To the GIRL:*) Right. Now this is something I know about. I know how tempting the GI can be, better dressed, money to flash around, always a pack of gum for the kids. But, you know, none of that makes him —

BOY: They're not picking up GIs. They're picketing the base.

MAN: What?

BOY: Women against Cruise. Yanks go home. You wi' me?

The GIRL looks exhausted. The MAN takes his time to think it through.

MAN (*nods*): Of course. (*Sadly:*) So that's why you're so antagonistic to me.

GIRL: What?

MAN: It's coming over in waves. Anti-American. (*Sighs.*) Have you any idea how such rejection hurts from a country we love?

GIRL: I'm not anti-American. It's just we don't have any say in our future.

MAN: What say do you want? Don't we have the same enemies? Aren't we fighting for the same freedoms? Aren't we allies?

GIRL: Perhaps, but, obviously you care about America, while we're much nearer to —

MAN: We don't care about you, is that what you're saying?

GIRL: What I'm saying is if we —

MAN: I'll show you how much we care. I'm going to make a complete ass of myself, right, but . . . If it convinces you of our sincerity.

He takes off his jacket and loosens his shirt.

At least you'll see what's next to our heart.

GIRL: Look, I'm not trying to attack you personally. It's not personal. It's just we ought to have the freedom —

MAN: It is personal. It's truly personal. It's what we value most dearly.

He reveals a Union Jack T-shirt, with THE EMPIRE STRIKES BACK across it.

MAN (*embarrassed*): Go on, laugh. Laugh if you want.

GIRL: I'm not laughing.

MAN: It's no joke what you wear across your chest. The T-shirt is the American tattoo. It's a way of making public our true feelings. I only wear my shirt over it so as not to embarrass you English. I know how reserved you are. So now I'm embarrassed. But that's OK if it makes you stop and think. Here it is. America, land of the brave, salutes the old empire.

GIRL (*quietly*): There in't no empire. That's all dead and gone.

MAN: Your people have rekindled its spirit.

GIRL: That's not true.

MAN: What do you want? To put the lion back to sleep again? No, rejoice, and point it in the right direction to secure the future.

GIRL: What direction's that?

MAN: Well, it sure as hell ain't into the arms of the commies.

GIRL: Who's arms is it, then? Yours?

MAN (*smiling*): Far be it from me to be forward, ma'am.

GIRL: Where's our choice in that?

MAN: 'No man's an island.' You have to be embraced by someone.

BOY: Not by men.

MAN: Don't misunderstand her, son. (*To the GIRL:*) Look, I don't doubt your sincerity, your desire for peace, but with an enemy as strong as the Russkies you have to argue from united strength. Power's all they comprehend, and if you women undermine our power, you strengthen theirs.

GIRL: So, best if we stay silent, then, is it? Just accept. Don't ask questions. Mum's the word.

MAN: What do you want?

GIRL: Just to make people think about what's happening, what we're letting happen to us.

MAN: And how do you do that?

GIRL: We have to make people notice us.

MAN: What people?

GIRL: Everybody. Americans as well. You go back with this film, at least they'll see that some of us —

MAN: Hold on. I'm not here just to give you a media trip.

GIRL: You said you'd tell the truth about us.

MAN: Truth, yes, not propaganda. I'm not out to make a film that'll drive a wedge between our nations. I want to bring them together. I believe in marriage guidance not divorce attorneys.

GIRL: Is that telling the truth?

MAN: You women have the priority on that now, do you?

GIRL: No, you do. Because you have the power.

MAN: Power, that's all your sort ever talk about.

BOY (*to* GIRL): You never used to talk like this.

GIRL: Like what?

BOY: Your voice even sounds different.

MAN: More strident?

BOY: Ye', that's it.

GIRL: But you don't listen to what I say!

BOY: I'm listening. Come on, tell me. I'm dying to know what I've done wrong out there, nearly getting killed for you. Come on, put me straight, and me mates, them who can't hear you no more. Come on!

Silence.

GIRL: How can I . . .?

BOY: Come on. Teach me!

GIRL (*almost in tears*): You're making it impossible for me to stay.

BOY: If you go, that's it. Finish. No way I'll take you back. You can't just stick me in a fridge, and take me out on a hot day. That's no way. Relationships mean you have to be together.

Silence. She half turns away. He grips her arm.

BOY (*desperate*): You can't go. I need you. I've got it all pictured. I've even got a photo of the quarters. I can see us there.

She looks at his hand on her. He releases his grip.

GIRL: Mick, I can't see any of us anywhere. Not if these bombs are —

BOY: Fuck the bombs! That's just an excuse. You're running away from me. Because you're shit scared of growing up, of marriage, of committing yourself for love. Look, I've done it. I've committed meself to you. Look.

He holds up a clenched fist. She involuntarily steps back.

BOY: No, look. Your name where the world can see. I'm proud to own you in public, I am.

GIRL (*nervous*): What does that mean?

BOY: What?

GIRL: My name on your knuckle. What you and your mates got on your T-shirts? Superman? What does that prove?

He slaps her across the face. She falls back over her bags.

MAN: Jesus Christ!

He turns away. Silence, as the GIRL *gets up into a kneeling position and sorts her possessions back together. She does not look up.*

BOY (*regretful*): Take the piss out of me, but not out my mates, right? They *were* supermen. Now they're froze under a blanket of snow.

GIRL: I won't calling the soldiers. I was calling all of us.

BOY (*slowly*): They fought for love. We all did. The chaplain said, don't kill out of hate, remember your loved ones, remember why you have to do these terrible things. I remembered. I remembered you. You were there with me.

GIRL: Yes.

BOY (*softly*): And now you spit on that love. What do you want I should do, shall I get my bayonet and cut your name right out?

She shakes her head.

I could, dead easy. Makes no difference to me. I'm bleedin' inside, anyway.

GIRL (*looking at him*): I'm sorry.

Pause.

BOY: I just need you to tell me what I did out there meant someat.

Silence. He sits on the bench, and does not look up, or appear to be listening. The GIRL *watches him. The* MAN *moves towards her.*

MAN (*gently*): He's been through a lot. You've no idea what war's like.

GIRL: I was there with him.

MAN: He thinks he's losing everything, so he over-reacts. But there was some provocation, yes? Not enough to warrant the level of aggression but, let's not escalate it out of all proportion.

She looks up at him. He crouches by her.

MAN (*nods*): Maybe we men have become too brutal, maybe we need to learn from you how to feel again. Then the world might become a better place to live in. That's what you're talking about, isn't it? (*Pause.*) But one thing's crystal clear, we won't learn anything from each other by polarising into some crazy war of the sexes. Real peace can only be found through love, in marriage, in the family. The *family.* (*Pause.*) That's why we men get so het up about these women's camps. Not because we feel challenged on the logic of defence, no, let's be truthful, it's because we fear you women trying to go it alone. *Separate.* That's not just male paranoia. No, it's because such acts directly threaten the very heart of our western democracy — the nuclear family. Now, God, I know that's not your intent, no more than you aim to play the commie propaganda game, but that's the potential result. And if you push, we men have to respond. We can hold the commies at the border but we can't let them rot us from within, like a cancer. We have to stand firm for freedom and refuse to be betrayed, even by those we love. (*Pause.*) Your boys fought for the same freedom on a clear front line.

Some made the supreme sacrifice. Don't knife the others when they limp home.

GIRL (*starts to gather her bags*): We're the front line now.

MAN: Listen, it's love we're talking about. Your hero's home. And he wants to sacrifice his freedom to marry you. What do you say?

She crosses to sit by the BOY.

GIRL (*quietly*): Mick? Mick, I'm goin'. We have to stop these maniacs killing us. (*Pause.*) I love you. Are you listenin' to me?

Getting no response, she stands. The MAN *blocks her path.*

MAN: If you really want peace, stand behind your soldier. Peace can only come in his shadow.

GIRL: There won't be any shadows. Not here. Not anywhere.

MAN: You're an innocent.

GIRL: 'Scuse me.

He steps aside. She leaves. He sits by the BOY.

MAN (*sighs*): That's the trouble with war. You go off to fight for your women and that means leaving them on their own. We had a hell of a time getting them to surrender their jobs after the last one. That's when all this women's nonsense began. (*Pause.*) They drone on and on about sexual politics, I say, OK, I'm willing to sacrifice the sex, but what I want to know is what about love? They only ever talk about the 'love' they make amongst themselves.

BOY: God, I hate her!

MAN: Make that your shield. (*Pause.*) You're still young. You've plenty of time to find a woman who'll really love you.

BOY: How can you trust any of 'em?

MAN: You can, believe me. My wife and I, we were like that. (*He holds up*

two fingers.) Like one. Indivisible. Except when I had to go away on business, of course. Oh, I love that woman now as much as I did when I first met her in the movies.

BOY: She was a film star?

MAN: An usherette. But she was Vivian Leigh to me. When she died, I . . . Well.

BOY: You still miss her?

MAN (*smiling*): We're still together, in a way. I kind of talk to her when I need a shoulder, you know. Sounds crazy? Well, it is, love is crazy. But it's the only thing worth possessing.

He holds up a fist. Silence.

(*Eventually:*) You plan to stay in the army?

BOY: I don't know.

MAN: Take a tip from me. Get out of the engineers. Look for an opening into signals, communications, especially satellite surveillance. Security is the future. Believe me. You see, everything has to intermesh to form a tight protective screen. If it doesn't, then the commies, either fronted by these women's groups or some ethnic, liberal whatever, will be through the gap in seconds. That's why we need men like you with eyes wide open.

BOY: What, you mean, to spy? To spy on our own people?

MAN: Does a doctor spy when he screens for cancer, in order to save lives? Security screening is just the same.

BOY: And these women are the cancer cells, are they?

MAN: You know she's the enemy. Fraternising just weakens morale, destroys security.

BOY: What do we do, we cut 'em do we? Get a sharp knife and away we go.

MAN: I never said anything about a knife.

BOY: That's what you meant though, in't it?

MAN: All I meant was the preservation of freedom.

BOY: She in't a cancer. I know she in't.

MAN: You're blinded. It takes time.

BOY: She loves me.

MAN (*angrily*): What the hell difference does that make?

BOY: It must make some.

MAN: She's really got in there, kid, hasn't she? She's way behind the fence.

The BOY *stands and gathers his gear together.*

So what are you going to do, pitch your tent across the road and hope she forsakes the arms of her sisters? *Your* sister.

BOY (*confused*): I don't know.

MAN: Don't you see how it's rotting the family? You've got to look to yourself, to your own future.

BOY: Won't that what she was saying?

MAN: She was talking about power. POWER.

Silence. The BOY *picks up the pamphlets.*

BOY: I don't know. I need time to think.

MAN: Come on. Let's go for a drink. Talk quietly.

BOY: No.

MAN: I want to help you. You remind me so much of . . . I'd like to help. We're allies, after all.

He packs the pamphlets. The MAN *offers his hand.*

There's nothing wrong with the hand of friendship, is there?

BOY (*quietly*): You shun't come pointin' out our cancer. (*Pause.*) Who says we're sick? (*Pause.*) Who says you're the doctor?

He exits. The MAN *clenches his fist in anger.*
Silence.

MAN (*furious*): Where the fuck's that crew?

WOMAN (*evenly*): Maybe they're searching for a parking lot. Space is a rare commodity, today.

MAN: They should park anywhere. Time the violation comes round, we'll have quit this waste land.

WOMAN: 'We are ambassadors. We must respect the law of the land.' Your words. I quote.

MAN: Ambassadors! They don't want ambassadors. They want to kick us out. They win one minor skirmish and go power-crazy. Who the hell do these Brits think they are?

WOMAN: Don't ask me. I'm an American citizen.

MAN: What kind of world is it where folks resent a helping hand? Well nigh bit it right off. Especially the girl. Pretty but twisted with hate. Stuck outside a base with a pack of witches. What a waste. When she's fifty and looks back on the beauty she's squandered. You should have been here. You'd have talked some sense into her.

WOMAN: Being a woman.

MAN: Exactly. And having some experience of life.

WOMAN: What's that worth?

He turns to look at her for the first time.

MAN: It's always been worth a lot to me, my love.

Silence. She takes off her sunglasses.

WOMAN: You're looking your age, Dick.

MAN: You don't look a day over forty.

WOMAN (*wrily*): I'm not. You never let me be.

MAN: You never wanted to be.

WOMAN: Oh, I did, Dick. The day I died, I'd have settled for being a hundred and forty for a few more minutes.

He sits by her.

MAN: You're still as beautiful to me as on our wedding day.

WOMAN (*with a southern accent*): Well, thank you, kind sir.

MAN (*smiling*): Scarlett O'Hara. Vivian Leigh.

He, gently, almost touches her face. Silence.

It could have been the make-up.

WOMAN: What?

MAN: They've found a lot of that old make-up was carcinogenic.

Pause. She laughs.

It's no laughing matter, Jane. I wept when I read that.

WOMAN: I never denied you had feelings, Dick.

MAN (*bitterly*): Ye', but what good does that do you? It didn't help me save you, or our boy from dying, any more than it'll stop these kids from throwing their lives away.

She opens her make-up bag, and with the aid of a mirror, removes her make-up.

WOMAN: Dick, did he remind you of anyone?

MAN: Who?

WOMAN: The soldier.

MAN: Well, myself, I guess.

WOMAN: Not our son? (*Pause.*) You never think about him?

MAN: All the time.

WOMAN: And what do you think?

MAN: What I always think. That he died a hero in a war that everyone betrayed.

WOMAN: We don't even know he wasn't bombed by his own side. It was the craziest of wars.

MAN: The Vietcong killed him.

WOMAN: Does it matter which side finally dropped the bomb?

MAN: It matters to me.

WOMAN: Would it matter to him, Dick?

MAN: Yes. Yes.

WOMAN: You don't think he might be more interested in who put him there?

MAN: He put himself there. He volunteered.

WOMAN: And we encouraged him?

MAN: We supported him.

WOMAN: How?

MAN: We gave him a decent upbringing with values. Values worth fighting for, dying for, even.

WOMAN: You never think it might have been a waste?

MAN (*turning away*): No. No. I won't listen to this liberal crap. Sacrifice has the highest meaning. He'd have understood, that it's an act of love. And we taught him that love. (*He smiles.*)

WOMAN: The richest country in the world. Love's bound to be expensive. Did we get a good deal, Dick?

MAN: What are you talking about?

WOMAN (*quietly*): What if what they sold us were lies? What if there were lies in our love? I often wanted to talk about it, but I kept it locked away, like a cancer.

MAN: I'm not buying any of this shit.

He walks away. She sighs and looks around. Silence.

WOMAN: I'd forgotten how the pavements are made from large slabs.

MAN: Sidewalks.

WOMAN: What?

MAN: You mean the sidewalks.

WOMAN: Pavements. Paving slabs. Like Slab Square in Nottingham. Used to meet my fellers there in front of the Council House. (*She attempts an English accent*.) 'Hey up, my love. How are you?' (*Slipping back into American*:) 'I'm fine, just fine.' No, that's not . . . 'I'm . . .' (*She smiles*.) I've forgotten how to speak my own language. Strange hearing it again.

MAN: You were keen enough to forget it. Couldn't drag you back even for a vacation. You loved everything American from drive-in movies to Madison Avenue.

WOMAN: True, but returning home again . . . (*She grins*.) You should have buried me under a slab.

MAN: You had a beautiful service. I still play the 16 mill. of it.

WOMAN: You didn't make me a star, though, did you, Dick?

MAN: What's that supposed to mean?

WOMAN: It was a joke. I think.

MAN (*turning*): I've had enough English irony for one day. Why can't you people just say what you want to say, instead of playing games? Just be sincere.

WOMAN: Sincere? (*She pauses*.) Yes, you're right. I never talked sincerely about our love, did I? Talked about sex a lot. (*She laughs*.) God, all I read in hospital were sex manuals to keep up the pretence of future contact between us. Shouldn't I have been reading something else, Dick? Something just for myself? *The Bible* or a do-it-yourself death manual, or what? I've no idea. You occupied all my thoughts. I worried and worried about you, composing the last words I'd say to you, as a comfort.

MAN: And they were a comfort.

WOMAN: 'Your dinner's in the oven.

I'm leaving you.'

MAN (*smiling*): You'd never have said that.

WOMAN: 'We'll always be together. Dick.'

MAN: Yes. And so we are.

WOMAN (*pauses*): Your dinner's in the oven. Your past is in the deep freeze. I'm leaving you, Dick.

Silence. The MAN *takes out a handkerchief and wipes his face and hands.*

Do you hear me, Dick?

MAN (*pauses*): What's with all this? What are you trying to do Jane? Smash up my most precious memories? Memories are all I have, to build a future out of.

WOMAN: I'm dead, Dick. I can't hear you. I'm dead. And I'd like to be left in peace. If I was alive, I figure I'd be saying the same thing. If you love me, let me go.

MAN: You can't leave me.

WOMAN: No. I'm not. (*Pause*.) I'm not leaving you.

MAN: Thank God.

WOMAN: You're going to have to leave me.

The MAN *stares at her in almost terror. She finishes taking off her make-up.*

WOMAN: I'm home, Dick. It's you who's goin' to have to wing his way back across the sea.

MAN: You're not her, you're not my wife. That witch of a gal has conjured you to curse me. My wife would never betray me like this. Never. I know her.

WOMAN: Is this betrayal? Asking for a bit of space for myself? I didn't even get six foot of earth 'cos you wanted me to grace the mantlepiece. I'm surprised you din't have me stuffed like Trigger.

MAN: She'd never talk like that.

WOMAN: She would, Dick. Oh, ye', she would. If she was sincere.

Silence.

MAN: So what's this? The British brushoff? Yanks go Home? Right. Sure as damn it, that's exactly what we'll do. We'll go. Your cry for help will fall on deaf ears. We don't need you. We never did. We protected you out of love, and respect, that's all.

WOMAN: Love for you must be all or nothing, eh?

MAN: I've always believed that.

WOMAN: I loved you.

MAN: This is not love.

WOMAN: Isn't it?

MAN: Love is sacrifice.

WOMAN (*mildly*): You always were stupid, Dick. Not vicious, but then again, you never needed to be. All you had to do was hold on to what you'd stored in the fridge. Keep screaming betrayal, and dreaming of love. That won't come between the finger and the button.

MAN: You're not the woman I married. (*He picks up his coat.*) I'll leave this ghost in this dead land. When I get home, it'll be all right. Jane will be waiting. I know that. I believe.

WOMAN (*pauses*): Here comes your crew, Dick. You'd better go. They'll be waiting to hear their orders.

He turns to go, and stops.

MAN: I loved you. Or somebody like you.

WOMAN (*as Clark Gable*): Frankly, my dear, I just don't give a damn.

The man exits.
She sits, looking out to sea. Her eyes fighting sleep.
She lies back on the bench, and closes her eyes.
A gun salute rouses her.

She stands, clearly angry.
The band breaks into 'Auld Lang Syne', with the crowd joining in.
She moves downstage to look down across the bay.
She runs her hand across her face, then slips off her shoes, feeling the earth beneath her feet. She stretches out to the sky.
She stands, ready, quiet, a sentinel.
Slow fade.

Methuen's Modern Plays

Michael Frayn	*Clouds*
	Alphabetical Order and Donkey's Years
	Make and Break
	Noises Off
	Benefactors
Max Frisch	*The Fire Raisers*
	Andorra
	Triptych
Jean Giraudoux	*The Trojan War Will Not Take Place*
Simon Gray	*Butley*
	Otherwise Engaged and other plays
	Dog Days
	The Rear Column and other plays
	Close of Play and Pig in a Poke
	Stage Struck
	Quartermaine's Terms
Peter Handke	*Offending the Audience* and *Self-Accusation*
	Kaspar
Kaufman & Hart	*The Ride Across Lake Constance*
	They Are Dying Out
	Once in a Lifetime, You Can't Take It With You and *The Man Who Came To Dinner*
Barrie Keeffe	*Gimme Shelter (Gem, Gotcha, Getaway)*
	Barbarians (Killing Time, Abide With Me, In the City)
	A Mad World, My Masters
Arthur Kopit	*Indians*
	Wings
John McGrath	*The Cheviot, the Stag and the Black, Black Oil*
David Mamet	*Glengarry Glen Ross*
David Mercer	*After Haggerty*
	The Bankrupt and other plays
	Cousin Vladimir and *Shooting the Chandelier*
	Duck Song
	Huggy Bear and other plays

	The Monster of Karlovy Vary and *Then and Now*
	No Limits To Love
Arthur Miller	*The American Clock*
Percy Mtwa, Mbongeni Ngema, Barney Simon	*Woza Albert*
Peter Nichols	*Passion Play*
	Poppy
Joe Orton	*Loot*
	What the Butler Saw
	Funeral Games and *The Good and Faithful Servant*
	Entertaining Mr Sloane
	Up Against It
Harold Pinter	*The Birthday Party*
	The Room and *The Dumb Waiter*
	The Caretaker
	A Slight Ache and other plays
	The Collection and *The Lover*
	The Homecoming
	Tea Party and other plays
	Landscape and *Silence*
	Old Times
	No Man's Land
	Betrayal
	The Hothouse
	Other Places (A Kind of Alaska, Victoria Station, Family Voices)
Luigi Pirandello	*Henry IV*
	Six Characters in Search of an Author
Stephen Poliakoff	*Hitting Town* and *City Sugar*
David Rudkin	*The Sons of Light*
	The Triumph of Death
Jean-Paul Sartre	*Crime Passionnel*
Wole Soyinka	*Madmen and Specialists*
	The Jero Plays
	Death and the King's Horseman
C.P. Taylor	*And a Nightingale Sang . . .*

	Good
Peter Whelan	*The Accrington Pals*
Nigel Williams	*Line 'Em*
	Class Enemy
Charles Wood	*Veterans*
Theatre Workshop	*Oh What a Lovely War!*
Various authors	*Best Radio Plays of 1978* (Don Haworth: *Episode on a Thursday Evening:* Tom Mallin: *Halt! Who Goes There?;* Jennifer Phillips: *Daughters of Men;* Fay Weldon: *Polaris;* Jill Hyem: *Remember Me;* Richard Harris: *Is It Something I Said?*)
	Best Radio Plays of 1979 (Shirley Gee: *Typhoid Mary;* Carey Harrison: *I Never Killed My German;* Barrie Keeffe: *Heaven Scent;* John Kirkmorris: *Coxcombe;* John Peacock: *Attard in Retirement;* Olwen Wymark: *The Child*)
	Best Radio Plays of 1982 (Rhys Adrian:*Watching the Plays Together;* John Arden: *The Old Man Sleeps Alone;* Harry Barton: *Hoopoe Day;* Donald Chapman: *Invisible Writing;* Tom Stoppard: *The Dog It Was That Died;* William Trevor: *Autumn Sunshine*)

Methuen's Theatrescripts

The Master Playwrights

Collections of plays by the best-known modern playwrights in value-for-money paperbacks.

John Arden **PLAYS: ONE**
Serjeant Musgrave's Dance, The Workhouse Donkey, Armstrong's Last Goodnight

Brendan Behan **THE COMPLETE PLAYS**
The Hostage, The Quare Fellow, Richard's Cork Leg, Moving Out, A Garden Party, The Big House

Edward Bond **PLAYS: ONE**
Saved, Early Morning, The Pope's Wedding
PLAYS: TWO
Lear, The Sea, Narrow Road to the Deep North, Black Mass, Passion

Noël Coward **PLAYS: ONE**
Hay Fever, The Vortex, Fallen Angels, Easy Virtue
PLAYS: TWO
Private Lives, Bitter Sweet, The Marquise, Post-Mortem
PLAYS: THREE
Design for Living, Cavalcade, Conversation Piece, and Hands Across the Sea, Still Life and Fumed Oak from Tonight at 8.30
PLAYS: FOUR
Blithe Spirit, This Happy Breed, Present Laughter and Ways and Means, The Astonished Heart and Red Peppers from Tonight at 8.30
PLAYS: FIVE
Relative Values, Look After Lulu, Waiting in the Wings, Suite in Three Keys

John Galsworthy **FIVE PLAYS**
Strife, The Eldest Son, The Skin Game, Justice, Loyalties

If you would like to receive, free of charge, regular information about new plays and theatre books from Methuen, please send your name and address to:

The Marketing Department (Drama)
Methuen London Ltd
North Way
Andover
Hampshire SP10 5BE